The Complete
Scorekeeping H;

MW00986760

Revised and Updated Edition

The Complete
Baseball Scorekeeping
Handbook
Revised and Updated Edition

ANDRES WIRKMAA

McFarland & Company, Inc., Publishers
Jefferson, North Carolina

Portions of the Official Baseball Rules appearing in this book have been reprinted by special permission of the Office of the Commissioner of Baseball. The copyright in the Official Baseball Rules is owned and has been registered by the Commissioner of Baseball. Any additional material contained in this book has not been endorsed by the Office of the Commissioner of Baseball.

LIBRARY OF CONGRESS CATALOGUING-IN-PUBLICATION DATA

Wirkmaa, Andres.
   The complete baseball scorekeeping handbook / Andres Wirkmaa.—Revised and updated edition.
      p.   cm.
   Includes index.
   ISBN 978-0-4766-6389-0 (softcover : acid free paper) ∞
   ISBN 978-1-4766-1525-7 (ebook)

   1. Baseball—Scorekeeping.   I. Title.
   GV879.W58 2015b
   796.357'021—dc23   2015028295

BRITISH LIBRARY CATALOGUING DATA ARE AVAILABLE

Cover image © 2015 Comstock

Printed in the United States of America

McFarland & Company, Inc., Publishers
  Box 611, Jefferson, North Carolina 28640
  www.mcfarlandpub.com

To my sons, Alex and Chris—two true boys of summer that I love very much.

And to all my many baseball friends, big and small.

And to my dear, darling and beautiful wife, Nancy, the flower of my heart whose love and affection have made me consider myself the luckiest man on the face of the earth.

Table of Contents

Preface

Some years ago, I wrote a book annotating Major League Baseball's rules governing scorekeeping. Titled *Baseball Scorekeeping: A Practical Guide to the Rules*, it was published in 2003. Four years later, however, in 2007, MLB revised a number of its rules. Consequently, I wrote this book with those changes in mind.

But *The Complete Baseball Scorekeeping Handbook* isn't a simple revision of the earlier book; rather, it is expanded to include the art of keeping score, and the sections of the book that deal with the rulebook have been rewritten from scratch and in an entirely new format that reflects my experience in answering the many hundreds of scorekeeping questions that I've received since publication of my previous book. The result of these changes is that the book you now hold in your hands bears little resemblance to *Baseball Scorekeeping*.

So how did I come to write either book?

Although it happened quite some time ago, I remember—quite clearly—the moment when I experienced the flash of insight and inspiration that led me to write about scorekeeping in baseball.

I could tell you—briefly—how it occurred, and go from there, but to understand fully what a true and sudden manifestation of the essence of this corner of baseball it was, and to appreciate the fundamental cognition it gave rise to and how it put me on the path that led me to where I've come, some context is necessary.

For starters, I've always been a baseball fan, but only in the broadest sense. In my time, I've watched and enjoyed more than my fair share of baseball games, and I've otherwise experienced baseball like any average American male, but I never idolized any particular players, nor have I ever lived or died depending on the fortunes of any particular team. That is to say, I've always enjoyed baseball just for what it is—fun to watch and play, fun to read and talk about—but I've never made baseball a central part of my life (although a number of my friends fit that description, and many of them are people for whom I have the highest regard and admiration).

Nor have I ever memorized statistics, or even the names of players or any considerable part of the universe of data associated with baseball like so many "die-hard fans" are wont to do, and to this day I care to do so not at all: I just like baseball, a lot.

Beginning around 1988, I was unwittingly drawn into baseball beyond my rather casual relationship with it because my two sons—both possessing and exhibiting considerable athletic skills, if I may say so—were actively involved in organized youth baseball. Trying to be a good father, and as a fan of the game, I found myself attending all their games.

Not being content to be a passive observer, I felt compelled to volunteer my time to "helping out." Consequently, I schooled myself in all the "how to properly hold a bat" and "how to take a good lead off first base" stuff, and all the other jock aspects of baseball by reading and studying anything and everything that I could lay my hands on. It wasn't long before I felt schooled enough to believe that the chances of my not making a fool of myself in front of parents and players were fairly good, and thereupon I became a bona fide baseball coach. (After all, there were then, as there are now, enough books to fill the Grand Canyon about that kind of stuff, and if you devote a fair amount of time to studying the requisite manuals and other materials, it doesn't take much more than a little nerve to convince anyone—including yourself—that you have real baseball savvy.)

However, in terms of scorekeeping, I was a dunce—close to clueless. In large part, that was because the universe of baseball literature was nearly devoid of any titles on the subject, and scorekeeping isn't central to actually playing the game, so it wasn't something with which I felt I needed to concern myself.

Granted, I knew that there were official scorers, and that some people kept score on their own, and I had a vague understanding of how that was done, but when—by chance—I purchased a copy of *The National* (a daily baseball newspaper that ceased publication many years ago) on October 17 of 1990, my eyes were opened, and I was amazed, delighted, awestruck and inspired by what I saw.

There, tacked onto the official box score and all the blah blah blah written about the first game of the 1990 World Series between the Oakland Athletics and the Cincinnati Reds, was what's shown on the following page.

I had glanced at scorecards before—made up mostly of what appeared to me to be chicken scratch scribbles that didn't seem to be of any consequence—but I'd never seen anything like this before. It drew me in, ignited a spark in me, and it took no time at all for me to realize and appreciate that it was something truly special.

Instead of a standard box score (which always had seemed to me to be dull, dry and dreary things), here was a comprehensive picture of an entire game from the first plate appearance of the first batter for the visiting team, down to the last out. And it wasn't some long and drawn-out narrative text either. Instead, everything was there to behold, take in and enjoy, set out in the most elegant, clear, clever and altogether marvelous manner that I could ever imagine.

Look at it!

Instantly, you can see that Cincinnati won, and by a good margin as well inasmuch as Oakland was obviously shut out and the first four batters in the lineup for the Reds scored seven times during the first five innings.

(I am, of course, referring to the fact that all the black

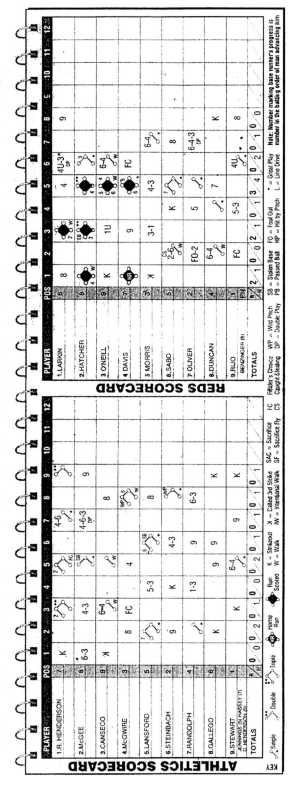

Oakland Athletics	AB	R	H	RBI
R. Henderson lf	5	0	3	0
McGee cf	5	0	1	0
Canseco rf	2	0	0	0
McGwire 1b	3	0	0	0
Lansford 3b	4	0	2	0
Steinbach c	4	0	1	0
Randolph 2b	4	0	1	0
Gallego ss	4	0	0	0
Stewart p	1	0	0	0
Jennings ph	1	0	1	0
Burns p	0	0	0	0
Nelson p	0	0	0	0
Hassey ph	1	0	0	0
Sanderson p	0	0	0	0
Eckersley p	0	0	0	0
D. Henderson ph	1	0	0	0
Totals	35	0	9	0

Cincinnati Reds	AB	R	H	RBI
Larkin ss	4	1	0	0
Hatcher cf	3	3	3	1
O'Neill rf	2	1	0	1
Davis lf	4	2	2	3
Morris 1b	4	0	1	0
Sabo 3b	3	0	1	2
Oliver c	4	0	1	0
Duncan 2b	3	0	1	0
Rijo p	3	0	1	0
Dibble p	0	0	0	0
Benzinger ph	1	0	0	0
Myers p	0	0	0	0
Totals	31	7	10	7

dots—representing runs scored—are on Cincinnati's side of the ledger, and none are to be found on Oakland's page.)

But that's far from all the magic of it: Employing no words, only symbols and succinct abbreviations, the scorecard tells a fairly long and complex story in considerable detail, and it can be read from left to right or top to bottom, start to finish or back to front.

Virtually everything is there, ready to be taken in as a whole, or in parts, and in any manner you wish. All you need is to possess the simple knowledge that the defensive players are referred to by numbers (1 for the pitcher; 2 for the catcher; 3 for the first baseman; 4 for the second baseman; 5 for the third baseman; 6 for the shortstop; 7 for the left fielder; 8 for the center fielder; and 9 for the right fielder), and comprehend the "key" that appears at the bottom of the scorecard, in order to have the entire game at your fingertips.

For example, the box score of the game tells you, among other things, that Oakland's first baseman, [Mark] McGwire went 0-for-3 with no RBIs. But the scorecard tells you in what innings he came to the plate, what the situations were when he did so, and the particulars of each out he made.

You can see—at a glance—by looking at the scorecard that McGwire (batting clean-up for the Athletics) was in fact the lead-off batter in the top of the second inning, and he hit the ball for an out to the Reds' center fielder (whom you know to be [Billy] Hatcher by referring to the other side of the scorecard where—among many other things—the fielding positions of the Cincinnati players are listed).

At the same time, you can also see that the next two outs made by McGwire (a groundout to shortstop [Barry] Larkin in the third inning and a fly out to second baseman [Mariano] Duncan in the fifth inning) both accounted for the last out of the inning, and in each case McGwire left at least one runner on base in scoring position. Moreover, you can also easily see that McGwire drew his walk with one out in the top of the eighth inning and he advanced as far as third base until [Willie] Randolph—playing second base for Oakland—grounded out to the Reds' shortstop (Larkin) with runners at second and third to end the inning for the Athletics.

That's a lot of information, but it's only a fraction of what can be gleaned from this scorecard, and it comes from focusing on only one of the 22 players that came to bat in this game!

Here's another example: Take a look at Hatcher, the #2 batter for the Reds. The box score tells you that he had a good game, going 3-for-3, scoring three runs and driving in a run. But again, the scorecard goes far beyond that.

Looking at the scorecard, you can easily see that two of Hatcher's three hits were doubles, and the first of the two doubles drove in Larkin all the way from first base to make a two-run lead a three-run lead for Cincinnati. Of the three runs that Hatcher scored, two were driven in by the Reds' left fielder ([Eric] Davis), and one was driven in by Cincinnati's right fielder ([Paul] O'Neill), facts that are altogether absent from the box score.

And it doesn't stop there.

A general impression of how many runners were left on base is readily had. Moreover, it's easy not only to count them, but to identify each runner and exactly which base he was "left on" and why.

Strikeouts are much the same, and those that were called strikeouts—as opposed to swinging strikeouts—are all there to be seen, easily and in full context.

Examples of how this graphic representation of the first game of the 1990 World Series speaks volumes are practically endless, but the bottom line is simply this: To spell out in sentences and paragraphs everything this scorecard tells you would take many thousands of words, and how any given event related to another would be difficult to surmise reading a narrative account of the game. At the same time, the box score gives you only the cumulative totals of what happened with little if any indication of context—of when what happened happened, and what the implications were when what happened happened.

But the scorecard tells the story of the game in context, and with remarkable detail—neatly, concisely and clearly.

Amazing!

The point is that when I first saw this scorecard, I recognized that it was something truly remarkable, and that realization led me to explore, study, analyze and generally immerse myself in this extraordinary aspect of baseball that I had stumbled upon.

As a result, I kept score in every game that I was involved in from then on, and I took on the duties of the official scorer whenever and wherever the opportunity presented itself.

In the process, I collected dozens and dozens of scorebooks of all shapes and sizes (some good, some not so good, some simply horrible), and in my zeal—and convinced that I could do better—I designed my own scorebook, employing the best features of the good scorecards in general circulation, getting rid of the garbage, and adding more than a few of my own ideas in the bargain.

At the same time, I made it my business to compare notes and otherwise commiserate with other scorekeepers and learn all that I could about scorekeeping from any source that I could find.

I also soon realized—doing what I was doing—that the Official Rules of Baseball contain myriad provisions concerning scorekeeping "technicalities," and that approximately 25 percent (!) of the rulebook is devoted to scorekeeping. At the same time, many of the provisions are difficult to deal with or even understand. Therefore (inasmuch as I have been a practicing attorney for many years, and consequently experienced in dealing with "vagaries" as bad as or worse than what MLB has managed to come up with), I wrote a book analyzing and explaining each and every section of the rulebook that deals with official scorekeeping, and the gratifying success that the book has enjoyed has confirmed to me that I am not alone in my love for, and fascination with, scorekeeping.

So, from a spark grew a flame, and it led to my putting this book together in hopes that it will serve to help scorekeepers everywhere perform the task of keeping score better, as well as add to the enjoyment that so many people find in scorekeeping.

At the same time, it's also my hope that this book will excite and inspire others in the same way that I have been, and give "the pastime within the pastime" some greater degree of the attention and respect that it deserves, but rarely gets.

After all, scorekeeping is vital to baseball: If no one bothered to record the seemingly countless things to be kept track of, there would be no statistics in baseball, and it's impossible to imagine baseball—as we know it—without its numbers. Furthermore, the integrity of the history of the game and its records are rooted in scorekeeping. Therefore, scorekeeping ought to be "done right," and this book is intended to facilitate and foster that as well.

In addition to that, there is a secret that scorekeepers know, and anyone who has never bothered to take a whack at keeping score most likely doesn't know: Short of wearing a uniform and being in the dugout or on the field of play, there is no better way to involve yourself in a game of baseball than to keep score. By keeping score, you elevate yourself from a mere observer to someone connected to the game, and—as if that weren't enough—a scorekeeper can take the game he or she scored home in his or her pocket.

Others who watched the game will remember this, that or the other thing about what happened. Nonetheless, those memories invariably fade over time, but a well-kept scorecard is a detailed portrait of the contest that will last long after time has caused memory to fade away.

All that said, it all comes down to this.

Baseball is an extraordinary game, and the fact that it lends itself so remarkably well to being "scored," the fact that scorekeeping gives rise to the universe of numbers that baseball statistics provide, and the fact that scoring baseball games can be pleasure all unto itself, makes baseball unique and an endless source of fun and gratification for anyone who chooses to partake of its pleasures with a pencil and a piece of paper, or the latest software designed to facilitate the joy of keeping score.

This revised edition of *The Complete Baseball Scorekeeping Handbook* is a result of the fact that in December of 2014, MLB's Playing Rules Committee (after the passage of very many years) chose to reorganize the order and placement of the rules that make up MLB's rulebook, beginning with the 2015 season. Consequently, citations to rules set forth in the original edition of this book were altered to comport with the new arrangement of MLB's official rules.

Introduction
The "Dying Art"

Since I became deeply interested and involved in scorekeeping a good many years ago, I've noticed something: Year after year, on a regular basis, a reporter somewhere will write a piece about how scorekeeping in baseball is a "dying art."

It's an easy topic to riff on. After all, there's a simple premise and an obvious punch line—all neat and tidy.

Invariably, the starting point is that in days gone by, everyone (or nearly everyone, or most people, or at least a significant number of people) attending baseball games kept a scorecard, but in modern times, next to no one keeps score, and the few that still do are peculiar individuals, akin to dinosaurs.

From that observation, the writer reasons that scorekeeping is nearing extinction.

Added to that will be some nostalgia and general exposition on the subject, with perhaps a pithy quote or two thrown in for good measure, but the end point of the article invariably will be to note sadly that the good old days when scorekeeping was performed by everyone attending a ball game are gone, and—like other things that are perceived to have faded away over time, such as good manners, clean jokes and well-behaved children—those days will be sorely missed.

Although I don't begrudge any writer tapping into any subject that easily lends itself to filling up space, I nevertheless think to myself each time I read yet another piece along those lines, just how trite and simple-minded the cliché of scorekeeping being something that once was, but is no more, really is.

(For whatever it's worth, it should be noted that if scorekeeping is in fact a dying art, its death is awfully protracted because as far back as 1950—ironically, the year that I was born—*The Sporting News* published an article about scorekeeping being a dying art.)

Granted, although there are no hard numbers regarding how many fans kept score at professional baseball games in the past as compared to how many do so these days, it's nonetheless apparent that scorekeeping by ordinary fans is less common than it may once have been. After all, it has been reported that the sales of "official" scorecards at major league venues (shoddy things for the most part, printed by the home team seemingly out of habit and not to actually promote or otherwise encourage scorekeeping by fans) are less than they once were, and that's understandable. After all, with all the electronic "bling" that fills almost every corner of professional ballparks these days, you don't need a scorecard to know who is up, what the score is, or what any given batter takes with him—in terms of past performance—into the batter's box. Add to that the countless distractions at major and minor league ballparks, and it's easy to understand why "old school" scorekeeping might not be as visible in the grandstands as it once was.

However, based on what I've observed over the years, scorekeeping itself is far from dead. In fact, it's not only as much a part of the game as it ever was, it's more so than ever before, and it's performed across a far wider spectrum—and far more diligently—than it ever was in the past.

Storks Might Deliver Babies, but Statistics Come from Scorekeepers

Consider the fact that until fairly recently, baseball statistics were by-and-large limited to relatively simple things like batting averages, earned run averages and the like. However, with the aid of computers and the insights gained by individuals such as Bill James and countless other "sabermetricians," statistics in baseball are now infinitely more sophisticated than they have ever been, and those statistics—however simple or complex they may be—all come from someone taking the time and making the effort to record (in detail) what occurred during the course of a baseball game. That being so, scorekeeping (although it may not be practiced by as many average fans just for the fun of it as it may have once been) not only continues to play a pivotal role in baseball, its importance to the game has grown tremendously, much more than anyone could ever have imagined way back when.

Consequently, although scorekeeping may appear to be less prevalent in the stands of professional baseball games these days than it may have once been, there is still a lot of scorekeeping going on in the world of baseball, and it's far more detailed than it ever was in the past.

As Baseball Grows, So Does Scorekeeping, and Baseball Is Growing

Think about it: It wasn't until relatively recent years that organized youth baseball and softball even existed, let alone their being the competitive big things that they are now. In addition, many leagues have come into existence for men and women of all ages, leagues that didn't even exist years ago. As a result of that—and other factors—scorecards are being kept by legions of individuals for tons of organized games that would not have even been played, let alone have been scored, back in the day (as they say).

Add to that the expansion of baseball and softball outside the borders of the United States: more players, more teams, more leagues, more scorekeeping.

Also, the attention to detail employed by scorekeepers to record games has increased as well throughout the universe of baseball. This is largely because only the most basic data was recorded in earlier times, like runs, hits, errors and outs. Now, in large part due to the widespread use of computers to process data and generate extraordinarily complex and sophisticated statistics at all levels of the game, scorecards (be they paper or electronic) are used to record so much more, like the number of pitches thrown during the course of a game, the nature and sequence of those pitches, where balls were hit, the position of runners when outs were logged, and on and on and on.

In short, the need and desire to "get it right" in scorekeeping has never been greater, and therefore scorekeeping is more vigorously performed than ever before.

As Long as There's Organized Baseball (and Softball), People Will Be Keeping Score

With the expansion of organized baseball and softball to virtually every age group, with baseball and softball expanding to an ever-increasing number of countries, and with scorekeeping being at the heart of the ever-expanding world of statistics in organized baseball and softball, scorekeeping is certainly not a dying art.

Perhaps because the high costs associated with attending MLB games these days has made going to a ball game akin to going on a family vacation to Bermuda, along with the factors previously mentioned and other reasons as well, ordinary fans generally don't want to bother with anything more than passively taking in the spectacle they've paid so much to see. They would rather not be bothered with paying the kind of sustained attention, or otherwise expending the effort necessary to keep even a simple scorecard, and therefore the percentage of people at any given game that engage in scorekeeping purely for pleasure is less than once was the case. However, keeping score in the broader sense has never been more widespread because organized baseball and softball have never been more widespread, and the demand for more and ever-increasingly sophisticated data has never been greater, and it continues to grow.

Consequently, scorekeeping is not dead, or even dying. It will die only when the game itself dies, and that day is far in the future because more people watch, play or otherwise participate in organized baseball and softball today than ever before, and the love of the game (and everything that goes with it) continues to be a cherished possession for countless individuals in the United States and all around the world.

◆ 1 ◆

Who's on First?

Finding Your Way Around the Scorecard

What (Exactly) Is Scorekeeping?

Here's something I'll wager has never occurred to you.

Anyone who has a basic understanding of baseball, and can write, can "keep score" without any special knowledge or expertise beyond those two things.

That's because keeping score is really nothing more than recording what happened during the course of a baseball game.

Adam struck out swinging for the first out of the inning. Then Bruce hit a ground ball that was fielded by the shortstop and thrown to the first baseman to retire Bruce. Next, with two outs, Charlie hit the ball over the wall in fair territory for a home run. Then David drew a walk. After that, Edgar drew a walk and David advanced to second base as a result. Then Fred hit a ground ball to the third baseman to force out David at third base to end the inning.

Now there's nothing wrong with "keeping score" that way. After all, the primary information is all there. However, actually "scoring" a game in that manner would be an incredibly daunting task (think writer's cramp), especially in a fast-moving game and/or when the plays are not as routine as those in the example given. Moreover, if the actions of the players were recorded in this fashion, something as simple as tallying how many times any given batter came to the plate during the course of the game, the number of base hits any given batter made, or anything else of that nature would require plowing through a long narrative text.

Consequently, a better way to record the events that make up a baseball game was devised quite early in the history of baseball: a relatively simple and satisfactory methodology.

The key is the recognition of the fact that the journey of each and every batter from the batter's box, back to the dugout or around the bases, can be graphically—and with little effort—recorded by employing a simple grid and terse abbreviations.

In sum, the aforementioned 91 words required to record what Adam, Bruce, Charlie, David, Edgar and Fred did can be distilled to the following.

Player	1
ADAM	K
BRUCE	6-3
CHARLIE	≡◆
DAVID	SU ↘⁵ BB
EDGAR	↘⁶ BB
FRED	FC

It's not unlike musical notation: rather than describing the notes that make up a composition in words (which would be a mind-boggling task even in the case of the most simple musical piece), a graphic representation of the sounds that constitute the music—employing symbols, abbreviations, and other "short-cuts"—is used, and it is far superior to employing words to do so.

Instead of writing that "in the key of C minor, in ¾ time, the piece begins with a ½-beat rest, followed by G natural above middle C played in three quarter notes, followed by an E flat above middle C that is held, and the motif is then repeated by sounding an F natural above middle C instead of the preceding G natural, followed by D natural above middle C instead of the preceding E flat," you simply have the following:

Consequently, those individuals who "keep score" in baseball universally make use of a tried and true system that (although subject to myriad variations in its fine points) is in essence a simple and straightforward approach that neatly accomplishes what it's designed to do.

Learning How to Keep Score (More Than One Way to Skin a Cat)

You can learn the fundamentals of keeping a scorecard in many ways, but basically, there are two approaches.

One way is to study it from the ground up: learn the ABCs and then apply them to basic and simple situations. From there, increasingly complex situations are dealt with and mastered until any and all occurrences that might take place during the course of a game are easily noted.

(Like a child, first you learn to crawl, then stand up, then walk and eventually run.)

The other approach is going from the top down: taking a completed scorecard and learning to read it (i.e. interpret the various symbols and abbreviations), and in doing so, "get it" and go from there.

(Like a child, first you hear the language spoken by the people that surround you without really understanding it. Then, little by little, you pick up on what they're saying and how they're saying it until, over time, you're able to fully understand and speak the language yourself).

Both approaches are valid, and one approach need not be employed to the exclusion of the other. In fact, many people who keep score learned to do so by alternating between the two approaches.

Inasmuch as both methods are sound and useful, I will employ them both to impart the essential knowledge necessary to keep score. But before anything else, the single most fundamental and essential concept in scorekeeping must be understood and learned: that fielders are referred to with numbers, and although almost every other aspect of scorekeeping is subject to all sorts of permutations and idiosyncrasies, the numbering of fielders (as set forth below) is as written in stone as anything you can imagine. It's the essential unifying precept in scorekeeping.

So here it is—the magic decoder ring of scorekeeping in baseball.

1 = Pitcher.	6 = Shortstop.
2 = Catcher.	7 = Left Fielder.
3 = First Baseman.	8 = Center Fielder.
4 = Second Baseman.	9 = Right Fielder.
5 = Third Baseman.	

(Note that when a tenth fielder is allowed under special rules—as is sometimes the case in certain levels of softball or youth baseball and the like—that tenth fielder [often called a rover, short fielder or roving fielder] is referred to with the number 10 on the scorecard, regardless of where that fielder might be positioned at any given time).

There is an inherent logic to this system: it begins with the player positioned in the middle of the diamond (the pitcher), goes around the infield from position to position—more or less—then continues from left to right across the outfield. However, why the numbering "skips" the shortstop while going around the infield counterclockwise (as base runners do) is somewhat curious.

For my part, I have never seen a definitive explanation for why the shortstop isn't designated as 5, and the third baseman isn't referred to as 6, and why it is that way has apparently been lost in the mists of time. No matter: it works, and it is inconceivable that it will ever change, as there is no compelling reason to change it. Doing so after all these years would only cause a great deal of confusion and consternation in the scorekeeping world.

In any case, with this numeric alphabet in hand, we can begin to examine how a scorecard is constructed by deconstructing the scorecard from an actual game.

A Scorecard Is Worth a Thousand Words

Here is a scorecard from the seventh game of the 2001 World Series between the New York Yankees and the Arizona Diamondbacks, played on November 4 of that year in Phoenix, Arizona.

This game is considered by many to be among the greatest baseball games ever played, for a host of reasons. In fact, entire books and numerous articles have been written about it and its significance in the history of baseball, as well as its place in modern American culture. At the same time, it is a fairly typical major league baseball game from the perspective of recording it on a scorecard, and therefore it serves our purposes quite well.

Without a doubt, if you were to look at the many scorecards from this game—drawn by many different scorekeepers—you would find some that are "clean" and easy to read. Others would be sloppy and/or poorly organized, and therefore difficult or impossible to disentangle. Also, they would have varying degrees of details in regards to the minutia—like the pitches that were

Player	Pos	1	2	3	4	5	6	7	8	9
JETER	6	⅄			9			3♦2 4-	×fc	
O'NEILL / KNOBLAUCH (B8)	9 / 7	⇐⅄= 9-4 5		K				3-6 /-	9	
WILLIAMS	8	8			⅄			⅄4 /fc		8
MARTINEZ	3		K		8		/-			6-3
POSADA	2		7		⅄		7			K
SPENCER (B8)	7 / 9		8		4		8			
SORIANO	4			9		K		E♦		
BROSIUS	5			3		K		K		
CLEMENS / STANTON (B7)	1 / 1			K		9		5-4 /- ×		
JUSTICE (T8) / RIVERA (B8)	PH / 1									

Player	Pos	1	2	3	4	5	6	7	8	9
WOMACK	6	8	K	4-3			2-6 (C5) /- ×		3⅄=	
COUNSELL	4	⅄3 3E1	⅄4 /-	6-3			3	×	⅄3 /HB	
GONZALEZ	7	3U	K	6-4 /E4			×	K	/-	
WILLIAMS	5	K	/-	/fc			K			
FINLEY	8	6-3	K		♦-		/-			
BAUTISTA	9	⅄7 /BB	8	8-6 5 /=			K			
GRACE / DELLUCCI (B9)	3 / PR	/-	/-	4-3			1-5 E1			
MILLER / CUMMINGS (B9)	2 / PR	K	K	K			♦9 fc			
SCHILLING / BATISTA (T8)	1 / 1	⅄	K	⅄			3♦fc			
JOHNSON (T8) / BELL (B9)	1 / PH									

thrown, where balls were hit, and other aspects of the game. However, for our purposes, I have drawn this scorecard with the minimum notations, and with the notations as clear and distinct as possible so as to convey the essence of a scorecard.

The finer points—the "advanced techniques," if you will—will be dealt with later in this book.

Inasmuch as we have already covered the method of referencing the fielders with numbers (see above), chances are that you can decipher much of the information that this scorecard contains without further explanation, but certainly not all of the information contained in it will be obvious unless you already know the basics of scorekeeping. Therefore, if you are not an experienced scorekeeper and you read the following narrative of the game while referring to the scorecard, you'll learn the essential things you need to know in order to understand the basics of scorekeeping and will thereby gain the aptitude to score a game yourself as well as interpret (at least at a fundamental level) the scorecards of other scorekeepers.

♦ ♦ ♦

Top of the First

SCHILLING PITCHING FOR THE DIAMONDBACKS.

Jeter (playing shortstop for the Yankees) struck out looking.

O'Neill (the Yankees' right fielder) doubled, but he was put out attempting to advance to third by a throw from the Arizona right fielder (Bautista) to the second baseman Counsell, followed by a throw to Williams, Arizona's third baseman.

The center fielder for New York (with the same surname as Arizona's third baseman—Williams) flied out to Arizona's center fielder, Finley.

Bottom of the First

CLEMENS PITCHING FOR THE YANKEES.

Womack (playing shortstop for Arizona) flied out to New York's center fielder, Williams.

Counsell (second baseman for Arizona) reached first on an error: a ground ball to the Yankees' first baseman, Martinez, thrown to but muffed by New York's pitcher (Clemens) covering first.

Gonzalez (left fielder for the Diamondbacks) grounded out to Martinez at first base, and Counsell advanced to second in the process.

Williams (playing third base for Arizona) struck out swinging.

Top of the Second

SCHILLING PITCHING FOR THE DIAMONDBACKS.

Martinez struck out swinging.

Posada (New York's catcher) flied out to Arizona's left fielder, Gonzalez.

Spencer (the left fielder for New York) flied out to Arizona's center fielder, Finley.

Bottom of the Second
CLEMENS PITCHING FOR THE YANKEES.

Finley (Arizona's center fielder) grounded out by hitting the ball to New York's shortstop (Jeter), who threw the ball to the first baseman (Martinez).

Bautista (right fielder for the Diamondbacks) walked.

Grace (playing first base for Arizona) singled, sending Bautista to second base.

Miller (the Arizona catcher) struck out swinging.

Schilling struck out looking.

Top of the Third
SCHILLING PITCHING FOR THE DIAMONDBACKS.

Soriano (New York's second baseman) flied out to Arizona's right fielder, Bautista.

Brosius (playing third base for the Yankees) popped out to the Diamondbacks' first baseman, Grace.

Clemens struck out swinging.

Bottom of the Third
CLEMENS PITCHING FOR THE YANKEES.

Womack struck out swinging.

Counsell singled.

Gonzalez struck out swinging.

Williams singled, sending Counsell to second base.

Finley struck out swinging.

Top of the Fourth
SCHILLING PITCHING FOR THE DIAMONDBACKS.

Jeter flied out to the right fielder, Bautista.

O'Neill struck out swinging.

Williams struck out looking.

Bottom of the Fourth
CLEMENS PITCHING FOR THE YANKEES.

Bautista flied out to the center fielder, Williams.

Grace singled.

Miller struck out swinging.
Schilling struck out swinging.

Top of the Fifth

SCHILLING PITCHING FOR THE DIAMONDBACKS.

Martinez flied out to the center fielder, Finley.
Posada struck out looking.
Spencer popped out to the second baseman, Counsell.

Bottom of the Fifth

CLEMENS PITCHING FOR THE YANKEES.

Womack grounded out, second baseman Soriano to the first baseman, Martinez.
Counsell grounded out, shortstop Jeter to the first baseman, Martinez.
Gonzalez reached first base on a fielding error by the second baseman, Soriano.
Williams grounded into a fielder's choice, shortstop Jeter to the second baseman, Soriano. Williams to first. Gonzalez out.

Top of the Sixth

SCHILLING PITCHING FOR THE DIAMONDBACKS.

Soriano struck out swinging.
Brosius struck out swinging.
Clemens flied out to the right fielder, Bautista.

Bottom of the Sixth

CLEMENS PITCHING FOR THE YANKEES.

Finley singled.
Bautista doubled. Finley scored. Bautista was put out attempting to advance to third, center fielder Williams to the shortstop, Jeter, to the third baseman, Brosius.
Grace grounded out, second baseman Soriano to the first baseman, Martinez.
Miller struck out swinging.

Top of the Seventh

SCHILLING PITCHING FOR THE DIAMONDBACKS.

Jeter singled.

O'Neill singled. Jeter to second.

Williams grounded into a fielder's choice, first baseman Grace to the shortstop, Womack. Williams to first. O'Neill out. Jeter to third.

Martinez singled. Williams to second. Jeter scored.

Posada flied out to the left fielder, Gonzalez.

Spencer flied out to the center fielder, Finley.

Bottom of the Seventh

CLEMENS PITCHING FOR THE YANKEES.

Schilling struck out looking.

Womack singled.

Stanton relieved Clemens.

Womack was put out at second base, "caught stealing" by the catcher, Posada, to the shortstop, Jeter.

Counsell popped out to the first baseman, Martinez.

Top of the Eighth

SCHILLING PITCHING FOR THE DIAMONDBACKS.

Soriano hit a home run.

Brosius struck out swinging.

Justice (batting for Stanton) singled.

Batista relieved Schilling.

Jeter grounded into a fielder's choice, third baseman Williams to the second baseman, Counsell. Jeter to first. Justice out.

Johnson relieved Batista.

Knoblauch (batting for O'Neill) flied out to the right fielder, Bautista.

Bottom of the Eighth

RIVERA PITCHING FOR THE YANKEES.

Knoblauch playing left field.

Spencer playing right field.

Gonzalez struck out swinging.

Williams struck out swinging.

Finley singled.

Bautista struck out swinging.

Top of the Ninth

JOHNSON PITCHING FOR THE DIAMONDBACKS.

Williams flied out to the center fielder, Finley.

Martinez grounded out, shortstop Womack to the first baseman, Grace.

Posada struck out swinging.

Bottom of the Ninth

RIVERA PITCHING FOR THE YANKEES.

Grace singled.

Dellucci substituted for Grace at first base.

Miller grounded into a fielder's choice. Dellucci to second on the pitcher Rivera's throwing error. Miller to first.

Bell (batting for Johnson) grounded into a fielder's choice, pitcher Rivera to the third baseman, Brosius. Dellucci out. Miller to second. Bell to first.

Cummings substituted for Miller at second base.

Womack doubled. Cummings scored. Bell to third.

Counsell hit by pitch.

Gonzalez singled. Counsell to second base. Womack to third base. Bell scored.

◆ 2 ◆

What Just Happened?
Getting the Basics Down

Filling in the Blanks: Understanding What Has Been "Scored," and How

If you've "read" the scorecard from Game 7 of the 2001 World Series, a great deal (if not most) of the methodology employed should be evident. Nonetheless, for the sake of being as comprehensive as possible, let's look at and analyze what we have.

First and foremost, note that the scorecard tells a somewhat extended and involved story, but the story is made up of a number of individual stories, each story telling the journey of each batter from the batter's box to wherever that batter ended up (be it scoring a run, being left on base or going back to the dugout without reaching base at all).

Strike Outs—Ground Outs—Fly Ball Outs

A batter's fate in any given plate appearance is most easily recorded when the batter is put out before reaching base at all, and the easiest of those instances to deal with is when the batter is put out on a strikeout: all that needs to be done is inscribe a "K" (or another symbol, such as "SO," as apparently was the practice of President Eisenhower when he often scored baseball games) in the box of the scorecard that corresponds to the batter's time at bat.

(See—for instance—Martinez in the top of the second inning.)

Note, however, that it is quite easy, and common, for a scorekeeper to differentiate between a "swinging" strikeout (where the last pitch is swung on and missed) from a "called" strikeout (where the last pitch is not swung at but the umpire calls it a strike nevertheless). Typically, a standard letter K is used to denote a swinging strikeout, and a reversed K (Я) is used for called strikeouts, (as is the case in Jeter's plate appearance in the top of the first inning). At the same time, some scorekeepers use the symbol "Kc" or other symbols to denote "called" strikeouts, or make no differentiation at all.

It bears mentioning that the genesis for the virtually universal practice of using the letter K—in one form or another—to denote strikeouts is one of the great mysteries in baseball. Endless speculation has been made about how K came to symbolize a strikeout (similar to speculation about why the shortstop is 6 and not 5, and the third baseman is 5 and not 6), and many theories have been put forward about it, but none that I know of is altogether conclusive to the exclusion of all other theories. From a scorekeeper's perspective it doesn't really matter where this abbreviation came from, and because it's so deeply ingrained in the lexicon of baseball, it's simple, effective, widely recognized and understood, and it is here to stay regardless of exactly what its origins may be. Therefore, I defer to the many baseball historians that have investigated the issue and suggest that their works be consulted in this regard by anyone inclined to do so.

Recording most every other manner in which a batter can be put out without reaching base is also simple and straightforward. All that needs be done is for the number or numbers of the fielder or fielders that put out the "batter-runner" to be written in the appropriate scoring box.

(For those unfamiliar with the terminology, note that a "batter-runner" is defined by the MLB rulebook as follows. **"BATTER-RUNNER is a term that identifies the offensive player** [no humor intended by the authors, as far as I know] **who has just finished his time at bat until he is put out or until the play on which he becomes a runner ends."**)

For instance, Bautista (leading off the bottom of the fourth inning for Arizona) flied out to the Yankees' center fielder. Consequently, an 8 is recorded in that box. The same holds true for Posada in the top of the second inning (having flied out to the Diamondbacks' left fielder—7) and Clemens in the top of the sixth inning (having flied out to Arizona's right fielder—9).

Note, however, that a "U" is added to the "3" that appears in the box representing Gonzalez's plate appearance in the bottom of the first inning. This is done to denote that Gonzalez's ground ball was fielded by the first baseman who then stepped on first base with the ball to put out Gonzalez before

Gonzalez could get there: In other words, it wasn't a fly out or a line drive caught by the first baseman.

Simply put, a fielder's number, all by itself, typically indicates that the batter was put out on a fly ball, a line drive or a pop-up by the fielder whose number is recorded. However, if a fielder puts out a batter without the assistance of another fielder, but the batted ball was not caught on the fly to do so, a "U"—standing for "unassisted"—in addition to the number representing the appropriate fielder is used to denote that fact.

Then there are the cases where one fielder throws to another fielder to put out a batter.

For instance, in the top of the ninth, Martinez hit a ground ball to the Arizona shortstop that was thrown to first base to put him out, 6–3. Alternatively, Grace (batting in the bottom of the sixth) hit a ground ball to the Yankees second baseman that was thrown to first base to put him out, 4–3.

In some cases, more than one fielder delivers the ball to the fielder who ultimately puts out a runner. (See, for example, the putout of Bautisia trying to advance from second to third in the bottom of the sixth inning, or O'Neil doing the same thing in the top of the first inning.) In those cases, the numbers of all fielders handling the ball are simply listed in sequence.

A Quick Aside Concerning "Double Plays"

I wish I had a nickel for every time that I've heard an announcer declare that a batter hit into a "6-4-3" or "4-6-3" (etc.) double play.

It's a common occurrence, and all the announcer is doing is using the parlance of scorekeeping to let his or her audience know that the double play being described was made by a certain fielder throwing the ball to another fielder who, in turn, threw the ball to yet another fielder to log two putouts on one pitch.

The point is that it would be more accurate to declare that it was (for example) a "6–4 / 4–3" double play, instead of a "6-4-3 double play" for the reason that a double play is—by definition—two separate outs made one after the other. Using the "X-Y-Z" shorthand for reference to double plays is commonly understood, and it does no real disservice to the game even though lumping the fielders together for descriptive purposes—as though the double play was in fact one play—is not altogether accurate.

Reaching Base

There are many ways for a batter to reach base. The most common—at least in the higher levels of play—are when a batter hits a single, double, triple or a home run.

Those occurrences are easily recorded by drawing a line in the appropriate box on the scorecard—as if the box framed the playing field itself—from "home plate" to the base where the batter ends up. (See, for example, Grace's single in the bottom of the second inning, Womack's double in the bottom of the ninth inning, or Soriano's home run in the top of the eighth inning.)

Note also that in addition to drawing a line around the "base path" in the appropriate scoring box, a marking is made to denote a single, double, triple, or home run in the appropriate quadrant of the scoring box.

In the scorecard of our sample game, this is done by using one or more "slashes" (as appropriate), but any other method (whether it is using dots, vertical lines, or anything else) that conveys the information will do.

Of course, there are ways for batters to reach base other than by of base hits. When that happens, the line from home plate to the base attained is drawn—as before—but instead of slashes (or the like) being employed, other symbols are used. For instance, Counsell reached base in the bottom of the ninth inning because he was hit by a pitch. Therefore, an HB (standing for "hit batsman") is used to record that fact in the lower right-hand quadrant of his scoring box in the ninth inning. Similarly, Bautista drew a walk in the bottom of the second inning. Consequently, a BB (representing a base on balls—a walk) is written in the appropriate portion of the appropriate box on the scorecard for him.

Counsell reached base on an error in the bottom of the first inning by virtue of a dropped throw from the first baseman to the pitcher covering first. Therefore, a 3-E1 appears in that box, showing that the first basemen made a throw to the pitcher that could/should have resulted in a putout (which means that the first baseman gets credit for an assist under Rule 9.10(a)(1)). At the same time, the pitcher's error in muffing the thrown ball accounted for Counsell reaching base safely, and therefore Counsell is properly considered as having reached base on an error.

Some scorers differentiate errors where a fielder fails to catch or otherwise properly field a batted or thrown ball that should have been caught or fielded, from those errors arising from a bad throw, by various means. A common methodology is to add a "T" to "throwing errors" (e.g.—"E6T" when the shortstop makes a wild throw to first base in an attempt to retire a batter, and a good throw would have put out the batter), and using no extra symbol when the error was not a throwing error (e.g.—"E6" when the shortstop should have caught the ball, but didn't, and that resulted in a blown opportunity to put out a runner or a batter, and/or otherwise allowed the advancement along the base paths by a runner or runners that would not have occurred but for the error.)

Advancement from Base to Base: Level One

Once on base, further advancement of a runner along the base paths is represented by continuing to draw lines from "base to base" in the scoring boxes of the runners who advance and indicating who/what accounted for the advancement.

For instance, Jeter reached base on a single to begin the top of the seventh inning. He advanced to second base as a result of O'Neill hitting a single as well. That is represented by the line drawn from "first base" to "second base" in Jeter's box and the number 2 inserted in the top right-hand quadrant of the scoring box (inasmuch as it was what the number two batter in the order— O'Neill—did that led to Jeter's advancement).

Then Jeter advanced to third base, as indicated by a line drawn from "second base" to "third base," and it can easily be seen that the advancement to third base was attributable to Williams (the third batter in the order) putting the ball into play because 3 appears in the top left-hand quadrant of Jeter's scoring box.

Finally, Jeter scored a run by virtue of the single that was hit by Martinez (batting fourth in the Yankees lineup). Therefore a line is drawn from "third base" to "home plate" and the number 4 appears in the lower left-hand quadrant of Jeter's scorekeeping box.

Note that the 4 in the lower left-hand quadrant also serves to indicate that the run Jeter scored was a run "batted in" by Martinez. However, if because of some technicality in the rules governing scorekeeping regarding when a batter is entitled or not to credit for a run batted in, Martinez would not be properly considered as having officially "batted in" Jeter, the 4 would still be appropriate, but an extra notation (such as putting the 4 in parentheses, as this portion of this very long sentence is in parentheses) would indicate that although Jeter scored as a result of Martinez's actions, it is not one officially counted as a run batted in by Martinez.

Note also that Jeter scoring a run is graphically represented by the middle portion of the "diamond" being filled in. This is a common scorekeeping technique and is widely employed, albeit with some variations. For instance, some scorekeepers will write the "number" of the run—that is, whether it's the first, second, third [or whatever] run scored by the scoring runner's team—into the middle of the box instead of filling in the area, so as to put a finer edge on the process of recording and keeping track of runs that score during the course of a game.

Advancement from Base to Base: Level Two

Trickier advancements/putouts require a little extra effort to make them clear.

For example, in the top of the first inning, O'Neill was put out (9-4-5) after he had made second base safely: he was put out trying to stretch a bona fide double into a triple. In order to make it clear how/when O'Neill was put out, an arrow in the scoring box from the top right-hand quadrant to the top left-hand quadrant indicates that the 9-4-5 putout was made after O'Neill hit his double.

Granted, you could figure that out without the arrow, as there is no other feasible way for O'Neill to have been put out "9-4-5" while Williams was in the batter's box, or as a consequence of Williams having flied out to the center fielder to end the inning, but the arrow serves to clarify how/when O'Neill was put out without the necessity of having to think through how/when that putout occurred.

The same holds true for Batista in the bottom of the sixth. Once again, you could figure out that the 8-6-5 putout must have happened when Batista (like O'Neill) tried to stretch a double into a triple, but the arrow makes doing so much easier.

In short, "connective" arrows are not altogether necessary to describe what transpired, inasmuch as one could infer what must have happened, but in terms of clarity, the arrows are not altogether superfluous: they serve to make the scorecard easier to "read," and in some cases—cases similar to those recounted here—using this technique (or something comparable) can be vital to having the scorecard "make sense."

Perhaps the most common situation when it's a good idea to employ this technique is when a batter hits a single, but advances to second base because the defensive team tries to put out a runner that was already on base: In other words, it's a single followed by a fielder's choice that got the batter to second base, and making that clear in some manner will serve to avoid having to think through how/when a particular batter advanced beyond first base.

Substitutions

Consider the bottom of the ninth in our sample game.

The leadoff batter (Grace) hit a single to get to first base. Dellucci came into the game to run for Grace. Then Miller reached first base on a fielder's choice (because the Yankees' pitcher [Rivera] chose to throw the ball that Miller put into play to second base instead of putting out Miller at first, and but for Rivera's throw to second base being a wild throw, Dellucci would have been forced out at second base).

That was followed by Bell coming in to bat for Johnson and reaching base on a fielder's choice (inasmuch as Dellucci was put out at third base [1–5] on the ball that Bell put into play).

Note also the Cummings took over running the bases for Miller, so when Womack doubled to drive in a run, it was Cummings who scored the run that tied the game, and it was Bell—who batted in place of Johnson—who ultimately scored the winning run for Arizona.

The point is, substitutions are the bane of a scorer's existence, especially when they occur during the course of an inning and not simply between innings when they are easier to deal with.

Anyone who has ever tried to score an All-Star Game will tell you it's a major headache to keep track of who leaves a game and who takes that player's place, what position changes (if any) are involved, and when (exactly) it happens, all while keeping track of everything else taking place during the course of a game. However, it's not too difficult to do if "shortcuts" are handy, and a few can be found on the sample scorecard.

For instance, in our sample game, there's Knoblauch coming in to bat for O'Neill in the top of the eighth inning, indicated by Knoblauch's name appearing directly below O'Neill's and the horizontal line drawn between the seventh and eighth inning in the row for the second batter in the Yankees' lineup.

In addition, the "B8" next to Knoblauch's name on the scorecard indicates that Knoblauch took the field to play on defense for the Yankees in the bottom of the eighth inning, and he was positioned in left field (inasmuch as the number 7 is listed as his position). At the same time, Spencer's shift from left field to right field in the bottom of the eighth inning is indicated in a similar fashion.

The same is true for Justice coming into the game in the top of the eighth as a pinch-hitter, as well as Dellucci and Cummings coming in as pinch-runners in the bottom of the ninth and Bell coming in as a pinch-hitter for Arizona in the same inning. At the same time, note that no vertical line is drawn in the case of Dellucci or Cummings because neither of them batted for the player that was substituted out of the game. However, a vertical line is drawn for Bell because he batted for Johnson.

Note also the "Xs" that appear in the top of the eighth inning, as well as the bottom of the seventh and eighth innings. They were drawn to indicate when pitching changes were made by the opposing team.

Abbreviations

There are a number of abbreviations commonly employed by scorekeepers on scorecards, as well as in the listing of the cumulative totals of various statistical categories.

A few of them (such as FC, BB and HB) appear on the sample scorecard. However, there are many others.

Listed below are a number of those used in scorekeeping.

2B = Double (two-base hit).
3B = Triple (three-base hit).
A = Assist.
AB = At-Bat (i.e., a plate appearance that did not result in a sacrifice bunt or fly, a walk or a hit by pitch or an award of first base because of obstruction or interference).
BB = Base on balls (walk).
BK = Balk.
BT = Bunt (or balls thrown, depending on context).
CS = Caught Stealing.
DH = Designated Hitter.
DI = Defensive Indifference.

DP = Double Play.

E = Error.

ER = Earned Run.

ERA = Earned Run Average.

F = Fly (ball) or Foul (ball).

FC = Fielder's Choice.

FO = Foul Out.

H = Hit or Hits.

HB = Hit Batsman (Hit by Pitched Ball).

HP = Hit by Pitched Ball (Hit Batsman).

HR = Home Run.

I = Interference.

IBB = Intentional Base on Balls (Intentional Walk).

IF = Infield Fly.

IH = Infield Hit.

IP = Innings Pitched.

IW = Intentional Walk (Intentional Base on Balls).

K = Strikeout (of any sort, but implicitly a strikeout on a swinging third strike if another abbreviation is used to signify a strikeout on a called third strike).

Ж or Kc = Strikeout on a called third strike.

Ks = Strikeout on a "swinging" third strike.

L = Line Drive.

LOB = (Runner or Runners) Left On Base.

OBS = Obstruction.

PA = Plate Appearance (not to be confused with an At-Bat).

PB = Passed Ball.

PH = Pinch Hitter.

PT = Pitches Thrown.

PO = Putout (sometimes "Pick-Off," depending on context).

R = Run.

RBI = Run Batted In.

SAC = Sacrifice.

SB = Stolen Base.

SF = Sacrifice Fly.

SH = Sacrifice "Hit" (a/k/a Sacrifice Bunt, inasmuch as SB could be confused with Stolen Base).

SO = Strikeout.

ST = Strikes Thrown.
TP = Triple Play.
TPT = Total Pitches Thrown.
U = Unassisted (putout).
W = Walk (base on balls).
WP = Wild Pitch.

♦ 3 ♦

Where and When Did It Happen?
Filling in the Details

Advanced Techniques

As bare bones as the sample scorecard employed up to this point might appear to be, consider the following: a scorecard from the 1912 World Series between the Boston Red Sox and the New York Giants (shown on the next page).

On one level, it's marvelous: With only one notation in each scoring box, it tells you what each batter ultimately achieved—he was either put out (as denoted by a 1, 2 or 3 representing the first, second or third out of the inning), scored a run (as denoted by an R), or was left on base (as indicated by an LB in the case of the Red Sox's side of the ledger, and an × in the case of the Giants).

It's remarkable in its own way, elegant in its simplicity. At the same time, the scorecard falls woefully short of what can be "scored" using a minimum of additional notations. It doesn't tell you—among many other things—how any given batter reached base, nor does it indicate whether a batter's arrival on base was by way of a single, double, triple, home run, error, fielder's choice, or any other manner.

Moreover, fielding is left entirely to the imagination, and what was done in terms of pitching is anyone's guess.

That said, we'll return to the seventh game of the 2001 World Series, only this time with a more comprehensive scorecard (shown on pages 35 and 36).

THE BASEBALL RESEARCH JOURNAL

October 9th 1912

BOSTON "RED SOX," Champions of the American League

	1	2	3	4	5	6	7	8	9	10	11	R	H	O	A	E
1. HOOPER, R. F.																
2. YERKES, 2nd B.																
3. SPEAKER, C. F.																
4. LEWIS, L. F.																
5. GARDNER, 3rd B.																
6. STAHL, 1st B.																
7. WAGNER, S. S.																
8. CADY, C.; 9. CARRIGAN, C.; 11. THOMAS, C.; 12. NUNAMAKER, C.																
14. WOOD, P.; 15. HALL, P.; 16. O'BRIEN, P.; 17. COLLINS, P.; 18. BEDIENT, P.; 22. PAPE, P.																
Total																

(Look for number on score board for pitcher and catcher)

23. BALL, Inf.; 31. ENGLE, Inf.; 43. KRUG, Inf.; 51. BRADLEY, Inf.; 61. HENRIKSEN, O. F.
UMPIRES—(1) RIGLER and (2) KLEM, National League. (3) EVANS and (4) O'LOUGHLIN, American League.

BATTING FOR FOUR HUNDRED FOR THIRTY YEARS

CUSHING PROCESS

TWO STORES

166 CANAL STREET, NEAR NORTH STATION AND WASHINGTON STREET, CORNER HAYWARD PLACE

NEW YORK "GIANTS," Champions of the National League

	1	2	3	4	5	6	7	8	9	10	11	R	H	O	A	E
1. Snodgrass																
2. DOYLE, 2nd B.																
3. Becker C. F.																
4. MURRAY, R. F.																
5. MERKLE, 1st B.																
6. HERZOG, 3rd B.																
18. HARTLEY, C.; 8. MEYERS, C.; 9. WILSON, C.																
7. FLETCHER, S. S.																
11. AMES, P.; 12. CRANDALL, P.; 14. MARQUARD, P.; 15. MATHEWSON, P.; 16. TESREAU, P.; 17. WILTSE, P.																
Total																

(Look for number on Score Board for Pitcher and Catcher)

22. BECKER, O. F.; 23. BURNS, O. F.; 21. McCORMICK, O. F.; 49. SHAFER, Inf.; 51. GROH, Inf.; 61. ROBINSON, Coach; 71. McGRAW, Mgr.
UMPIRES—(1) RIGLER and (2) KLEM, National League. (3) EVANS and (4) O'LOUGHLIN, American League.

IN BASEBALL, THE QUESTION IS, WILL IT BE THE "RED SOX" OR "GIANTS"? BUT IN HEADWEAR THERE IS NO QUESTION

THE CHAMPION HAT OF THE WORLD

IS, HAS BEEN, AND ALWAYS WILL BE

THE AMERICAN HAT   A "STETSON"   FOR AMERICAN MEN

Here, a myriad of details missing from the basic scorecard are recorded. For starters, the date of the game, its location, the start and end time and the identity of the scorekeeper are indicated. Moreover, the at-bats, runs scored, hits, doubles, triples, home runs, walks, hit by pitch, strikeouts, sacrifices, stolen bases and runs batted in for each batter are tallied, as well as the putouts, assists and errors for each player.

In addition, the pitchers are catalogued, along with notations regarding the number of innings each one pitched, as well as the number of batters faced, how many of those batters had official at-bats (as opposed to plate appearances that do not count as at-bats, such as walks, sacrifices and the like), the number of strikeouts each pitcher achieved, the runs (overall) charged to each pitcher (as well as the earned runs), the number of wild pitches, balks, strikes and balls thrown, and the total pitches thrown by each pitcher.

	R	H	E			
Visitor YANKEES	0 0 0 0 0 0 1 1 0	2	6	3	Date: 11/__ Scored By: AW	
Home DIAMONDBACKS	0 0 0 0 0 1 0 0 2	3	11	0	Place: PHOENIX Game Start 6:28 Game End 9:48	

PLAYERS ① ② ③ ④ ⑤ ⑥ ⑦ ⑧ ⑨

1. WOMACK (L) 6
2. COUNSELL (L) 4
3. GONZALEZ (L) 7
4. WILLIAMS 5
5. FINLEY (L) 8
6. BAUTISTA 9
7. GRACE (L) 3 / DELLUCCI (B9) 8
8. MILLER / CUMMINGS (B9) R
9. SCHILLING 1 / BATISTA 1 / JOHNSON 1 / BELL (B9) 8

PITCHERS	W-L	IP	BF	AB	K	BB	H	R	ER	WP	HP	BK	ST	BT	TPT
CLEMENS		6.1	28	27	10	1	7	1	1	0	0	0	75	39	114
STANTON (L)		0.2	1	1	0	0	0	0	0	0	0	0	3	1	4
RIVERA	L	1.1	10	9	3	0	4	2	1	0	1	0	21	7	23

SCORER'S NOTES: 3-E1 CHANGED FROM E3 @ B2. CUMMINGS ENTERS GAME AFTER [9] B9. INFIELD & OUTFIELD IN FOR [2] & [3] ~ B9.

At the same time, the runs, hits, errors and runners left on base are tallied for each team in each inning, and comments are noted about the weather, the attendance, and other aspects of the contest that do not readily lend themselves to being recorded in the scoring boxes.

Moreover, the putouts are noted by the numbers 1, 2 or 3 (circled in the appropriate scoring boxes), and the scoring boxes that are not used have lines drawn through them to clarify which batters did not come to the plate in any given inning.

On top of all that, "stars" are included to denote outstanding fielding plays, and notations—vis-à-vis where balls that resulted in batters reaching base were hit—are employed.

Also, balls caught on the fly are more precisely described, with the letter "F" used to indicate a fly ball (as opposed to a line drive, where the letter "L" would be appropriate), and balls caught in foul territory to put out a batter are indicated with the letters "FO," representing a "foul out."

Recording Where Balls Are Hit

When a ball is put into play and the batter—and/or a runner or runners on base—is put out, it's easy to discern where the batter hit the ball.

In other words, a 6–3 putout on the scorecard tells you that the ball was hit to the shortstop, a 3U means that the ball was hit to the first baseman, and an 8 (or F8 or L8) indicates that the ball was hit to the area of the playing field where the center fielder is typically stationed.

However, when a batter reaches base, where the ball was hit to is not recorded when the scorecard reflects only the fact that a batter reached base.

One way to indicate where balls were hit (when one or more putouts don't arise from the ball being put into play) that many scorers use is to draw lines on the scorecard to depict the flight of the ball. Some scorers employ fairly elaborate coding systems to do so, and other scorers even employ different colored pens or pencils to further "fine tune" where pitches were hit (as well as other aspects of the game).

Regardless, all those techniques are valid in their own way, and anyone comfortable using them cannot be fairly criticized. However, the system employed in this "expanded" scorecard of the seventh game of the 2001 World Series has considerable merit, in a number of ways, because it is relatively simple yet highly descriptive, and it doesn't require artistic skills, complex notations, or otherwise make any given scoring box too "busy" or complicated.

Here, the numbering of fielders is employed to designate the areas of the playing field where balls were hit. In other words, a ground ball that was hit between the second baseman and the first baseman goes into the book as a single, with the notation "43" beneath the symbol (dash) representing a single. See, for example, Womack's single in the bottom of the seventh inning.

Balls hit to the outfield are dealt with in a similar fashion. See, for example, Grace's single to left field in the bottom of the second inning, Miller's single to center field in the bottom of the ninth, or Bautista's double into the gap between left field and center field in the bottom of the sixth inning.

A finer edge can be put on this by recording balls hit down the lines of the playing field by using the symbol "+," as in the case of Womack in the bottom of the ninth.

Also, balls that never leave the infield, but nevertheless count as hits, can be dealt with by including the symbol "IH" (Infield Hit) with the number of the fielder or fielders in whose direction the ball was hit (as in the case of Williams in the bottom of the third).

When Things Happen

Most of what happens during the course of a baseball game happens in a natural progression, and it's therefore usually easy to decipher when one thing occurred in relationship to another.

For example, in the top of the second inning, it is obvious that the inning began with Martinez striking out, followed by Posada flying out to left field, then Spencer flying out to center field. In fact, aside from the employment of an arrow to indicate that O'Neill was put out trying to reach third base after hitting a double in the top of the first inning, and Bautista doing the same thing in the bottom of the sixth inning, no special notations are required to keep the chronology of this sample game straight.

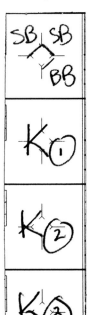

However, consider the following hypothetical half-inning.

Here, you know that the first batter reached on a walk, and thereafter stole second base, then third base, and ended up at third base at the conclusion of the inning after the three batters that followed him each struck out in turn.

Inasmuch as great attention is given these days to what batters do with runners "in scoring position" (that is, when there is a runner at second base and/or third base, as opposed to when there are no runners on base at all or only a runner at first base), when the runner on base stole second base and third base becomes important.

From the way this sample half-inning is laid out, it could very well be that the runner remained at first base while the next two batters came to the plate, and therefore it was only the third batter who left a runner in scoring position. By the same token, the runner could have advanced to second, and maybe even third base, while the first batter following him was at the plate striking out, and therefore all three batters made outs with a runner in scoring position.

Consequently, a scorer is well served to be cognizant of

situations such as this and make sure that some system is employed to denote when things happen on the field when there is call to do so.

In this case, a simple solution is to write down which batter was at the plate when the runner stole second, and when the runner stole third (using the batter's number in the batting order), as follows.

Now it's clear that when the second batter in the inning struck out, there was no runner in scoring position, but that was not the case for the other two batters.

Another way to keep straight when things happen, when it isn't obvious, is simply to make a note on the scorecard to clarify the progression of events (akin to the notation made on the Diamondbacks' side of the scorecard in the sample game about when Cummings entered the game for Arizona as a pinch-runner—not right after Miller reached base, but after Bell's plate appearance).

♦ 4 ♦

How Did It Happen?

Digging Deeper

Recording Pitches

One way to record pitches is to indicate in the batter's scoring box what the count was when the batter's plate appearance ended.

For example, "2–2" could be written into the scoring box of Jeter in the top of the first inning to indicate that he struck out after having had two balls and two strikes delivered to him. Of course, the sequence of the pitches is left to the imagination using that system, and whether the strikes were called strikes, foul balls or pitches swung at and missed is also overlooked. Moreover, situations like Soriano's in the top of the eighth inning, where four pitches—none of them balls—were delivered to him before he hit a home run, would be reflected only as an "0–2" count, and an accurate "pitch count" would be impossible to discern from a scorecard that employed that methodology.

However, many commercial scorecards have boxes in each batter's scoring box in which balls and strikes can be recorded. Usually, there are two for strikes and three for balls. Typically, scorers will simply "fill in" those boxes as pitches are made. However, the sequence of pitches is impossible to discern using that method, as well as the types of strikes, and foul balls struck after a two-strike count are overlooked entirely.

Inasmuch as the rulebook does not require the official scorer to report the number of pitches thrown during the course of a game—let alone the results of each and every pitch, or their sequence—any approach taken vis-à-vis this issue is fine, including ignoring the topic altogether. But the system employed on the sample scorecard here is simple, easy and accurate, though exactly how it works is not entirely self-evident, so here's the explanation.

Although strikes can arise in three ways—called strikes, fouled-off pitches or pitches swung on and missed—pitches thrown for balls are all the same in terms of describing them: they were all delivered outside of the strike zone and the batter didn't swing at them. Consequently, only one symbol is required to record balls, and the one that makes the most sense (because doing so will serve as a key to deciphering all the pitches in any given sequence, as explained later) is using the number of the pitch thrown. In other words, if the first pitch thrown is a ball, the number 1 is recorded. If the next called ball is the third pitch in the sequence, a number 3 is employed to record that pitch (the second ball delivered to the batter), and so on.

As far as strikes are concerned, a dot is used to denote a called strike. (Note that this represents the most passive of symbols, reflecting the batter's inaction when the umpire calls a strike.)

A ball struck at and missed is denoted with an X. (Note that this represents the batter's failure to make contact, so the box is—in a sense— "nullified" by being crossed out entirely.)

Foul balls are reflected by a check mark. (Note that this is—in a way—a graphic representation of the ball hitting the bat and flying off in a wayward direction.)

In passing, note also that no special notation is used for foul tips—balls that come off the bat and go directly into the catcher's mitt and are caught— inasmuch as foul tips are really the same as balls struck at and missed altogether under the playing rules. However, an additional symbol of some kind may of course be used for foul tips, if desired.

Note also that strikes are written in the boxes reserved for them beginning in the top left-hand corner, then going across, then from left to right in the next row, and so on.

Employing this system, you can see that Posada (in the top of the ninth) swung at the first pitch and missed. He fouled off the next two pitches and ultimately struck out swinging on the fourth and final pitch.

Then there is Womack in the bottom of the seventh. The first pitch was a called strike. The second pitch was swung at and missed. The third and fourth pitches were called balls. The fifth and sixth pitches were fouled off, but the seventh and final pitch was grounded between first and second base for a single.

Of course, some plate appearances consist of only one pitch, as is the case of Brosius in the top of the third, O'Neill in the top of the seventh, Jeter in the top of the eighth, Bautista in the bottom of the sixth and Bell in the bottom of the ninth. They are in marked contrast to Martinez in the fifth, who went to a full count after five pitches, fouled off the next five pitches, and finally flied out to center field on the 11th and final pitch.

A Note About Using Notes

Because almost everything that happens during the course of a baseball game lends itself so easily to being recorded by abbreviations and symbols, some scorekeepers feel that everything that could possibly happen needs to be codified into some sort of hieroglyphic. Consequently, those scorekeepers will conjure up special symbols for things as rare as a runner being called out for running too far outside the baseline to avoid being tagged out, for passing a preceding runner, or just about anything along those lines you could care to imagine.

There is nothing wrong with doing that, per se. In fact, a scorer going that far is worthy of some degree of admiration for trying to be so thoroughly comprehensive. However, it has its drawbacks, at least in two significant ways.

First, because of the rarity of those sorts of things happening, it's difficult and taxing to recall just how to record those occurrences with the ease one would have for something far more common, such as using SB to signify runner advancement by a stolen base.

Perhaps even more troublesome is that using "special" abbreviations for odd and unusual happenings makes it difficult for other people to read the scorecard. Any deviation from the simple vocabulary of scorekeeping symbols and abbreviations leads to someone (who does not have knowledge of the special "language" being used) struggling to understand what is being referred to on the scorecard in those special cases.

Although it is a matter of personal choice, my feelings are that the better way to record things that are divorced from the norm is to write simple notes somewhere on the scorecard that explain any unusual set of circumstances that arose.

In other words, using standard symbols and abbreviations to record routine plays is logical and efficient. However, employing esoteric symbols and abbreviations for rare occurrences is not necessary because a few words written in the margins of a scorecard are sufficient to convey what happened.

All that said, there are some things that cry out to be recorded about a game that just don't fit in the score boxes of a scoring sheet, things that may not be altogether connected directly to the official data generated during the course of the game, but including them in the record of the game adds something to the scorecard, not unlike a sprig of parsley on a dinner plate—a garnish that is not intended to be eaten but nevertheless makes the meal more interesting and enjoyable.

A good illustration of that—and my personal all-time favorite—occurred when I noted on my scorecard the fact that a full lunar eclipse occurred during the final game of the 2004 World Series, when the Boston Red Sox finished their four-game sweep of the St. Louis Cardinals to win the World Series for the first time in 86 years.

The bottom line is that using notes to supplement a scorecard makes sense, and doing so (in many ways) is superior to resorting to the use of symbols and abbreviations that are cryptic to the point of being unintelligible to anyone other than the person who invented them and used them on his or her scorecard.

A Decidedly Different Approach to Scorekeeping (Scorekeeping in "Foreign Lands," and Why Every Scorekeeper Considers His Or Her Way of Keeping Score to Be the Best)

You may have noticed that in the preceding sections of this book regarding how to keep a scorecard, nothing—except referring to the fielders with the numbers one through nine—is absolute. It's all suggestions and recommendations, and deciding exactly how to score a baseball game is ultimately up to the person doing it.

In other words, you can keep score—effectively and "properly" —in any manner that works for you, as long as the essential game data can be gleaned from the completed scorecard. In fact, even using alternative numbers or symbols for the fielders is not prohibited (although I have never seen a scorecard where that's the case, or even heard a rumor of anyone ever doing so). It's the "American Way" of scorekeeping: rugged individualism through and through, with no constraints, rules or regulations.

That comes in large part from the fact that the rulebook calls upon the official scorer to do nothing more than report statistical tallies, like the names of the players who appeared in the game, the number of hits, the names of the pitchers, the number of innings pitched, and so forth, but how the official scorer records and collects that data is of no concern or consequence. All that is submitted to the league by an official scorer after a game is the official scorer's report, and the scorecard can be kept or discarded after the official scorer's report is filed because the scorecard is not considered an official record of the game. Therefore, there are no instructions, let alone mandates, in terms of what the official scorer's scorecard should look like in MLB's rulebook.

I believe that scorekeeping practices in America are pretty much a casual affair because baseball is so ingrained in American culture that there is no perception that anyone needs to be told how to watch, enjoy or appreciate the cumulative events that make up a baseball game, let alone how to record them. But baseball is played beyond the borders of the United States, and when it is—in an official and organized fashion—it is usually governed by the "IBAF" (the International Baseball Federation). When it comes to scorekeeping in the IBAF, a radically different approach is taken: As much as there is a lack of formal rules when it comes to how scorecards are drawn in the USA, even those kept by official scorers at the highest levels of the game, the IBAF is that much strict and rigid in mandating exactly how an official scorer fills in the scorecard of any given game.

Consider the following.

Although roughly 25 percent of the Official Rules of Baseball is dedicated to scorekeeping, not one word instructs the official scorekeeper in regards to how to record a hit, putout, error or anything else. On the other hand, the IBAF has a "Scoring Manual" that goes on for nearly 200 pages with the most detailed instructions imaginable regarding how—exactly—an official scorer *must* record the events that make up a baseball game.

Perhaps because baseball is somewhat alien and unfamiliar to those who don't have it woven into their fundamental cultural fabric, there is a perceived need to leave nothing to the imagination. However, scorekeeping in the IBAF is not altogether different from scorekeeping in baseball's homeland. The fielders are numbered 1 through 9 in the traditional manner, a grid is used as the basic framework, and the time-honored conventions of scorekeeping are followed in general. However, while scorers in the United States are free to do it as they deem best (as long as all the data called for in the official scorer's report can be culled from the scorecard by the scorer), a scorer in the IBAF is called upon to adhere strictly to a complex, rigid and elaborate methodology.

One of the most extreme examples can be found in the Australian Baseball Federation. There's no scorer's report. Rather, the scorecard is the official record of the game. Consequently, not only is the official scorer required to use the scorebook that the federation has deemed to be the only scorebook that can be used, but he or she must also use a host of super-precise abbreviations and symbols in a highly regulated manner, and make notations using a rainbow of different colored pencils: green (for hits and earned runs); blue (for strikeouts, walks, wild pitches and sacrifices); red (for errors, passed balls and unearned runs); orange (for double plays, the end of innings and out numbers); purple (for stolen bases) and plain lead (for fielded outs and bases advanced). RBIs are marked with a yellow highlighter.

On top of that, sometimes a mix of colors is employed when, for example, a batter strikes out but reaches first base by way of a passed ball (where blue is used to denote the strikeout and red is used to denote the passed ball), and as if that weren't enough, a detailed batter by batter, inning by inning pitch count is required, among a number of other things.

Given all that, it is not surprising that the Australia Baseball Federation has sanctioned a group—the Council of Australian Baseball Scorers—not only to train scorekeepers, but also to set up and administer examinations for achieving levels of accreditation—of which there are five!

For someone like me who has scored many games using a far simpler system, it is hard to understand why such a complex system is used by anyone, a system that requires far more effort than is necessary to achieve what is sought to be achieved. However, my personal perceptions are doubtless biased by my experiences and background, and I certainly do not wish to judge how other baseball organizations deal with scorekeeping. I would be greatly remiss in criticizing any organization that wants to really "get it right," so I will make no further comment other than to point out that one laudatory goal is achieved by mandating exactly how an official scorekeeper's scorecard is drawn: anyone who is familiar with the system employed can read any official scorecard without having to guess at what one or more idiosyncratic symbols or abbreviations might mean. Therefore, in that regard, "international baseball scorekeeping" is far superior to the more relaxed and loose techniques employed in the United States because it standardizes the scorekeeper's vernacular in much the same fashion that dictionaries and treatises on grammar standardize language, and it thereby facilitates orderly and accurate communication of baseball data.

All that aside, there is an old scorekeeping adage that comes from the largely unstructured world of scorekeeping here in the United States: every scorekeeper believes that the way that he or she keeps his or her scorecard is the best way to do it.

I've certainly found that to be the case, but the question is, why is that so?

The answer is that it's because the manner in which a scorekeeper (unfettered by an regulatory system) keeps his or her scorecard is the way that works best for that scorer in terms of getting down what that scorer feels is important (giving little attention to or perhaps even ignoring what others might consider important), and it's what he or she is used to and comfortable with. Therefore, it's natural for individual scorekeepers to consider their way of keeping score as being "the best."

It's much like someone having a favorite recipe for a dish that he or she loves, and that affection is not based on any objective standard. Rather, it comes from personal preferences and from using that recipe with good results (from the perspective of the individual using it) over an extended period of time.

It all comes down to the simple fact that what works, works, and as long as it works, everything is fine and the world of baseball will accommodate anyone and everyone that cares to join in the fun in any manner that they may choose.

♦ 5 ♦

Getting to Know Rule 9

The Rules of Scoring
(A Brief Overview of Baseball's Rulebook)

Baseball's official rulebook is published annually under the auspices of the Office of the Commissioner of Baseball. It governs "the playing of baseball games by the professional teams of Major League Baseball and the leagues that are members of the National Association of Professional Baseball Leagues" (the NAPBL being comprised of professional leagues that compete at levels below that of Major League Baseball and have agreements to operate as affiliates of Major League Baseball: the "Minor Leagues," in common parlance).

Although other baseball leagues may have rules that differ in some aspects from those rules found in MLB's rulebook, the "Official Baseball Rules" are followed—for the most part—universally.

♦ ♦ ♦

Prior to 2015, MLB's rulebook was divided into ten sections, with the rules governing scorekeeping being Rule 10, but beginning in 2015, MLB's rulebook was reorganized and divided into nine sections (as follows) with a separate section entitled Definition of Terms, and the scorekeeping rules being found in Rule 9.

The first section (Rule 1.00) is labeled "Objectives of the Game."

Rule 2.00 covers "The Playing Field."

Rule 3.00 addresses "Equipment and Uniforms."

Rule 4.00 is entitled "Game Preliminaries."

Rule 5.00's subject matter is "Playing the Game."

Rule 6.00 is dedicated to "Improper Play, Illegal Action and Misconduct." Rule 7.00 concerns itself with "Ending the Game." Rule 8.00 covers "The Umpire."

That leaves Rule 9—"The Official Scorer"—and the fact that Rule 9.00 constitutes a lot more than one-ninth of the rulebook in verbiage gives some indication of how involved the rules governing scorekeeping are, as well as the importance of scorekeeping in baseball.

Rule 9

Rule 9 is divided into 23 sub-sections, as follows.

9.01—Official Scorer (General Rules).

Here, the duties and responsibilities of an official scorer are laid out (among other things that do not necessarily fit into the more specific sub-sections that follow).

9.02—Official Score Report.

Here, the specific data that an official scorer is called upon to report to after each game are set forth in detail.

9.03—Official Score Report (Additional Rules).

Here, further instruction is given to the official scorer in terms of preparing the score report. In addition, how to "prove a box score" is laid out, how to deal with a player or players batting out of turn is dealt with, and issues attendant to called and forfeited games are covered.

9.04—Runs Batted In.

Here, as the title suggests, the rules regarding when to credit a batter with one or more runs batted in—and when not to do so—are set out.

9.05—Base Hits.

Here, the general principles and policies to be used to determine whether to credit a batter with a base hit, or not, are delineated, along with the technicalities that arise in a number of situations.

9.06—Determining Value of Base Hits.

Once it is determined that a batter is properly credited with a base hit, the question of whether to award credit for a single, double, triple or a home run arises. Inasmuch as Rule 9.06 addresses that question in the context of a number of situations, it is in reality an extension of Rule 9.05.

9.07—Stolen Bases and Caught Stealing.

9.08—Sacrifices.

9.09—Putouts.

9.10—Assists.

9.11—Double and Triple Plays.

9.12—Errors.

9.13—Wild Pitches and Passed Balls.

9.14—Bases on Balls.

9.15—Strikeouts.

9.16—Earned Runs and Runs Allowed.

9.17—Winning and Losing Pitcher.

9.18—Shutouts.

9.19—Saves for Relief Pitchers.

9.20—Statistics.

Note that this section does not directly impact scorekeeping per se. Rather, it concerns itself primarily with the league's appointment of an official statistician, and the duties and responsibilities of same. However, this sub-section also touches on how the official scorer is to credit players for "appearances" in games.

9.21—Determining Percentage Records.

Here, the formulas used to calculate win/loss percentages, batting averages, slugging percentages, fielding averages, earned run averages and on-base percentages are set forth.

9.22—Minimum Standards for Individual Championships.

Here, the methodologies employed for determining seasonal batting, pitching and fielding champions are spelled out.

9.23—Guidelines for Cumulative Performance Records.

This final sub-section of Rule 9 establishes the criteria for determining how long a given player's consecutive hitting streak, or consecutive-game hitting streak, or consecutive-game playing streak continues, and when it is properly considered as broken.

♦ ♦ ♦

All of Rule 9's provisions are covered in the following sections of this book, and examples—together with an analysis of each example—are given to clarify or otherwise explain those provisions and put them into context. In doing so, it is hoped that a complete and comprehensive picture of the rules governing scorekeeping will be had. However, not every possible situation (especially those that are rare, extraordinarily quirky, odd or otherwise bizarre) can be addressed specifically. Nevertheless, given the volume of text devoted by the rulebook to scorekeeping, coupled with what this book may add to it, situations where a logical and valid solution to a scorekeeping question cannot be readily found should be few and far between.

A Short Postscript

Although Rule 9.00 remained virtually unchanged for decades, in 2006, MLB's Rules Committee revised and otherwise modified a number of Rule 9's provisions, which revisions and modifications took effect in 2007.

For the sake of expediency, the discussion and analysis of Rule 9.00 that follows will not concern itself with exactly what changes were made, or otherwise make reference to the pre–2007 version of Rule 9, except when doing so contributes to a better understanding of the concepts and policies behind any given aspect of a rule or rules.

◆ 6 ◆

Speaking in Generalities
Rules 9.01–9.03

The rulebook begins, quite logically, with an index for the rules governing scorekeeping.

While being helpful in locating specific provisions pertaining to any given scorekeeping issue, it also evidences the attention that was given to Rule 9 by MLB's Rules Committee in its 2007 modifications, inasmuch as a specific index to Rule 9 did not exist prior to the 2007 revisions.

(In passing, it may be noted that the references that make up this index were for the most part simply moved from the rulebook's pre-existing general index at the back of the rulebook to the front of Rule 9, and those references that were not simply "relocated" appear in italics below.)

Appeal of scoring decision, 9.01(a)
Assists, 9.10
Base hits, 9.05, 9.06
Bases on balls, 9.14
Batting out of turn, 9.01(b)(4), 9.03(d)
Box scores, 9.02, 9.03(b)
Box scores, how to prove, 9.03(c)
Called game, 9.03 (c)
Caught stealing, 9.07(h)
Defensive indifference, 9.07(g)
Determining value of hits, 9.07
Double plays, 9.11
Earned runs, 9.16

Errors, 9.12
Forfeited game, 9.03(e)
Game-ending hits, 9.06(f), 9.06(g)
Individual championships, how determined, 9.22
League President, definition, DOT
Official Scorer, 9.01
Ordinary effort, definition, *DOT*
Oversliding, definition, DOT
Passed balls, 9.13
Percentages, how determined, 9.21
Protested game, 9.01(b)(3)

51

Rule 9.01—Official Scorer (General Rules)

Rule 9.01(a)   The Office of the Commissioner, with respect to Major League games, and the Minor League President, with respect to Minor League games, shall appoint an official scorer for each league championship, post-season or all-star game.

The term "league championship" (describing a game or games) is arcane, inasmuch as that terminology is hardly ever used these days in any context.

What's being referred to are simply regular season games.

The official scorer shall observe the game from a position in the press box.

This is the first of many examples where the rulebook seeks to achieve uniformity in scorekeeping: placing all official scorers in more or less the same physical proximity to the game being scored.

It also appears to be an attempt to insulate—to some degree—the official scorer from outside influences (and make sure that the official scorer gets a good seat from which to observe the game as well, although that isn't always the case).

The official scorer shall have sole authority to make all decisions concerning application of Rule 9 that involve judgment, such as whether a batter's advance to first base is the result of a hit or an error.

Note that this was "the last word" on the subject before the 2007 revisions, but it's not altogether accurate anymore by virtue of the "appeal" process delineated later in Rule 9.01(a).

The official scorer shall communicate such decisions to the press box and broadcasting booths by hand signals or over the press box loudspeaker system and shall advise the public address announcer of such decisions, if requested.

After all, the media, as well as the public that the media serves, have a right to know what's going on when it's going on.

Club officials and players are prohibited from communicating with the official scorer regarding any such decisions.

In other words, the official scorer is not to be subjected to outside influences—for obvious reasons—but there is no indication of what the consequences of violating this rule are.

The official scorer shall make all decisions concerning judgment calls within 24 hours after a game concludes or is suspended.

Here's another throwback to earlier times inasmuch as the statistics of games these days are routinely "finalized" and "official" within far less than 24 hours after the conclusion of a game. Still, this provision does (technically) afford an official scorer some opportunity for reflection, at least as far as the rulebook is concerned.

A Major League player or club may request that the Executive Vice President for Baseball Operations review a judgment call of an official scorer made in a game in which such player or club participated, by notifying the Office of the Commissioner in writing or by approved electronic means within 72 hours of the conclusion or suspension of such game, or within 72 hours of the official scorer's call, in the event the official scorer changes a call within 24 hours after a game concludes or is suspended, as provided in this Rule 9.01(a). The Executive Vice President for Baseball Operations shall have access to all relevant and available video and, after considering any evidence he wishes to consider, may order a change in a judgment call if he determines that the judgment of the official scorer was clearly erroneous. No judgment decision shall be changed thereafter. If the Executive Vice President for Baseball Operations determines that a player or club has abused the appeals process by repeatedly filing frivolous appeals, or acting in bad faith, he may, after providing a warning, impose reasonable sanctions on the club or player. A Minor League player or club may request that the League President review a judgment call of an official scorer in accordance with league rules.

This rule evidences recognition of how important statistics have become, not only for the fans and the media at large, but also for teams and the players themselves.

Note also that a good deal of deference is given to the scorer's original judgment call, and that the official scorer's call will be changed only if it is deemed to be "clearly erroneous."

After each game, including forfeited and called games, the official scorer shall prepare a report, on a form prescribed by the Office of the Commissioner, with respect to Major League games, and the Minor League President, with respect to Minor League games, listing the date of the game, where it was played, the names of the competing clubs and the umpires, the full score of the game and all records of individual players compiled according to the system specified in this Rule 9. The official scorer shall forward this report to the Office of the Commissioner, with respect to Major League games, and the league office, with respect to Minor League games, as soon as practicable after the game ends. The official scorer shall forward the report of any suspended game as soon as practicable after the game has been completed, or after it becomes a called game because it cannot be completed, as provided by the Rule 7.02.

Note that further specifics in regards to what the official scorer is to include in his or her report are set forth in Rule 9.02.

Rule 9.01(a) Comment: The official scorer shall forward the official score report to the league statistician instead of to the league office, if requested to do so by the league. In the event of any discrepancy in records maintained by a league statistician and the rulings by an official scorer, the report of such official scorer shall control. League statisticians and official scorers should consult cooperatively to resolve any discrepancies.

Currently, the "league statistician" for all of MLB and its affiliates is the Elias Sports Bureau, founded in 1913 and well established as a reliable and formidable repository of data for many sports, including—but not limited to— the NFL, NBA, NHL, MLs, and many other professional leagues.

Rule 9.01(b)(1)   In all cases, the official scorer shall not make a scoring decision that is in conflict with Rule 9 or any other Official Baseball Rule. The official scorer shall conform strictly to the rules of scoring set forth in this Rule 9.

Some things do not necessarily have to be said, but ought to be said (nevertheless) to keep everything "on the up and up," and that is the case here: the rules were made to be followed.

The official scorer shall not make any decision that conflicts with an umpire's decision.

For example, a batter reaches first base well ahead of the throw made to put him out. Nevertheless, the umpire inexplicably calls the batter out.

Although the umpire's call was blatantly wrong, the scorer cannot credit the batter with a base hit; the scorer must consider the batter as having been put out without reaching base, regardless of how unfair to the batter that may be.

The official scorer shall have authority to rule on any point not specifically covered in these rules.

Although this sentence is buried in the text of Rule 9.01, and no attention of any kind is drawn to it by the rulebook, it is nonetheless a critical and highly important provision that acknowledges the fact that the nature of baseball is such that situations unforeseen by anyone—including the authors of the rulebook—will inevitably arise from time to time, and sometimes no completely satisfactory resolution of whatever scorekeeping issue may be involved can be found within the covers of the rulebook. Therefore, a "last line of defense" is necessary, and it is altogether appropriate that the rulebook expressly recognizes that fact.

However, it would be a disservice to the rules governing scorekeeping in baseball—and baseball in general—to look to this provision each and every time a "knotty problem" comes along. To use this provision as an easy way out of thoroughly analyzing a situation that's hard to figure out easily, damages the integrity of scorekeeping, because doing so tends to make scorekeeping a "shoot from the hip" proposition, a "make it up as you go along" contrivance instead of the measured exercise in objectivity that official scorekeeping strives to be.

The Office of the Commissioner, with respect to Major League scorers, and the League President, with respect to Minor League scorers shall order changed any decision of an official scorer that contradicts the rules of scoring set forth in this Rule 9 and shall take whatever remedial actions as may be necessary to correct any statistics that need correction as a result of such mistaken scoring decision.

Note that this portion of the rule addresses a scorekeeping decision that is contrary to the rules of scorekeeping per se, not judgment calls (as dealt with earlier in the text of Rule 9.01).

Rule 9.01(2)   If the teams change sides before three men are put out, the official scorer shall immediately inform the umpire-in-chief of the mistake.

This is the only provision in all of Rule 9 that puts the official scorer in a position to engage directly or actively with the game being played. In all other instances, the scorer—although central to gathering the data generated by a game, and therefore critical to the generation of baseball statistics that form such an important part of baseball as we know it—is a passive observer.

Rule 9.01(3)   If the game is protested or suspended, the official scorer shall make a note of the exact situation at the time of the protest or suspension, including the score, the number of outs, the position of any runners, the ball-and-strike count on the batter, the lineups of both teams and the players who have been removed from the game for each team.

Rule 9.01(b)(3) Comment: It is important that a suspended game resume with exactly the same situation as existed at the time of suspension. If a protested game is ordered replayed from the point of protest, the game must be resumed with exactly the situation that existed just before the protested play.

Note that the comment to Rule 9.01(b)(3) explains why it's important for the official scorer to abide by the instructions contained in the main text of Rule 9.01(b)(3), all of which is largely self-evident.

Rule 9.01(4)   The official scorer shall not call the attention of any umpire or of any member of either team to the fact that a player is batting out of turn.

Allowing an inning to end with less than three outs would cause havoc, statistically and otherwise. Therefore, Rule 9.01(b)(2) calls upon the official scorer to intercede and do something to prevent that from happening. However, here we have the opposite of Rule 9.01(b)(2)—the scorer is to remain silent when a batter or batters come to bat out of turn, and that is because a team's batting out of turn will not harm the statistics of a game (as made clear in the provisions of Rule 9.03(d), where how to deal with that is spelled out in detail).

Moreover, this section of Rule 9.01 conforms to the fact that it is the duty and responsibility of the teams themselves to keep track of who is properly in the batter's box at any given point in the game (as stated in the "playing rules"). Therefore, even the umpires are instructed by the rulebook [pursuant to Rule 6.03] to remain silent when a player comes to bat "out of order."

Rule 9.01(c)   The official scorer is an official representative who is entitled to the respect and dignity of his office and shall be accorded full protection by the Office of the Commissioner, with respect to Major League scorers, and the League President, with respect to Minor League scorers. The official scorer shall report to the appropriate league official any indignity expressed by any manager, player, club employee or club officer in the course of, or as the result of, the discharge of official scorer duties.

To some extent, this portion of Rule 9.01 harkens back to stories of official scorers in the distant, and the not-so-distant past, being sometimes violently confronted in one way or another by irate players, managers, or others who may have disagreed with how a given play was scored. (Truth be told, it still happens, but not often as rough and tumble as in days gone by.)

Although the rough edges that baseball is said to have once had may no longer exist (at least to the degree they did in the past), it can nevertheless be a source of solace for scorekeepers to know that the rulebook expressly recognizes that they are "entitled" to "respect and dignity," and "shall be accorded full protection" (whatever that means) by rule.

As if that weren't enough, scorers are not only expressly allowed to "blow the whistle" on anyone who gets out of line with them, but they are also mandated to do so. Nevertheless, it is a well-known and often repeated joke in official scorekeeping that scorers are paid one dollar to keep score, and the rest of their compensation represents payment for the aggravation that comes with the job.

♦ ♦ ♦

Rule 9.02—Official Scorer's Report

Rule 9.02's entire purpose is to set out the specific categories of data that the official scorer is obliged to catalog and ultimately report at the conclusion of a game.

On the following page is what one team's part of an MLB official score report looks like.

Here are the particulars.

The official score report prepared by the official scorer shall be in a form prescribed by the league and shall include:

Rule 9.02(a) the following records for each batter and runner:

(1) Number of times batted, except that no time at bat shall be charged when a player

   (A) hits a sacrifice bunt or sacrifice fly;
   (B) is awarded first base on four called balls;
   (C) is hit by a pitched ball; or
   (D) is awarded first base because of interference or obstruction;

Perhaps the most inarticulate and misleading bit of nomenclature in common day-to-day baseball parlance is referring to every time a batter comes to bat as being an "at-bat."

HOME CLUB PLAYERS — PUT SUBS IN PROPER BATTING ORDER	Pos	AB	R	H	Total Bases	2B	3B	HR	RBI	Sac Bunt	Sac Fly	HB	BB Tot	BB Int	SO	SB	CS	Grnd into F DP	PO	A	E	DP
1 Craig Counsell	SS	3	1	1	1								2			1		1	1	1		1
2 Eric Byrnes	CF	4	2	1	4			1	2				1		1				2			
3 Jose Valverde	P	0																	1			
4 Chad Tracy	3B	5	2	3	3				1				1						2			
5 Luis Gonzalez	LF	5	1	1	4			1	3				2						2			
6 Conor Jackson	1B	4	1	2	2								1						6			1
7 Luis Vizcaino	P	0																				
8 Jeff DaVanon	CF	1		1	1														1			
9 Shawn Green	RF	5		2	2														3		1	
10 Orlando Hudson	2B	3		2	3	1			2										2		1	
11 Casey Daigle	P	0																				
12 Tony Clark a)	PH/2B	1		1	1																	
13 Tony Clark	1B	1																	2			
14 Chris Snyder	C	4													3				9			
15 Johnny Estrada b)	PH	1													1							
16 Miguel Batista	P	1																	1	1		
17 Andy Green c)	PH/2B	3	2	1	4			1	1				1				1		1	1		
18																						
19																						
20																						
21																						
22																						
23																						
24																						
25																						
26																						
27																						
TOTAL		41	9	15	25	1	0	3	9	0	0	0	4	0	10	1	1	0	27	8	2	1

BATTED FOR (Tell how, as: - 'doubled for Smith in 5th')

HOW		NAME	inn.	RAN FOR		inn.
a) Singled	for	C. Daigle	in 6th	1) for		in
b) Strike out	for	C. Snyder	in 9th	2) for		in
c) Homered	for	M. Batista	in 5th	3) for		in
d)	for		in	4) for		in
e)	for		in	5) for		in

Number out when winning run scored ____
DP ↑ Team Total
1st Base on Interference ____
Passed Balls ____ 2
Home Run with Bases full ____

DOUBLE PLAYS Hudson, Counsell, and Jackson (Vizquel off Batista)

(Give Names)

HOME CLUB PITCHER'S SUMMARY (OPPONENTS)

	W L S	IP	H	AB	Total Bats to Face Pitch'r	R	ER	HR	Sac Bunt	Sac Fly	HB	BB Tot	BB Int	SO	WP	BK
M. Batista		5.0	11	25	29	7	6		1	1		2	1	6	2	
C. Daigle		1.0	3	3	3	0								2		
L. Vizcaino		1.2	5	6	6	1	1			1		1	1			
J. Valverde	L	1.1	2	4	8	2	2	1	1	1		2	1	1		

Comparison made of Home Pitching vs. Visiting Batting Totals ☐

9.0 | 13 | 37 | 46 | 10 | 9 | 1 | 2 | 2 | 0 | 5 | 2 | 10 | 2 | 0

Note: When total earned runs differ from team total, enter team total and circle it.

Check One

BOX SCORE PROOF
Runs	9	At Bat 41
LOB	9	Bases on Balls 4
		Sacrifices 0
Opponents Put Outs 26		Hit by Pitcher & 1st by Interference 0
TOTAL 44		TOTAL 45

Totals should equal

STARTING TIME & DATE MUST BE DUPLICATED ON HOME TEAM'S SHEET

SCORE BY INNINGS
	1	2	3	4	5	6	7	8	9	10	11	12	13	14	15	16	17	18	19	Total
Visiting Club San Francisco Giants	2	2	3	0	0	0	0	2	1											10
Home Club Arizona Diamondbacks	0	0	0	1	4	4	0	0	0											9

OFFICIAL REPORT OF BASEBALL GAME (Sheet 2)
Home Club Sheet
Played in City of Phoenix, AR   on April 17   20 06
Between San Francisco Giants & Arizona Diamondbacks
Visiting Club   Home Club

Game Started at 06:42 PM
Elapsed Time of Game 03 HR 28 Min
Paid Attendance 21,610

It's repeated over and over again by announcers, managers, commentators—you name it—and the vast majority of those who hear it don't give it a second thought because it sounds altogether accurate, appropriate and proper. However, technically speaking, always referring to a batter's turn at bat as being an "at-bat" is fundamentally wrong.

For example, it's common to hear that "he'll have at least one more at-bat before the game is over" or "until he recovers from his injury, he's going to miss a lot of at-bats."

You might even hear someone say, "His last at-bat resulted in a walk."

What's wrong with all that is that an "at-bat" is a specific statistical category in scorekeeping, and it is not always analogous to stepping into the batter's box and having a turn at the plate.

Simply put, each time a batter comes to bat, it's a "plate appearance," but not every plate appearance is an "at-bat." That's because every time a batter's turn to bat results in the batter drawing a walk, being awarded first base by virtue of being hit by a pitch, executing a sacrifice bunt or sacrifice fly, or reaching base on an umpire's call of obstruction or interference, it's properly considered a "plate appearance," but it's not an "at-bat."

That being so, it's preferable to refer to a batter's trips to the batter's box as "plate appearances," and only official at-bats as "at-bats" for the sake of accuracy.

(Now in case one might think that all this is an exercise in hair-splitting, think again, because calculating a number of statistics turns on whether only official at-bats are counted, as opposed to whether all plate appearances are factored in. Consequently, it would serve the game far better if references to plate appearances were not all loosely labeled as being at-bats, and care be taken to differentiate between the two.)

 (2) **Number of runs scored;**
 (3) **Number of safe hits;**
 (4) **Number of runs batted in;**
 (5) **Two-base hits;**
 (6) **Three-base hits;**
 (7) **Home runs;**
 (8) **Total bases on safe hits;**
 (9) **Stolen bases;**
(10) **Sacrifice bunts;**
(11) **Sacrifice flies;**
(12) **Total number of bases on balls;**
(13) **Separate listing of any intentional bases on balls;**
(14) **Number of times hit by a pitched ball;**
(15) **Number of times awarded first base for interference or obstruction;**

(16) Strikeouts;
(17) Number of force double plays and reverse-force double plays grounded into;

Rule 9.02(a) (17) Comment: The official scorer should not charge a batter with grounding into a double play if the batter-runner is called out due to interference by a preceding runner.

Putting the ball into play, and having it result in a double play, is not enough to warrant a player having his name appear in this portion of the official scorer's report; specific criteria must be met.

For starters, Rule 9.02(a)(17) applies only to a batter hitting a ground ball that leads to a double play. A line drive or fly ball that brings about a double play is something altogether different.

It would seem that the emphasis put on grounding into a double play, to the exclusion of other ways of hitting into a double play, comes from the fact that any double play that may arise after a batter hits a line drive or fly ball is most likely the result of poor base-running on the part of a player or players on base, as opposed to a failure on the part of the batter to accomplish anything more than make it easy for the defensive team to log two outs in quick succession.

In addition, Rule 9.02(a)(17) is limited to "force" double plays and "reverse force" double plays. Therefore, it's important to understand and appreciate what those terms mean.

Specifically, as stated in the Definition of Terms, a force double play is a double play in which "both putouts are force plays." That is to say, if one of the putouts in back-to-back putouts is made on a runner who was not forced to advance, the double play is not a force double play.

For example, with a runner at second base, and less than two outs, the batter hits a ground ball to the shortstop. The runner at second base is tagged out by the shortstop while trying to advance to third, and the batter is thereupon put out at first base.

That's a double play, but it's not a force double play because the first out was made on a runner that was not forced to advance when the ball was put into play.

In contrast, consider a classic "6–4–3" double play (a "6–4" putout immediately followed by a "4–3" putout) where a runner on first base, forced to advance from first base to second base when the batter puts the ball into play, is forced out at second base by a throw from the shortstop to the second baseman, and the batter is thereupon forced out at first base by a throw from the second baseman to the first baseman.

Both putouts were force-outs. Therefore, the batter in this case is properly considered as having grounded into a double play.

Then there are reverse-force double plays. Although it may sound somewhat tricky—and hyper-technical—it really isn't all that hard to understand or recognize.

Simply put, a reverse-force double play (as set forth in the Definition of Terms) is a double play where "the first out is a force play" and the second out "is made on a runner for whom the force is removed by reason of the first out."

A good example of this is when you have a runner at first base, the batter hits a ground ball to the first baseman, the first baseman steps on first base to put out the batter, and thereupon throws the ball to second base to put out (on a tag out) the runner attempting to advance from first base to second base on the play.

The first out was made on a runner (the batter-runner) who was "forced" to advance (to first base) after putting the ball into play. The second out was made on a runner who was initially forced to advance, but was no longer forced to advance after the batter was put out.

All that said, as far as the comment to Rule 9.02(a)(17) is concerned, reference needs to be made to Rule 6.01(a)(6), which states (in relevant part) that "**If, in the judgment of the umpire, a base runner willfully and deliberately interferes with a batted ball or a fielder in the act of fielding a batted ball with the obvious intent to break up a double play, the ball is dead. The umpire shall call the runner out for interference and also call out the batter-runner because of the action of his teammate.**"

That being so, one might assume that it's a double play, but because the batter might have reached first base on a fielder's choice but for the actions of the runner who was on base, the batter gets the benefit of the doubt and is not charged with having grounded into a force double play.

(18) Number of times caught stealing.

◆ ◆ ◆

Rule 9.02(b)   the following records for each fielder:

(1) Number of putouts;
(2) Number of assists;
(3) Number of errors;
(4) Number of double plays participated in; and
(5) Number of triple plays participated in.

Note that each of these categories has an entire subsection of Rule 9 devoted to it (with the exception of double plays and triple plays, which are combined into one subsection).

Rule 9.02(c)   The following records for each pitcher:

(1) Number of innings pitched;

Rule 9.02(c)(1) Comment: In computing innings pitched, the official scorer shall count each putout as ⅓ of an inning. For example, if a starting pitcher is replaced with one out in the sixth inning, the official scorer shall credit that pitcher with 5⅓ innings. If a starting pitcher is replaced with none out in the sixth inning, the official scorer shall credit that pitcher with 5 innings and make the notation that that pitcher faced _ batters in the sixth, noting the number of batters faced. If a relief pitcher retires two batters and is replaced, the official scorer shall credit that pitcher with ⅔ of an inning pitched. If a relief pitcher enters a game and his team initiates a successful appeal play that results in one out, the officer scorer shall credit such relief pitcher with ⅓ of an inning pitched.

Measuring "how much" a pitcher pitched by counting the number of putouts made while the pitcher was on the mound is a somewhat dubious methodology because it can be quite misleading and can otherwise lead to some rather curious results.

Consider the fact that one pitcher might spend a considerable amount of time facing batter after batter, throwing dozens and dozens of pitches, but get credit for only one inning pitched, while another pitcher might spend virtually no time on the mound, throw only a few pitches, and nevertheless be considered as having pitched just as much as the former pitcher, at least in terms of "innings pitched."

It's even more odd when you consider that a pitcher can get credit for ⅓ of an inning pitched, or more, and not even throw a pitch (for example, by coming into the game and picking off one or more runners on base).

Regardless, participation in a game is measured in outs, at least as far as the rulebook is concerned. However, the relatively recent and seemingly ever-increasing use of "pitch counts" would appear to denote a growing realization of the flaws inherent in measuring how much a pitcher "works" by simply counting putouts.

(2) Total number of batters faced;

(3) Number of batters officially at bat against pitcher, computed according to Rule 9.02(a)(1);

As regards 9.02(c)(2) and (3), reference can once again be made to the comments concerning the difference between plate appearances and at-bats that can be found in connection with Rule 9.02(a)(1).

(4) Number of hits allowed;
(5) Number of runs allowed;
(6) Number of earned runs allowed;
(7) Number of home runs allowed;
(8) Number of sacrifice hits allowed;
(9) Number of sacrifice flies allowed;
(10) Total number of bases on balls allowed;
(11) Separate listing of any intentional bases on balls allowed;
(12) Number of batters hit by pitched balls;
(13) Number of strikeouts;
(14) Number of wild pitches; and
(15) Number of balks.

Once again, as noted in the case of fielding data, some of the terms set forth here (like "earned runs") have entire subsections of Rule 9 devoted to them.

Rule 9.02(d)   **The following additional data:**

(1) Name of the winning pitcher;
(2) Name of the losing pitcher;
(3) Names of the starting pitcher and the finishing pitcher for each team; and
(4) Name of pitcher credited with a save, if any;

Rule 9.02(e)   **Number of passed balls allowed by each catcher;**

Rule 9.02(f)   **Name of players participating in double plays and triple plays.**

Rule 9.02(f) Comment: For example, an official scorer would note: "Double Plays—Jones, Roberts and Smith (2). Triple Play—Jones and Smith."

Rule 9.02(g)   **Number of runners left on base by each team. This total shall include all runners who get on base by any means and who do not score and are not put out. The official scorer shall include in this total a batter-runner whose batted ball results in another runner being retired for the third out.**

For example, with the bases loaded and two outs, the batter hits a ground ball to the third baseman, who steps on third base to put out the runner forced to advance from second base, and the inning ends with no run scoring. Although, in a sense, the batter never reached first base, the inning is nevertheless considered as having ended with three runners left on base, not two. This is because, in the "accounting system" that is used to score baseball games and compute statistics, every completed turn at bat must be categorized as the player in question either being put out, scoring, or being left on base. Otherwise, the "books" would not "balance."

(In this regard, see Rule 9.03(c)—How to Prove a Box Score.)

Rule 9.02(h)   **Names of batters who hit home runs with the bases full.**

Rule 9.02(i)   **Number of outs when winning run scored, if the game was won in the last half-inning.**

Rule 9.02(j)   **The score by innings for each team.**

Rule 9.02(k)   **Names of umpires, listed in this order: plate umpire, first-base umpire, second-base umpire, third-base umpire, left-field umpire (if any) and right-field umpire (if any).**

Rule 9.02(l)   **Time required to play the game, with delays deducted for weather, light failure or technological failure not related to game action.**

Rule 9.02(l) Comment: A delay to attend to the injury of a player, manager, coach or umpire shall be counted in computing time of game.

Rule 9.02(m)   **Official attendance, as provided by the home club.**

Note that a lot of things that are commonly kept track of in the world of baseball these days are not even mentioned in Rule 9.02, things like counting the number of pitches thrown or crediting middle relief pitchers with "holds."

It would seem that the reason the things listed in Rule 9.02 are there, and the things that aren't listed aren't listed, is because (for the most part) it's been that way for a long time and baseball has, throughout its history, consistently exhibited a profound reluctance and resistance to change. However, over time, things nevertheless do change, and the "powers that be" will react. This is displayed by the fact that Rule 9.02(a)(17), as well as the last sentence found in the comment to Rule 9.02(c)(1), Rule 9.02(i), 9.02(j) and 9.02(m), were all added to the rulebook in the revisions to Rule 9 made in 2007, and the language found in Rule 9.02(l) was substantially expanded as well. Consequently, it would be safe to assume that additions to what is required to be included in the official score report will be made over time, and the day may come when the number of pitches thrown, holds, and things that have not yet even been conceived of in baseball's ongoing history will someday become "official."

◆ ◆ ◆

Rule 9.03—Official Score Report (Additional Rules)

Before launching into the more substantive subsections of Rule 9, the rulebook employs Rule 9.03 to deal with five items of miscellany: (1) identifying what positions were played by the participants in the game, (2) addressing issues attendant to substitute batters and runners, (3) proving a box score, (4) dealing with players batting out of turn, and (5) instructions in regards to called and forfeited games.

Rule 9.03(a)   In compiling the official score report, the official scorer shall list each player's name and fielding position, or positions, in the order in which the player batted, or would have batted if the game ended before the player came to bat.

Rule 9.03(a) Comment: When a player does not exchange positions with another fielder but is merely placed in a different spot for a particular batter (for example, if a second baseman goes to the outfield to form a four-man outfield, or if a third baseman moves to a position between the shortstop and second baseman), the official scorer should not list this as a new position.

Rule 9.03(a), and its comment, are quite simple and straightforward, and therefore need no comment, as such. However, it can be noted that Rule 9.03(a) does not address the fact that a player can come into a game as neither a fielder, nor as a designated hitter. That is to say, a player might participate in a game merely as a substitute hitter or runner, and leave the game without assuming any fielding position. Moreover, a player can be "announced" into a line-up but never leave the dugout at all. Therefore, those instances are addressed in Rule 9.03(b).

Rule 9.03(b)   The official scorer shall identify in the official score report any player who enters the game as a substitute batter or substitute runner, whether or not such player continues in the game thereafter, in the batting order by a special symbol that shall refer to a separate record of substitute batters and runners. The record of substitute batters shall describe what the substitute batter did. The record of substitute batters and runners

shall include the name of any such substitute whose name is announced, but who is removed for another substitute before he actually gets into the game. Any such second substitute shall be recorded as batting or running for the first announced substitute.

Rule 9.03(b) Comment: Lower case letters are recommended as symbols for substitute batters and numerals are recommended as symbols for substitute runners. For example, an official score report may note as follows: "a-Singled for Abel in third inning; b-Flied out for Baker in sixth inning; c-Hit into force for Charles in seventh inning; d-Grounded out for Daniel in ninth inning; 1-Ran for Edward in ninth inning." If a substitute's name is announced but the substitute is removed for another substitute before he actually gets into the game, the official scorer report shall record the substitute, for example, as follows: "e-Announced as substitute for Frank in seventh inning."

Rule 9.03(c) How to Prove a Box Score   A box score shall balance (or is proven) when the total of the team's times at bat, bases on balls received, hit batters, sacrifice bunts, sacrifice flies and batters awarded first base because of interference or obstruction equals the total of that team's runs, players left on base and the opposing team's putouts.

It's curious and odd that the rulebook does not say that "proving a box score" is something that the official scorer must do, or even ought to do: it's just there. Nevertheless, one can glean from its presence in the rulebook, and from the fact that it appears as a section of MLB's scorer's report form, that going through the exercise of counting the things that Rule 9.03(c) inventories, after a game is completed, is a good idea, and (implicitly) doing so is part of the official scorer's responsibilities.

At the same time, Rule 9.03(c) is also a bit long-winded inasmuch as all that it is saying is that the completed plate appearances of each team must total that team's runs, runners left on base, and players on that team that were put out.

Also unstated, but clearly implied, is that if the completed plate appearances of a team do not match the runs, runners left on base and players put out, it means that something was overlooked or miscounted, and therefore proving a box score is a good way to make sure everything is properly accounted for, not unlike balancing a checkbook.

Note however that a formula for making sure that other statistics, such as stolen bases, assists, errors and the like, are properly tallied is not provided by the rulebook, and consequently the official scorer is left to his or her own devices in that regard.

Note also that Rule 9.03(c) stands for the proposition that there are only three ways for a batter's plate appearance to end (not counting incomplete plate appearances, such as when, for example, a pitcher commits a balk that scores a game-ending run, and the player in the batter's box at the time therefore doesn't get to finish his plate appearance), and those three ways are (as previously stated) to score a run, be left on base, or be put out.

Rule 9.03(d) When Player Bats Out of Turn   When a player bats out of turn and is put out, and the proper batter is called out before the ball is pitched to the next batter, the official scorer shall charge the proper batter with a time at bat and score the putout and any assists the same as if the correct batting order had been followed. If an improper batter becomes a runner and the proper batter is called out for having missed his turn at bat, the official scorer shall charge the proper batter with a time at bat, credit the putout to the catcher and ignore everything entering into the improper batter's safe arrival on base. If more than one batter bats out of turn in succession, the official scorer shall score all plays just as they occur, skipping the turn at bat of the player or players who first missed batting in the proper order.

Few things in baseball cause more confusion than when a team deviates from its batting order.

There is little doubt that the reason for that is that even individuals with many years of experience in baseball are altogether unfamiliar with how the rulebook deals with those situations, because those situations don't come up all that often.

Be that as it may, in order to understand and properly apply Rule 9.03(d), a scorekeeper is well served to be familiar with the underlying playing rule: Rule 6.03(b)

> **Rule 6.03(b)—Batting Out of Turn**
>
> **(1) A batter shall be called out, on appeal, when he fails to bat in his proper turn, and another batter completes a time at bat in his place.**
>
> **(2) The proper batter may take his place in the batter's box at any time before the improper batter becomes a runner or is put out, and any balls and strikes shall be counted in the proper batter's time at bat.**
>
> **(3) When an improper batter becomes a runner or is put out, and the defensive team appeals to the umpire before the first pitch to the**

next batter of either team, or before any play or attempted play, the umpire shall (1) declare the proper batter out; and (2) nullify any advance or score made because of a ball batted by the improper batter or because of the improper batter's advance to first base on a hit, an error, a base on balls, a hit batter or otherwise.

(4) If a runner advances, while the improper batter is at bat, on a stolen base, balk, wild pitch or passed ball, such advance is legal.

(5) When an improper batter becomes a runner or is put out, and a pitch is made to the next batter of either team before an appeal is made, the improper batter thereby becomes the proper batter, and the results of his time at bat become legal.

(6) When the proper batter is called out because he has failed to bat in turn, the next batter shall be the batter whose name follows that of the proper batter thus called out;

(7) When an improper batter becomes a proper batter because no appeal is made before the next pitch, the next batter shall be the batter whose name follows that of such legalized improper batter. The instant an improper batter's actions are legalized, the batting order picks up with the name following that of the legalized improper batter.

Rule 6.03(b)(7) Comment: The umpire shall not direct the attention of any person to the presence in the batter's box of an improper batter. This rule is designed to require constant vigilance by the players and managers of both teams. There are two fundamentals to keep in mind: When a player bats out of turn, the proper batter is the player called out. If an improper batter bats and reaches base or is out and no appeal is made before a pitch to the next batter, or before any play or attempted play, that improper batter is considered to have batted in proper turn and establishes the order that is to follow.

It's not really about batting out of turn, inasmuch as the player who bats when it isn't properly his turn to bat is *not* the player who is penalized. Rather, it's the player who failed to bat when it was his turn to bat who is penalized: that player is the one who is called out.

Given that, there are basically three situations in this context that a scorer may be called upon to deal with, as follows.

1. The first sentence of Rule 9.03(d) envisions an "improper" batter coming to bat and being put out, but the fact that the batter in question batted

out of turn is brought to the attention of the umpire in a timely manner and, as a result, the player who should have batted is called out for failure to bat in proper turn. In that case, the player who was called out for failure to come to bat properly is charged with having been put out, and whatever happened that resulted in the improper batter being put out goes into the scoring box of the batter who failed to bat in proper turn.

For example, in the top of the first inning, the visiting team's leadoff batter fails to come to the plate to start the game. Rather, the visiting team's #2 batter does, and that batter strikes out. The umpire's attention is drawn to the fact that the leadoff batter missed his turn at bat before another pitch is thrown or a play is made or attempted, and the leadoff batter is called out with the #2 batter returning to the plate to bat (just as he would had the leadoff batter made the first out of the inning in the usual course).

In this case, the leadoff batter is charged with the strikeout and the pitcher receives credit for a strikeout in the same manner as if the pitcher had actually struck out the leadoff batter.

By the same token, if the #2 batter had been put out on (say) a ground ball to the second baseman, the leadoff batter would be charged with having grounded out, the second baseman would be credited with an assist and the first baseman with a putout, just as though the leadoff batter had actually grounded out, "4–3."

2. The second sentence of Rule 9.03(d) envisions an "improper" batter coming to bat and reaching base, and (as before) the fact that the batter in question batted out of turn is brought to the attention of the umpire in a timely manner. As a result, the player who should have batted is called out for failure to bat in proper turn. In that case, the player who was called out for failure to come to bat properly is charged with having been put out, the catcher is credited with having put out the player who missed his turn at bat, and whatever gave rise to the improper batter reaching base is considered as never having happened.

3. The third sentence of Rule 9.03(d) addresses situations where more than one player bats out of turn in succession, but without penalty because an appeal wasn't made to the umpire in a timely manner, and it instructs the scorer simply to leave the scoring box of any player who missed his proper turn at bat blank.

In other words, it is only when a player is called out for failing to come to bat in proper turn that the provisions of the first two sentences of Rule 9.03(d) are applicable.

For example, as before, the leadoff hitter for the visiting team in the top of the first inning fails to come to bat and the #2 batter in the lineup subsequently becomes the initial batter in the inning. The batter singles, but (as Yogi Berra might say) nobody says nothing.

Next, the #3 batter on the lineup card comes up and grounds out to the first baseman, advancing the runner on base to second base.

Next, the #4 batter in the line-up fails to come to the plate and the #5 batter—batting when the #4 batter ought to have been in the batter's box—hits a home run.

At this point, before another pitch is thrown or play is made or attempted by the defensive team, the fact that the #5 batter came to bat when it was the #4 batter's turn to bat is brought to the attention of the umpire.

Properly applying Rule 6.03(b), the umpire calls the #4 batter in the visiting team's lineup out and returns the runner to second base, thereby nullifying the two runs that scored on the "home run" hit by the #5 batter, and directs the #5 batter to return to the plate to bat (inasmuch as the #5 batter properly follows the #4 batter in the lineup).

Thereupon, the #5 batter proceeds to strike out.

Applying the provisions of Rule 9.03(d), the scoring box of the #1 batter's box is left blank. The #2 batter gets credit for a single because the #2 batter became a "proper batter" as soon as a pitch was delivered to the next batter. The #3 batter's scoring box reflects him being put out by the first baseman for the first out of the inning and advancing the runner on base in the process. The scoring box of the #4 batter shows him as being "put out" "by the catcher" for the second out of the inning (for failing to bat when it was his turn to bat), and the scoring box of the #5 batter shows him striking out for the third and final out of the inning.

When all is said and done, it isn't all that convoluted or perplexing, but as can be seen from this last example, things can get a bit twisted, and it can be difficult to score without a good grasp of both Rule 9.03(d) and Rule 6.03(b).

In passing, note also that under Rule 9.01(b)(4), the official scorer is prohibited from calling to the attention of any umpire or member of either team that a player is batting out of turn, even though the official scorer is in the best position to do so, because—as stated in Rule 6.03(b)—the intention of Rule 6.03(b) is to require "constant vigilance by the players and managers of both teams." It's their job to keep track of whose turn it is to bat, and no one else's.

Rule 9.03(e) Called and Forfeited Games

(1) If a regulation game is called, the official scorer shall include the record of all individual and team actions up to the moment the game ends, as defined in Rules 7.01 and 7.02. If the game is a tie game, the official scorer shall not enter a winning or losing pitcher.

The pertinent parts of the playing rules text in this regard can be found in Rule 7.01, as follows.

A regulation game consists of nine innings, unless extended because of a tie score, or shortened (1) because the home team needs none of its half of the ninth inning or only a fraction of it, or (2) because the umpire-in-chief calls the game.

If a game is called, it is a regulation game: (1) If five innings have been completed; (2) If the home team has scored more runs in four or four and a fraction half-innings than the visiting team has scored in five completed half-innings; (3) If the home team scores one or more runs in its half of the fifth inning to tie the score.

In addition, the rulebook defines a "called game" as follows.

A Called Game is one in which, for any reason, the umpire in chief terminates play.

Fair enough.

Rule 9.03(e) does little more than state the obvious: if a game ends "early" but it is nevertheless a "regulation game," all the hits, errors, putouts and other events that occurred in the game are to be included in the official scorer's report. However, (by implication) if a game is terminated before meeting the criteria for a regulation game, it's as though the game never happened at all, and any hits, errors, putouts and the like are not reported in the official scorer's report because there would be (officially) no game to report.

Rule 9.03(e)—continued

(2) If a regulation game is forfeited, the official scorer shall include the record of all individual and team actions up to the time of forfeit. If the winning team by forfeit is ahead at the time of forfeit, the official scorer shall enter as winning and losing pitchers the players who would have qualified as the winning and losing pitchers if the game had been called at the time of forfeit. If the winning team by forfeit is behind or if the score is tied at the time of forfeit, the official scorer shall not enter a winning or losing pitcher. If a game is forfeited before it becomes a regulation game,

the official scorer shall include no records and shall report only the fact of the forfeit.

Rule 9.03(e) is easy to understand and apply. However, the comment attached to Rule 9.03(e) might cause you to scratch your head a little bit.

Rule 9.03(e) Comment: The official scorer shall not consider that, by rule, the score of a forfeited game is 9 to 0, notwithstanding the results on the field at the point the game is forfeited.

This comment addresses the fact that the rulebook defines a forfeited game as being "a game declared ended by the umpire in chief in favor of the offended team by the score of 9 to 0, for violation of the rules," and the comment to Rule 9.03(e)(2) instructs the official scorer to ignore the "score of 9 to 0" portion of the definition and report any runs that scored in a forfeited game in the same manner as the scorer would do if the game had not ended in a forfeit.

That's strange, to say the least, and why—as part of the 2007 revisions— the rulebook's "by the score of 9 to 0" language was simply not deleted instead of adding the comment to Rule 9.03(e)(3), and why "by the score of 9 to 0" was included in the rulebook's definition of a forfeited game in the first place, are not explained or otherwise discussed anywhere in the rulebook.

♦ 7 ♦

Batter Up!

Rules 9.04–9.06

Rule 9.04—Runs Batted In

A run batted in is a statistic credited to a batter whose action at bat causes one or more runs to score, as set forth in this Rule 9.04.

(a) The official scorer shall credit the batter with a run batted in for every run that scores

(1) unaided by an error and as part of a play begun by the batter's safe hit (including the batter's home run), sacrifice bunt, sacrifice fly, infield out or fielder's choice, unless Rule 9.04(b) applies.

For example: With a runner at third and two outs, the batter hits an easy ground ball directly to the first baseman. The ball goes under the first baseman's glove and between his legs for an error, allowing the batter to reach first base safely and the runner at third base to score a run.

Although the batter's "action at bat" gave rise to the run scoring, it's not a run batted in for the batter. That's because if the first baseman had not committed the error, he would have been able to force out the batter at first base for the third out of the inning, and inasmuch as under Rule 5.08 a run cannot score on a play where the third out is made "by the batter-runner before he touches first base," the run would not have counted.

The run is ultimately the product of the first baseman's error, not the batter having put the ball into play. Consequently, it's not a run batted in for the batter because it was "aided" by an error.

What it means: Broadly speaking, every time a batter puts the ball into play and a run scores, that run is credited to the batter as a run batted in, and

73

if two or three or four runs score, credit for each run batted in is properly awarded to the batter.

That's the bedrock premise when it comes to RBIs.

Therefore, if—in the same situation set forth above—the batter had grounded the ball sharply down the first base line, out of the reach of the first baseman for a clean base hit, it's an RBI for the batter. The same would hold true in almost every instance where the batter puts the ball into play and a run or runs score, even if the batter, or a runner or runners on base, were put out in the process. But if a run, or runs, would not have scored but for the commission of an error, the run, or runs, are not considered as having been batted in.

That said, note that there are a number of instances where a batter might put the ball into play and not qualify for an RBI, even in the absence of an error, which instances are addressed in Rule 9.04(b).

(Note also that the term, "action at bat causes" in the introductory verbiage of Rule 9.04 might be better phrased "plate appearance results in," as witnessed by the following section of Rule 9.04.)

You Don't Necessarily Need a Bat to "Bat In" a Run

Rule 9.04(a)(2)   The official scorer shall credit the batter with a run batted in for every run that scores … by reason of the batter becoming a runner with the bases full (because of a base on balls, an award of first base for being touched by a pitched ball or for interference or obstruction).

For example: With the bases loaded, the batter is hit by a pitch and consequently awarded first base.

As a result, all three runners on base advance one base with the runner at third scoring a run in the process, and that run is properly counted as a run batted in by the batter who was hit by the pitch.

What it means: This provision of Rule 9.04 evidences the fact that the term "runs batted in" is somewhat misleading, inasmuch as a run can be "walked in" or "hit by a pitch in" or "interfered or obstructed in" and still count as a run "batted in."

In any case, given the fact that a batter's plate appearance in these situations leads to a run scoring, credit for a run batted in is appropriate and fair, regardless of the fact that the run was not actually "batted" in per se.

Sometimes, Errors Don't Count

Rule 9.04(a)(3)   The official scorer shall credit the batter with a run batted in for every run that scores ... when, before two are out, an error is made on a play on which a runner from third base ordinarily would score.

For example: With a runner at third, less than two outs and the infielders positioned at normal depth (not positioned any closer to home plate than they would be if the bases were empty), the batter hits an easy ground ball to the shortstop, who fields the ball cleanly and throws it to first with the intent of retiring the batter there. However, the shortstop's throw is wild, and consequently the batter ends up safe at first.

In the meantime, the runner at third (having had a good lead off third base at the time of the pitch) scores a run.

Although the shortstop is properly charged with an error, and the batter is considered as having reached base on the error, it's nevertheless an RBI for the batter because the run that scored would have scored even if the shortstop's throw had been on the money and the batter had been put out.

What it means: This rule makes perfect sense: why should the batter be deprived of credit for an RBI just because the defensive team messed up? In other words, if the defensive team had done what it was supposed to do properly, the runner at third would have scored anyway, and the batter would have received credit for an RBI even though he was put out at first base.

Note, however, that the run in question must be scored by "a runner at third." This means, for example, if a runner at second base advances to home plate on an error like the one given in the example above, that run would not properly be considered an RBI.

Also, Rule 9.04(a)(3) applies only to situations where there are less than two outs, inasmuch as a run that scores while the defensive team fails to end an inning—fails to log the third out—by committing an error would ordinarily not score but for the commission of that error.

In any case, Rule 9.04(a)(3) conforms with the underlying premise that, in the broadest of terms, every time a batter puts the ball into play and a run scores, that run is credited to the batter as a run batted in.

However (as stated before), there are exceptions, and those exceptions are delineated in Rule 9.04(b).

LOSING CREDIT FOR AN RBI BY GROUNDING INTO A FORCE DOUBLE PLAY, OR A REVERSE FORCE DOUBLE PLAY

Rule 9.04(b)   The official scorer shall not credit a run batted in (1) when the batter grounds into a force double play or a reverse-force double play.

FOR EXAMPLE: With the bases loaded and no outs, the batter hits a ground ball to the pitcher, who fields the ball and throws it to the third baseman covering third base to force out the runner who is forced to advance from second base. Then the third baseman throws the ball to the second baseman covering second base, and the runner forced to advance from first base is put out at second base.

While all this is going on, the runner at third scores a run. Although the batter's putting the ball into play led to the run scoring, the batter does not get credit for an RBI because the batter grounded into a force double play.

In the same situation, assume that the ball is again hit to the pitcher, only this time, the pitcher fields the ball and throws to the shortstop covering second base to put out the runner forced to advance from first base. The shortstop throws the ball to third base, where the runner coming from second base—no longer forced to advance by virtue of the putout at second base—is tagged out.

In the meantime, as before, the runner at third scores a run.

Once again, although the batter's putting the ball into play led to the run scoring, the batter does not get credit for an RBI, this time because the batter grounded into a reverse-force double play.

WHAT IT MEANS: To fully understand Rule 9.04(b)(1), reference needs to be made to the definition of a "double play" as well as the definition of a "force double play" and a "reverse-force double play," as set forth in the rulebook.

A DOUBLE PLAY is a play by the defense in which two offensive players are put out as a result of continuous action, providing there is no error between putouts.

(a) A force double play is one in which both putouts are force plays.

(b) A reverse-force double play is one in which the first out is a force play and the second out is made on a runner for whom the force is removed by reason of the first out. Examples of reverse-force plays: runner on first, one out; batter grounds to first baseman, who steps

on first base (one out) and throws to second baseman or shortstop for the second out (a tag play). Another example: bases loaded, none out; batter grounds to third baseman, who steps on third base (one out); then throws to catcher for the second out (tag play).

Understanding what constitutes a force double play is not difficult inasmuch as the definition is quite simple and easy to visualize. (Think routine 6–4/4–3 double play.) At the same time, although the concept of a reverse-force double play is somewhat more involved, it too is readily comprehensible.

That being so, it's relatively easy and simple to apply the dictates of Rule 9.04(b)(1) to game situations, but the question remains: why is the batter in these instances denied credit for an RBI when his "action at bat" lead to a run scoring?

Although the rulebook doesn't provide an answer to that question, one can surmise that in cases like this, the batter's serving up a ground ball that gives rise to a relatively easy double play generally does more harm to the cause of the batter's team (by precipitating two outs) than the scoring of a run in the process benefits the batter's team. Therefore, from that perspective, a statistical award for the batter (in the form of an RBI) is inappropriate.

At the same time, if the run that scores makes what had been a two-run deficit for the home team in the bottom of the ninth...

Be that as it may, Rule 9.04(b)(1) is nonetheless clear in its mandate, whatever the thinking behind it may be, and therefore it should not be a source of consternation or bewilderment.

Losing Credit for an RBI Without Actually Grounding into a Force Double Play

Rule 9.04(b)(2) The official scorer shall not credit a run batted in ... when a fielder is charged with an error because the fielder muffs a throw at first base that would have completed a force double play.

For example: With runners on third and first, and no outs, the batter hits a ground ball to the second baseman, who flips the ball to the shortstop covering second base, forcing out the runner who's forced to advance to second base from first base. In turn, the shortstop delivers the ball to the first baseman covering first base. Although the shortstop's throw is right on the money and arrives at first base well ahead of the batter, the first baseman drops the ball and the batter is safe. In the process, the runner who had been at third base at the beginning of the play scores a run.

Despite the fact that the batter put the ball in play, a run scored, and there was no double play, the run is not an RBI for the batter.

WHAT IT MEANS: One of the most repeated platitudes in scorekeeping is that "you can't assume a double play." It comes from the fact that Rule 9.12(d)(3) states that "The official scorer shall not charge an error against ... any fielder who makes a wild throw in attempting to complete a double play." However, what is often overlooked is that Rule 9.12(d)(3) goes on to say (in its comment) that "When a fielder muffs a thrown ball that, if held, would have completed a double play ... the official scorer shall charge an error to the fielder who drops the ball and credit an assist to the fielder who made the throw."

Consequently, it is more accurate to say that a potential double play that's blown by a bad throw is overlooked (in other words, not "assumed") in terms of charging an error, but a potential double play that is botched by the failure to make a catch for the second out is not.

This ties in with Rule 9.04(b)(2), in the following manner.

There is the underlying premise that a batter who grounds into a force double play—or reverse-force double play—does not get credit for a run that scores while that double play is being executed, but a batter is nevertheless entitled to an RBI if only the batter is forced out at first base, or if only one runner on base is forced out, and a run scores in the process.

Add to that another premise: that a fielder is not to be charged with an error for failing to make a good throw to complete a double play, inasmuch as that throw is often quite difficult to execute cleanly, with—among other things—a runner often sliding into base hard to break up a potential double play. It is difficult for a scorekeeper to judge if a "good" throw in those instances would have actually completed a double play. Therefore, errors are not charged on wild throws made in an attempt to complete double plays.

(Note that a wild throw made in an attempt to complete a double play can be deemed an error if the wild throw leads not only to a failure to complete the double play, but additional runner advancement. However, that's not really relevant to this topic, and that issue is addressed in the section covering Rule 9.12(d)(3).)

With all that in mind, consider the fact that if a good throw is made to turn a double play, and the fielder receiving the throw mishandles the throw, in those cases it is obvious that the double play could have been executed if the catch necessary to complete the double play had not been botched: there's no guessing. Accordingly, in those instances, one can "assume a double play" as a double play would have been made if it weren't for the commission of the error on a muffed catch.

As a result, Rule 9.04(b)(2) identifies the situation where a batter, even though he didn't actually ground into a force double play, is nonetheless treated (in terms of crediting RBI) as if the batter had in fact grounded into a force double play, and credit for an RBI is withheld.

(Note that Rule 9.04(b)(2) does not—by definition—apply to batters grounding into a reverse-force doubleplay. In those instances, a double play that is blown by a fielder failing to competently handle a thrown ball to get the second out of a potential reverse-force double play does not disqualify the batter from being credited with an RBI, no doubt because the second out in a reverse-force double play is a tag play [which is relatively difficult] and not a force play [which is relatively easy]. Nor does Rule 9.04(b)(2) apply to any other type of double play that a batter might hit into, such as a caught line drive followed by a tag-out. Moreover, any botched catch in blown force double play situations must occur at first base—as opposed to second, third or home plate—for Rule 9.04(b)(2) to apply.)

CASES WHERE A RUNNER'S ACTIONS DETERMINE WHETHER OR NOT TO CREDIT THE BATTER WITH AN RBI

Rule 9.04(c)   The official scorer's judgment must determine whether a run batted in shall be credited for a run that scores when a fielder holds the ball or throws to a wrong base. Ordinarily, if the runner keeps going, the official scorer should credit a run batted in; if the runner stops and takes off again when the runner notices the misplay, the official scorer should credit the run as scored on a fielder's choice.

FOR EXAMPLE: With a runner at first base, the batter hits the ball over the head of the right fielder for a clean base hit.

The runner at first dashes to second base, then third base, but stops at third and sees that the right fielder—confused for some reason as to what to do next—has yet to return the ball to the infield. As a result, the runner starts up again and darts home to score a run. The run is not an RBI for the batter.

On the other hand, if everything had happened in exactly the same manner, but the runner advanced all the way to home plate oblivious to and unaware of the right fielder's brain freeze, the run scored would properly be considered a run batted in for the batter.

WHAT IT MEANS: In the first instance, it is indisputable that the runner's observation of the right fielder's indecision led to his advancement to home plate. Therefore, that advancement is primarily ascribable to the right fielder's actions, not the batter's putting the ball into play. Therefore, no RBI.

On the other hand, in the second instance, the aggressiveness of the base runner, coupled with the batter's putting the ball into play, accounted for the run scoring, and the right fielder's actions (or lack thereof) were of little consequence in that regard. Therefore, it's an RBI for the batter.

Special note should be taken of the fact that Rule 9.04(c) is not intended to apply to a run scoring by virtue of the commission of an error. That is why the rule is phrased the way it is: "holds the ball or throws to the wrong base." Those actions by a fielder do not constitute official fielding errors, and—as stated before—if a run scores that would not have scored but for an error, that run cannot be an RBI under any circumstances given Rule 9.04's primary text: a run must have scored "unaided by an error" in every case in order to be considered a run batted in.

A QUICK ASIDE: WHAT EXACTLY IS A "FIELDER'S CHOICE"?

Note that Rule 9.04 is the first time that the term "Fielder's Choice" is mentioned in Rule 9.00.

Inasmuch as the term is utilized many more times in the provisions of Rule 9.00 that follow, and it is a fundamental concept in scorekeeping, the definition of the term that appears in the rulebook is set forth here.

FIELDER'S CHOICE is the act of a fielder who handles a fair grounder and, instead of throwing to first base to put out the batter-runner, throws to another base in an attempt to put out a preceding runner. The term is also used by scorers (a) to account for the advance of the batter-runner who takes one or more extra bases when the fielder who handles his safe hit attempts to put out a preceding runner; (b) to account for the advance of a runner (other than by stolen base or error) while a fielder is attempting to put out another runner; and (c) to account for the advance of a runner made solely because of the defensive team's indifference (undefended steal).

◆ ◆ ◆

Rule 9.05—Base Hits

THE BEGINNING PREMISE

A base hit is a statistic credited to a batter when such batter reaches base safely, as set forth in this Rule 9.05.

(a) The official scorer shall credit a batter with a base hit when:
(1) the batter reaches first base (or any succeeding base) safely on a fair ball that settles on the ground, that touches a fence before being touched by a fielder or that clears a fence.

FOR EXAMPLE: With the bases empty, the batter hits a solid ground ball squarely between, and well out of the reach of the third baseman and shortstop, and reaches base safely.

Because the ball could not have been caught on the fly to put out the batter, nor could the ball have been fielded and delivered to first base in time to put out the batter, the batter is properly credited with a base hit.

WHAT IT MEANS: Logically, Rule 9.05 begins by setting forth the fundamental concept of what constitutes a base hit. However, although it is fairly clear in terms of what it intends to convey, Rule 9.05(a)(1) could be phrased in an alternate fashion that would be more to the point and useful to a scorer.

Specifically, if a batter puts the ball in play and reaches any base safely, and the batter's doing so is not attributable to a fielding error or a fielder's choice, the batter is properly credited with a base hit.

In other words, if a batter reaches base without batting the ball (by virtue of walk, being hit by a pitch, or because of interference or obstruction, or on a third strike passed ball or wild pitch, or the like), it's never a base hit for the batter. But if the ball is put into play, and the batter reaches base, that batter either reached base on an error, a fielder's choice, or a base hit: those are the three categories available to categorize the batter's reaching base after having hit a pitch; there are no other categories in scorekeeping from which to choose. Consequently, this alternative definition works as well—if not in some respects better—than Rule 9.05(a)(1) in helping a scorer determine what is, and what is not, a base hit.

(Note that determining whether a batter's base hit is properly scored a single, double, triple or home run is the subject of a section of the rulebook that's devoted entirely to that issue—Rule 9.06.)

A Somewhat Mysterious Turn of Phrase

Rule 9.05(a)(1)—continued   Note that Rule 9.05(a)(1) states that a base hit is to be scored when a batter reaches base safely on a fair ball that touches a fence "before being touched by a fielder."

This appears to be a curious choice of words because one cannot fairly read into that wording that a batter could be entitled to credit for a base hit if his fair ball hits a fence in fair territory after the ball merely touches a fielder.

It would seem that the words "before being touched by a fielder" in Rule 9.05(a)(1)—as well as the same words in Rule 9.05(a)(3), and the words "that has not been touched by a fielder" that appear in Rule 9.05(a)(4) and in Rule 9.05(a)(5)—are there to imply that if a fielder commits an error that allows a batter to reach base, no base hit is properly awarded.

However, if that is the case, the words serve their purpose poorly because the comment affixed to Rule 9.12(a)(1) (which is the first portion of the rulebook that specifically deals with errors) states quite emphatically that it is not necessary for a fielder to touch a ball to be charged with an error.

Given all that, one can only guess at why the rulebook has this repeated phrase in Rule 9.05. Nevertheless, it does seem to serve a legitimate purpose in the context of Rule 9.05(a)(3), as discussed in the commentary addressed to that section.

Not All Base Hits Are "Clean"

Rule 9.05(a)(2)   The official scorer shall credit a batter with a base hit when ... the batter reaches first base safely on a fair ball hit with such force, or so slowly, that any fielder attempting to make a play with the ball has no opportunity to do so.

FOR EXAMPLE: With the bases empty, the batter hits a ground ball directly to the second baseman. However, the ball has so much velocity, spin, force and fury on it that the second baseman cannot field the ball cleanly. In fact, Ryne Sandberg, Joe Morgan and Jackie Robinson—combined, well rested and at the peak of their prime—could not have made any play, let alone a successful one, on this ground ball. As a result, the batter reaches first base safely.

The next batter hits a pathetically weak ground ball in the general direction of the third baseman. By the time the third baseman is able to run in and pick up the ball, the batter is only a step or two from first base, and the third baseman—wisely recognizing the futility of trying to put out the batter at this point, or trying to put out the runner advancing from first base to second base—does not even bother to make a throw to either base, and the batter ends up safe at first.

In both cases, it's a base hit for the batter.

WHAT IT MEANS: A "clean" base is one where there is no doubt that the batter is entitled to credit for a base hit: the ball is hit well and into an area of the playing field where it's impossible for the fielders to put out the batter or any runner that might be on base at the time. However, Rule 9.05(a)(2) recognizes that sometimes a batter will not produce a clean base hit, but will nevertheless be entitled to credit for a base hit even though the batter didn't "hit it where they ain't" or make anything even remotely resembling good contact with the ball.

That said, note that Rule 9.05(a)(2) fits in well with the idea [outlined under Rule 9.05(a)(1)] that if a batter's safe arrival on base is not the product of an error, nor the result of a fielder's choice, a base hit is—if for no other reason, by default—appropriate.

Simply put, in the two instances dealt with in the example set forth above, no fielder did anything wrong or committed an error. At the same time, neither batter reached base because of the fielder's attempting to make a play on a runner that was already on base. Consequently, there is no other alternative than to credit each batter with a base hit.

GETTING CREDIT FOR A BASE HIT ON A FIELDING "MISTAKE"

Rule 9.05(a)(2) Comment: The official scorer shall credit a hit if the fielder attempting to handle the ball cannot make a play, even if such fielder deflects the ball from or cuts off another fielder who could have put out a runner.

FOR EXAMPLE: The batter hits a line drive in the direction of the shortstop. In all likelihood, the ball will be caught by the shortstop on the fly to put out the batter, but the pitcher (ill-advisedly, because it would border on a miracle for the pitcher to actually catch the ball) leaps at the ball in hopes of catching the ball himself, can manage only to deflect the flight of the ball and ruin the shortstop's ability to snag the line drive or otherwise put out the batter, and (as a result) the batter gets on base.

The following batter hits the ball in the same direction, but this time on the ground. Once again, if the ball were allowed to continue its progress to the shortstop, chances are the shortstop could put out the batter at first base, or the runner forced to advance from first base, or both, but the pitcher (as before) decides to take a crack at fielding the ball himself instead. This time, the pitcher actually gets the ball into his glove, but his momentum towards third base makes it impossible for him to turn around and get off a good throw to either first base or second base for an out.

Once again, as before, the batter is credited with a base hit.

WHAT IT MEANS: On the one hand, in both instances, it was more likely than not that if the pitcher had let the ball go to the shortstop, a putout would have resulted, but in both instances, what the pitcher did was not an error (inasmuch as there was no mechanical misplay of the batted ball in the form of a bad catch or throw). Moreover, in both cases, one cannot know for certain exactly what would have occurred but for the actions of the pitcher.

Given that, the rulebook chooses to give the batter the benefit of the doubt in these situations and award the batter credit for a base hit because the safe arrival of the batter at first base in each instance was not the product of an official scoring error, or a fielder's choice, but only the result of imperfect play on the part of a fielder.

BAD HOP AND LUCKY BOUNCE BASE HITS

Rule 9.05(a)(3)   The official scorer shall credit a batter with a base hit when ... the batter reaches first base safely on a fair ball that takes an unnatural bounce so that a fielder cannot handle it with ordinary effort, or that touches the pitcher's plate or any base (including home plate) before being touched by a fielder and bounces so that a fielder cannot handle the ball with ordinary effort.

FOR EXAMPLE: The batter hits a routine ground ball to the first baseman. The ball hits something (perhaps a divot in the major leagues, or perhaps a rock in a league where the playing fields do not resemble the top of a brand-new pool table), and that causes the ball to carom out of the first baseman's reach.

As a result, the batter arrives at first base safely and properly gets credit for a base hit.

WHAT IT MEANS: Notice the logical progression of topics.

Rule 9.05(a)(1) is all about clean base hits.

Rule 9.05(a)(2) deals with base hits that are not altogether clean, but base hits nonetheless.

Rule 9.05(a)(2)'s comment envisions base hits that are a product of fielding indiscretions (as opposed to official fielding errors).

Here, Rule 9.05(a)(3) goes on to address the concept of a base hit arising from a "bad hop," or a "lucky bounce."

As before, this sub-section of Rule 9.05 presents a situation where the batter put the ball into play, and the batter's reaching base cannot be fairly attributed to an error or a fielder's choice. Therefore, once again, it's a base hit (by default, in a manner of speaking).

(By the way, the "pitcher's plate"—in case you didn't already know, or hadn't guessed—is more commonly called the "rubber," the rectangular slab of whitened rubber set atop the pitcher's mound that the pitcher is obliged to be in contact with when he delivers a pitch to the batter).

A Mysterious Turn of Phrase, Revisited

Rule 9.05(a)(3)—continued   Rule 9.05(a)(3) states (in salient part) that "The official scorer shall credit a batter with a base hit when ... the batter reaches first base safely on a fair ball ... that touches the pitcher's plate or any base (including home plate) before being touched by a fielder and bounces so that a fielder cannot handle the ball with ordinary effort."

The key words here [that might go unnoticed because they are somewhat buried in the surrounding text of Rule 9.05(a)(3)], are "before being touched by a fielder."

What this can be taken to mean is that if a ball's path is diverted by coming in contact with the pitching rubber, a base, or home plate, after the ball has touched a fielder, and that spoils any reasonable chance of the ball being fielded cleanly, the batter is not entitled to credit for a base hit, and—applying the "it's got to be a base hit or an error or a fielder's choice" logic that underlies Rule 9.05—the batter in those instances ought to be considered as having reached base on an error, but whether that is truly the case is far from obvious or certain, given the manner in which Rule 9.05(a)(3) is worded.

A Brief Aside: Ordinary Effort

Rule 9.05(a)(3)—continued   The words "ordinary effort" are arguably the most well known and repeated in baseball scorekeeping, and they appear for the first of many times in Rule 9 in the text of Rule 9.05(a)(3).

Before the 2007 rule revisions, the phrase (as important as it is) was not defined by the rulebook, but now a definition is set out in the rulebook's Definition of Terms.

Given its importance, an extended portion of the section in this book dealing with Rule 9.12 (Errors) is devoted to the topic, and reference ought to be made to it for a better understanding of the phrase and its implications throughout Rule 9. However, for the time being, the phrase can be read simply to mean "average athletic competence" in the sense that if a fielder cannot make a given play or otherwise properly execute a fielding skill while exhibiting no more than the average athletic competence routinely exhibited by players in the league in question, that failure is not to be considered as an error.

BALLS HIT TO THE OUTFIELD

Rule 9.05(a)(4)   The official scorer shall credit a batter with a base hit when ... the batter reaches first base safely on a fair ball that has not been touched by a fielder and that is in fair territory when the ball reaches the outfield, unless in the scorer's judgment the ball could have been handled with ordinary effort.

FOR EXAMPLE: The batter hits a fly ball to the gap between the center fielder and the right fielder, where no one has a chance of catching the ball on the fly. The ball drops to the ground in fair territory, uncaught, and the batter, having reached first base safely, is credited with a base hit.

WHAT IT MEANS: This section of Rule 9.05 is one of the more obtuse and otherwise poorly worded provisions in all of Rule 9.

It suffers from the "not been touched by a fielder" phrase [as noted and discussed under Rule 9.05(a)(1)]. In addition, it really doesn't add anything to the provisions that precede it. All that it achieves is to reference formally the fact that if a ball in fair territory goes uncaught on the fly, but the ball could have been caught with "ordinary effort" to put out the batter who hit the ball, then the batter is properly considered and counted as having reached base on an error, and therefore not deserving of the statistical benefit of a base hit. However, if the ball wasn't caught, and no error was committed, it's a base hit for the batter.

TECHNICAL BASE HITS

Rule 9.05(a)(5)   The official scorer shall credit a batter with a base hit when ... a fair ball that has not been touched by a fielder touches a runner or an umpire, unless a runner is called out for having been touched by an Infield Fly, in which case the official scorer shall not score a hit.

FOR EXAMPLE: With a runner at first, the batter hits a ground ball between first and second base, but the ball hits the runner on the base path.

Under Rule 5.05(b)(4), the runner is declared out. At the same time, the batter is awarded first base.

Under Rule 9.05(a)(5), the batter's advancement from the batter's box to first base is deemed a base hit.

(Note that there are situations where a runner [or umpire] may come into contact with a batted ball, but the runner is not called out and the ball remains in play, but in those instances, Rule 9.05(a)(5) does not apply.)

WHAT IT MEANS: In cases like this, the rulebook is simply giving the batter the benefit of the doubt.

In other words, if the batted ball had not struck the runner, the batter may have been put out or may have reached base on a fielder's choice. At the same time, the batter may have reached base on a base hit. Consequently, rather than leave it up to the individual scorer to decide what would have happened but for the ball/runner contact (which would create a degree of subjectivity that might lead to some degree of inconsistency in scorekeeping), the rulebook opts to see it one way, to the exclusion of the other, and to side with the batter.

Note that application of Rule 9.05(a)(5) would be an awful way to ruin a potential no-hitter, and one can only guess what revisions of Rule 9.05(a)(5) might be made if that were ever to happen in a MLB game.

(By the way, there's that "not been touched by a fielder" language again, but here it makes sense because the playing rule that Rule 9.05(a)(5) is connected with Rule 5.05(b)(4) which specifically states that the ball in question cannot have been touched by a fielder before it hits a runner or umpire in order for the provisions of the playing rule to come into effect.)

Lastly, it may be noted that the final portion of Rule 9.05(a)(5) is a classic non sequitur, inasmuch as any batter who hits an infield fly is automatically declared out by the umpire, and therefore that batter would never be considered as having made a base hit, regardless of whether or not the batted ball hit a runner.

DON'T BE TOO QUICK TO SCORE A FIELDER'S CHOICE

Rule 9.05(a)(6)   The official scorer shall credit a batter with a base hit when … a fielder unsuccessfully attempts to put out a preceding runner and, in the official scorer's judgment, the batter-runner would not have been put out at first base by ordinary effort.

FOR EXAMPLE: With a runner at second base, the batter hits the ball through the middle of the diamond, and the runner at second base races for third.

The shortstop is able to field the ball, but a good distance behind second base. He chooses to try to put out the runner attempting to advance to third base instead of throwing the ball to first base in hopes of retiring the batter there. The throw is a good one, but the runner arrives at third base ahead of the throw and makes third base safely.

In the meantime, the batter makes first base easily.

If the scorer judges that the batter would have been put out at first base if the shortstop had thrown to first base, the batter is denied credit for a base hit, and the batter's arrival at first base is considered as being the product of a fielder's choice. On the other hand, if it is judged that the batter would have made it safely to first even if the shortstop had made a throw to first, the batter is properly credited with a base hit.

WHAT IT MEANS: Rule 9.05(a)(6) is an important rule to understand and be conscious of, because it is easy to assume that a batter—in cases where a play is made on a runner on base—should always be considered as having reached base on a fielder's choice because (in large part) that's what a fielder's choice is all about: a fielder "instead of throwing to first base to put out the batter-runner, throws to another base in an attempt to put out a preceding runner," as stated in the rulebook's Definition of Terms. But the thrust of Rule 9.05(a)(6) is that just because a play is attempted on a runner already on base, the batter is not automatically disqualified from getting credit for a base hit.

Note, however, that if a play made on a preceding runner is successful, or would have been successful but for an error, Rule 9.05(b)(3) applies and the batter (in virtually every case) is properly considered as having reached base on a fielder's choice, regardless of whether or not the batter could/would have been put out at first base if a play had been made on him.

The same is true in the case of any runner forced to advance, as stated in Rule 9.05(b)(1).

Note also that Rule 9.05(a)(6) is mirrored by Rule 9.05(b)(4), wherein what is stated in the positive in Rule 9.05(a)(6) is restated in the negative in Rule 9.05(b)(4).

AN EXTREMELY IMPORTANT PROVISION, ALBEIT OFTEN OVERLOOKED: THE SIMPLE ANSWER TO THE BIG QUESTION, WHAT TO DO WHEN IN DOUBT VIS-À-VIS SCORING A BASE HIT VERSUS AN ERROR

Rule 9.05(a) Comment: In applying Rule 9.05(a), the official scorer shall always give the batter the benefit of the doubt. A safe course for the official scorer to follow is to score a hit when exceptionally good fielding of a ball fails to result in a putout.

Little attention is ever given to Rule 9.05(a)'s comment. That is to say, few are aware of the existence of this presumption in favor of a base hit, a presumption much like the presumption of innocence in criminal law.

(Have you ever heard a broadcaster refer to Rule 9.05(a)'s comment on a play where opinions differ as to whether to score a base hit or an error, and if you have, how many times?)

However, despite its undeserved obscurity, Rule 9.05(a)'s comment can be quite useful to a scorer deciding between a base hit and error on truly close calls, and it is hard to argue against the benefit of the doubt being afforded batters in those instances inasmuch as scorekeeping ought not to be about second-guessing fielders.

Simply put, one of the main policy goals of Rule 9 is to promote consistency in scorekeeping among diverse scorers, so as to advance the integrity of scorekeeping and—as a consequence—the integrity of baseball's statistics. Therefore, Rule 9.05(a)'s comment serves an altogether laudable purpose because it attempts to steer all scorekeepers in the same direction (so to speak), like a compass or the North Star.

Reaching Base When a Runner on Base Is Put Out on a Force-Out

Rule 9.05(b)(1)   The official scorer shall not credit a base hit when a … runner is forced out by a batted ball, or would have been forced out except for a fielding error.

For example: With no outs and runners at first and second, the batter hits a routine ground ball to the third baseman.

The third baseman fields the ball and steps on third to force out the runner forced to advance from second base.

While this is going on, and with no further play attempted, the runner at first advances to second and the batter ends up safe at first.

Although the batter put the ball into play, no errors were committed, and the batter reached base, it's not a base hit for the batter. Rather, the batter is properly considered as having reached base on a fielder's choice.

What it means: For starters, despite how the text of Rule 9.05(b)(1) reads, a batted ball does not force out a runner: a fielder in possession of the ball does that. In addition, while directing the scorer not to credit a base hit, Rule 9.05(b)(1) doesn't indicate what ought to be scored instead. Aside from all that, Rule 9.05(b)(1) states a simple proposition: that a batter cannot be rightly credited with a base hit if a runner is forced out following the batter putting the ball into play, no matter what.

Consider—for instance—that (with no runner at first) a ball batted past the pitcher and up the middle of the diamond would often result in the batter reaching base on a base hit because it would be difficult for either of the middle infielders in that situation to field the ball and deliver it to first base in time to put out the batter. However, if there's a runner at first, it's often not difficult—in the same situation—for the ball to be tossed to second base to put out the runner forced to advance from first base, and thereby deny the batter credit for a base hit.

The point is, regardless of whether a particular batter might have managed a base hit if no runner had been on base, that batter does not get credit for a base hit if any runner on base is forced out as a consequence of the batter putting the ball into play.

No exceptions.

The same holds true if the attempted force-out didn't happen because a fielding error was committed. In other words, if the attempt to put out a runner forced to advance was spoiled by a fielding error, the batter is nevertheless denied credit for a base hit in the same manner as if the force-out had actually been made.

Note that situations where a runner on base who is not forced to advance is put out (or would have been put out but for an error) are dealt with in Rule 9.05(b)(3).

When a Runner on Base Is "Forced Out" on an Appeal Play—No Base Hit

Rule 9.05(b)(2)   The official scorer shall not credit a base hit when a ... batter apparently hits safely and a runner who is forced to advance by reason of the batter becoming a runner fails to touch the first base to which such runner is advancing and is called out on appeal. The official scorer shall charge the batter with a time at bat but no hit.

FOR EXAMPLE: With a runner at first, the batter smacks the ball all the way to the fence in right-center field. The runner at first advances to third, and the batter ends up safe at second base.

After the ball is returned to the infield, the defensive team makes an appeal play at second base, claiming that the runner that had been at first base failed to touch second base on his way to third. The appeal is successful, and the runner is called out.

Although the batter obviously hit the ball well enough to deserve credit for a base hit (a double, no less), the batter is properly considered as having reached base on a fielder's choice, just the same as if the runner at first had been forced out at second base in a more conventional manner (where Rule 9.05(b)(1) would apply).

WHAT IT MEANS: Here, the rulebook is ruthless, inasmuch as a rather harsh standard is applied to the innocent batter. Nonetheless, some degree of logic justifies the rulebook's approach to the issue.

As was the case in Rule 9.05(b)(1), the quality of the batter's "hit" is secondary to the fact that the defensive team was able to get a "force-out" (in an manner of speaking) from the batter having put the ball in play. Inasmuch as it's the same bottom line as it is in those circumstances where Rule 9.05(b)(2) applies, the same result is justified.

Granted, it's far from fair to do so, but the promotion of consistency in scorekeeping is the paramount concern of Rule 9, even if it sometimes comes at the cost of fairness.

Simply put, a reoccurring theme in the rulebook is that it's always better to score a play (such as this one) in a consistent manner, rather than leave it to the scorekeeper's discretion, because the less discretion that a scorekeeper has, the more uniform—and otherwise objective and valid—the records generated by the data accumulated by official scorers will be.

All that said, note that if, in the same situation described above, the runner had advanced to home plate, but was nevertheless called out because he failed to touch third base, the batter would get credit for a base hit because Rule 9.05(b)(2) applies only to a failure on the part of the runner to touch the "first base" to which such runner was advancing.

REACHING BASE WHEN A RUNNER ON BASE, WHO WAS NOT FORCED TO ADVANCE, IS PUT OUT

Rule 9.05(b)(3) **The official scorer shall not credit a base hit when a ... pitcher, the catcher or any infielder handles a batted ball and puts out a preceding runner who is attempting to advance one base or to return to his original base, or would have put out such runner with ordinary effort except for a fielding error. The official scorer shall charge the batter with a time at bat but no hit.**

FOR EXAMPLE: With a runner at second base, the batter hits a hard ground ball down the third base line. The third baseman hurls himself to the ground to smother the ball.

The runner at second—thinking that the ball will travel to the outfield, and that he can easily advance to third base safely—attempts to advance. However, having snagged the ball, the third baseman scrambles to his feet and manages to tag the runner coming from second base before the runner can reach third, and the runner is called out.

Although the batter—without a doubt—hit the ball well enough to warrant credit for a base hit, the batter is nonetheless properly considered as having reached base on a fielder's choice because of the putout at third base.

WHAT IT MEANS: Again, the text employed by the rulebook to convey a not-so-complex idea leaves a good deal to be desired, as is often the case, but the underlying concept is nonetheless understandable.

Rule 9.05(b)(1) concerns itself with runners being put out on force plays. In contrast, Rule 9.05(b)(3) addresses itself to runners who are not forced to advance being put out, but leading to the same result for the batter in question: no base hit.

Note, however, that Rule 9.05(b)(3) is limited to runners "attempting to advance one base." Therefore, if the runner in the example had not been put out at third, but had been put out trying for home plate instead, Rule 9.05(b)(3) would not apply, and the batter would qualify for a base hit.

In addition, note that Rule 9.05(b)(3) also applies to a runner "attempting ... to return to his original base." Therefore, if the runner in the example above had changed his mind about advancing on the play, had turned around to return to the safety of second base, and had been put out while trying to do so, Rule 9.05(b)(3) would again apply and the batter would not be credited with a base hit.

At the same time, Rule 9.05(b)(3) is limited to plays made by fielders other than outfielders. In other words, if the ball in the example given had been fielded by the left fielder instead of the third baseman, and the runner on base had been put out at third base, the batter would be considered as having reached base on a base hit and not on a fielder's choice (as long as it is clear that the batter would not have been put out at first base if the play had been made on the batter and not on the runner at third base).

Lastly, note that Rule 9.05(b)(3) follows the principle that is often repeated in Rule 9; if a putout is spoiled by the commission of an error, it is nonetheless deemed to have the same consequences as a successful putout would have led to, in terms of scorekeeping. It's what should/could have happened (absent the error) that counts, not necessarily what actually happened.

A Runner on Base Is Not Put Out, but the Batter Could Have Been Put Out at First Means No Base Hit

Rule 9.05(b)(4)   The official scorer shall not credit a base hit when a ... fielder fails in an attempt to put out a preceding runner and, in the scorer's judgment, the batter-runner could have been put out at first base.

For example: With a runner at third, the batter hits a ground ball to the second baseman.

Instead of throwing the ball to first base to retire the batter, the second baseman throws to home plate in an attempt to put out the runner trying to score. The throw is fine, and the catcher fields the throw cleanly, but the runner adroitly slides into home plate, avoiding the catcher's tag, and scores a run.

In the meantime, the batter reaches first base.

Although the batter put the ball into play, no error was committed, and no runner on base was put out, the batter does not get credit for a base hit. Rather, the batter is considered as having reached base on a fielder's choice because if the second baseman had chosen to put out the batter at first base, that play would have been successful—without a doubt—absent an error: a routine 4–3 putout.

What it means: Rule 9.05(b)(4) is simply the mirror image of Rule 9.05(a)(6).

Both sub-sections of Rule 9.05 recognize the fact that a batter ought not to be credited with a base hit merely because the defensive team tried to put out a runner on base instead of the batter, because doing so would give credit where no credit is due.

What Constitutes an "Attempt to Put Out a Preceding Runner"?

Rule 9.05(b) Comment: Rule 9.05(b) shall not apply if the fielder merely looks toward or feints toward another base before attempting to make the putout at first base.

For example: With a runner at third, the batter hits a ground ball back to the pitcher.

The pitcher fields the ball cleanly, with ample time and opportunity to throw the ball to first base to retire the batter, but the pitcher hesitates in doing so for fear that the runner at third base may advance to home plate and score a run while the batter is being put out at first.

In large part because the pitcher did not immediately deliver the ball to first base, the batter reaches first base safely.

The batter is credited with a base hit, or the batter is considered as having reached base on a fielder's choice, depending on the scorer's interpretation and application of Rule 9.05(b)'s comment.

WHAT IT MEANS: In point of fact, Rule 9.05(b)'s comment is actually applicable only to Rule 9.05(b)(4), and not all the provisions under Rule 9.05(b), but it is still an important provision of the rulebook because it addresses a common (and often vexing) scorekeeping quandary.

Specifically, Rule 9.05(b)(4) does not define what "an attempt to put out a preceding runner" means. Does the fielder actually have to make a throw to constitute an "attempt"? At the same time, is it necessary for the fielder to ignore the preceding runner altogether for the fielder to be considered as not having made an "attempt"?

As difficult as the far more common decision regarding whether to score an error or a base hit is, situations such as the one addressed here can be just as troublesome, if not even more so. Fortunately, the "comment" here gives some guidance, but it falls short of being altogether clear, and therefore leaves a great deal of latitude for interpretation.

When all is said and done, the best that one can glean from this comment to "Rule 9.05(b)" is that some sort of overt and obvious action on the part of a fielder must occur in order for the scorer to consider the fielder in question as having attempted to make a play on a runner. Therefore a batter is properly denied credit for a base hit in situations such as this only if some sort of overt and obvious attempt to put out a preceding runner is made. Otherwise, without that overt and obvious action on the part of the fielder, the batter deserves credit for a base hit, even though the batter's arrival on base may have been— at least to some degree—the product of the fielder devoting time and attention to a runner on base, to the exclusion of the batter.

That said, making a decision in situations like the one here is inherently difficult because of the subjectivity involved. Therefore, there is no absolute right or wrong, and the scorekeeper called upon to judge the issue can only use his or her best judgment and leave it at that.

A RUNNER ON BASE IS "PUT OUT" BY VIRTUE OF AN INTERFERENCE CALL: YOU MAKE THE CALL

Rule 9.05(b)(5)   The official scorer shall not credit a base hit when a ... runner is called out for interference with a fielder attempting to field a batted ball, unless in the scorer's judgment the batter-runner would have been safe had the interference not occurred.

FOR EXAMPLE. With a runner at second base, the batter hits a ground ball to the shortstop. The runner at second base intentionally barrels into the shortstop, knocking the shortstop down. The runner is called out for doing so, but the batter arrives at first base safe.

Whether to credit the batter with a base hit is a function of whether the scorer believes that the batter would have been retired at first base had the interference not occurred.

WHAT IT MEANS: In virtually every case, if a runner on base is put out when the batter puts the ball into play, the batter is denied credit for a base hit. However, Rule 9.05(b)(5) plainly gives the scorer discretion to decide if the batter would have been put out if the interference had not occurred (in which case the batter would properly be considered as having reached base on a fielder's choice), or if the batter would have reached base if the interference had not occurred (in which case the batter is properly credited with a base hit).

Note that here—as contrasted with other provisions of Rule 9—the goal of uniformity in scorekeeping that is advanced by limiting the official scorer's discretion as much as possible is not followed, but given the rarity of the requisite circumstances arising, Rule 9.05(b)(5) is a small concession to fairness over uniformity.

◆ ◆ ◆

Rule 9.06— Determining Value of Base Hits

THE BEGINNING PREMISE: ALL BASE HITS ARE NOT CREATED EQUAL

The official scorer shall score a base hit as a one-base hit, two-base hit, three-base hit or home run when no error or putout results, as follows:

(a) Subject to the provisions of Rules 9.06(b) and 9.06(c), it is a one-base hit if the batter stops at first base; it is a two-base hit if the batter stops at second base; it is a three-base hit if the batter stops at third base; and it is a home run if the batter touches all bases and scores.

FOR EXAMPLE: Legend has it that on October 1, 1932, Babe Ruth pointed in the direction of the center field fence at Wrigley Field in Chicago and proceeded to hit the ball on a 2–2 pitch delivered by the Chicago Cubs pitcher that day—Charlie Root—sending the ball over 436 feet from home plate and clearing the center field fence in the third game of that season's World Series, which series was ultimately swept by the New York Yankees.

(The legend part is the pointing; the rest is fact.)

Inasmuch as Ruth reached base safely, without the aid of an error or by virtue of a fielder's choice, he was properly credited with a base hit. Moreover, because he touched all the bases and scored, it was a four-base hit—a home run—for Ruth (and the last home run he hit in a World Series game).

WHAT IT MEANS: The premise that Rule 9.06(a) sets out would seem to be so self-evident that the authors of the rulebook could have chosen to skip it altogether, but it serves to introduce the idea that different base hits have varying "values."

In addition, there is far more to determining the value of any given base hit than simply going by how many bases a batter reached as a result of the base hit—as evidenced by the following sub-sections of Rule 9.06—and Rule 9.06(a) serves as a starting point for laying out the finer points of the task.

HOW FAR A BATTER ADVANCES ON A BASE HIT DOES NOT NECESSARILY DETERMINE THE ULTIMATE VALUE OF THE BASE HIT

Rule 9.06(b)   When, with one or more runners on base, the batter advances more than one base on a safe hit and the defensive team makes an attempt to put out a preceding runner, the scorer shall determine whether the batter made a legitimate two-base hit or three-base hit, or whether the batter-runner advanced beyond first base on the fielder's choice.

FOR EXAMPLE: With a runner at second base, the batter hits a line drive some distance (but not very far) down the right field line.

Believing he has a chance at putting out the runner who was at second when the ball was put into play (and who is in the process of trying to score a run), the right fielder fields the ball and immediately fires it to the catcher at home plate.

Seeing that, the batter takes second base on the right fielder's throw.

Although the batter [in the words of Rule 9.06(a)] "stops at second base," the batter is entitled to credit for only a one-base hit (a single), and the advancement to second base is considered as advancement on a fielder's choice.

WHAT IT MEANS: There is a fundamental fairness and logic at work here, inasmuch as if there had been no runner on base, the batter would doubtless have advanced no further than first base (absent a fielding error). It was the defensive team's attempt to put out a runner on base that gave rise to the batter advancing past first base.

ADDITIONAL FACTORS IN MEASURING THE VALUE OF BASE HITS

Rule 9.06 Comment: The official scorer shall not credit the batter with a three-base hit when a preceding runner is put out at home plate, or would have been out but for an error.

The official scorer shall not credit the batter with a two-base hit when a preceding runner trying to advance from first base is put out at third base, or would have been out but for an error.

The official scorer shall not, however, with the exception of the above, determine the value of base hits by the number of bases advanced by a preceding runner.

A batter may deserve a two-base hit even though a preceding runner advances one or no bases; a batter may deserve only a one-base hit even though he reaches second base and a preceding runner advances two bases.

For example:

(1) Runner on first. Batter hits to right fielder, who throws to third base in an unsuccessful attempt to put out runner. Batter takes second base. The official scorer shall credit batter with one-base hit.

(2) Runner on second. Batter hits fair fly ball. Runner holds up to determine if ball is caught and then advances only to third base, while batter takes second base. The official scorer shall credit batter with two-base hit.

(3) Runner on third. Batter hits high, fair fly. Runner takes a lead, then runs back to tag up, thinking the ball will be caught. The ball falls safe, but runner cannot score, although batter has reached second. The official scorer shall credit batter with a two-base hit.

Although the examples here sound like Tarzan wrote them, this "comment" to Rule 9.06(b) neatly carries forward the policy underlying the main text of Rule 9.06(b). Moreover, it represents one of the best portions of Rule 9 because it sets forth three cogent examples of situations where the dictates of the comment come into play and how those mandates are properly applied.

THE CONSEQUENCES ARISING FROM A BATTER-RUNNER BEING PUT OUT AFTER OVERSLIDING A BASE

Rule 9.06(c)　When the batter attempts to make a two-base hit or a three-base hit by sliding, he must hold the last base to which he advances. If a

batter-runner overslides and is tagged out before getting back to the base safely, he shall be credited with only as many bases as he attained safely. If a batter-runner overslides second base and is tagged out, the official scorer shall credited [*sic*] him with a one-base hit; if the batter-runner overslides third base and is tagged out, the official scorer shall credit him with a two-base hit.

FOR EXAMPLE: The batter hits a fly ball that carries over the head of the left fielder.

There is no doubt that the batter will get to first base easily, which he does, but there's a chance that the batter can make it safely to second base as well, so he rounds first base, hoping to "stretch" a single into a double.

The throw from left field arrives at second base at more or less the same time as the batter. When the batter slides into second, he avoids the tag of the shortstop covering second base. However, the momentum of the slide carries the batter past the bag, and he is tagged out before he can regain contact with second base.

Although the batter reached second base before being tagged out, he is nevertheless limited to credit for only a single.

WHAT IT MEANS: On top of the provisions that preceded it, Rule 9.06(c) adds another dimension, and the policy it embodies is easily understood.

A runner (a batter-runner is this case) cannot fairly be considered as having attained a base unless that runner "holds" the base. That is to say, although a runner may have technically reached a base safely—not having been tagged out or forced out before making contact with the base in question—it is of no consequence if that runner is put out at that base nonetheless.

From the perspective of the game, the runner may have just as well been put out before reaching the base as having been put out a second or two after technically reaching that base. Therefore, Rule 9.06(c) logically denies credit for that base in valuing any given base hit.

Note that Rule 9.06(c) addresses oversliding at second base and third base only because a runner cannot be put out at home plate after touching home plate safely, and the same holds true at first base—at least when the batter does not attempt to advance to second base after touching first base safely. (This also applies to Rule 9.06(c)'s comment limiting itself to plays at second and third base.)

In addition, note that Rule 9.06(c) is mirrored in Rule 9.07(e) and Rule 9.07(h)(3) in the context of a runner oversliding a base in an attempt to steal a base.

Note also that the grammatical error in the third sentence of Rule 9.06(c)—"scorer shall credited him"—appears in the official text of the rulebook, and that all the rulebook text quoted throughout this book is quoted verbatim, although some minor modifications in terms of punctuation and spacing have been made for the sake of clarity.

THE CONSEQUENCES ARISING FROM A BATTER-RUNNER BEING PUT OUT AFTER OVERRUNNING A BASE

Rule 9.06(c) Comment: If the batter-runner overruns second or third base and is tagged out trying to return, the official scorer shall credit the batter-runner with the last base he touched. If a batter-runner runs past second base after reaching that base on his feet, attempts to return and is tagged out, the official scorer shall credit the batter with a two-base hit. If a batter-runner runs past third base after reaching that base on his feet, attempts to return and is tagged out, the official scorer shall credit the batter with a three-base hit.

FOR EXAMPLE: In the same situation given in the example for the main text of Rule 9.06(c), the left fielder has trouble delivering the ball to second base because the ball takes a peculiar bounce off the outfield wall. As a result, the batter comes into second base standing up. Not only that, but the batter takes a few steps toward third base, thinking that he might have a chance to advance even further. However, the batter soon realizes that third base is not a viable option, and he attempts to return to second base.

Unfortunately (for the batter), the left fielder fires the ball to second base and the second baseman tags the batter out.

In this case, unlike the first case, the batter is credited with a two-base hit even though he was put out at second base.

WHAT IT MEANS: Here's the flip side of Rule 9.06(c)'s main text.

The difference between the two scenarios may be subtle, and arguably inconsequential. Nonetheless, one can understand why the rulebook takes this opposite approach here.

In the first case (oversliding), you can question whether the batter really hit the ball well enough to warrant credit for a two-base hit; after all, the fact that the batter chose to slide into the base in question would indicate a close play where the batter could easily have ended up being put out. However, in this case (overrunning), there is no doubt that the ball was hit well enough to justify the batter being credited with a double; after all, the fact that the batter didn't slide would lead one to conclude that it was a solid two-base hit.

In any case, regardless of whatever rationale may be behind it, the distinction is there and its application is clearly mandated.

APPEAL PLAYS: WHAT HAPPENS WHEN THE BATTER-RUNNER IS CALLED OUT FOR FAILING TO TOUCH A BASE

Rule 9.06(d) When the batter, after making a safe hit, is called out for having failed to touch a base, the last base the batter reached safely shall determine if the official scorer shall credit him with a one-base hit, a two-base hit or a three-base hit.

If a batter-runner is called out after missing home plate, the official scorer shall credit him with a three-base hit.

If a batter-runner is called out for missing third base, the official scorer shall credit him with a two-base hit.

If a batter-runner is called out for missing second base, the official scorer shall credit him with a one-base hit.

If a batter-runner is called out for missing first base, the official scorer shall charge him with a time at bat, but no hit.

As was the case with the comment attached to Rule 9.06(b), here we have another example where the rulebook leaves little—if anything—to be desired in terms of clarity.

ASCRIBING VALUE TO "TECHNICAL" BASE HITS

Rule 9.06(e) When a batter-runner is awarded two bases, three bases or a home run under the provisions of Rules 5.06(b)(4) or 6.01(h), the official scorer shall credit the batter-runner with a two-base hit, a three-base hit or a home run, as the case may be.

FOR EXAMPLE: The batter crushes the ball for a line drive headed into the gap in left-center field.

Ill-advisedly, the shortstop throws his glove at the ball as it's going by him, knocking the ball to the ground.

Although the batter may have only reached second base, or perhaps even only first base in the ordinary course of events, the batter is nonetheless awarded third base by the umpire under the provisions of Rule 5.06(b)(4), and the official scorer is obliged to credit the batter with a three-base hit.

WHAT IT MEANS: The playing rules mentioned in Rule 9.06(e), [Rules 5.06(b)(4) and 6.01(h)], address themselves to a number of situations where runners and/or batters are awarded bases because of rule infractions committed by the opposing team in the field, as in the example given above.

Rather than have the scorer judge how many bases the batter would have advanced if the infraction had not been committed, Rule 9.06(e) simply directs the scorer to value the "base hit" based on the number of bases awarded. This cut and dried approach is doubtless another manifestation of the rulebook's policy to promote consistency in scorekeeping by limiting—as much as possible—judgment calls on the part of official scorers.

VALUING GAME-ENDING HITS

Rule 9.06(f)   Subject to the provisions of Rule 9.06(g), when a batter ends a game with a safe hit that drives in as many runs as are necessary to put his team in the lead, the official scorer shall credit such batter with only as many bases on his hit as are advanced by the runner who scores the winning run, and then only if the batter runs out his hit for as many bases as are advanced by the runner who scores the winning run.

FOR EXAMPLE: In the bottom of the ninth, with the scored tied and the potential winning run at third base, the batter hits the ball to the fence in right field and the runner at third base scores the winning run to end the game.

There is no doubt that the ball was hit well enough for the batter to make at least second base under any set of circumstances. However, Rule 9.06(f) limits the batter to credit for a single.

WHAT IT MEANS: It's altogether logical.

Once a game is lost, the defensive team doesn't care how many extra bases the final batter in the game may advance on his base hit. That being so, judging the value of game-ending hits based on how many bases the batter reached often has no real validity, and Rule 9.06(f) is a simple recognition of that fact.

As far as the requirement that the batter "runs out his hit," as well as the proviso that Rule 9.06(f) is subject to Rule 9.06(g), please refer to the discussion of Rule 9.06(g) that follows.

RULE 9.06 (F) TRUMPS RULE 9.06(E) IN THE CONTEXT OF GAME-ENDING HITS

Rule 9.06(f) Comment: The official scorer shall apply this rule even when the batter is theoretically entitled to more bases because of being awarded an "automatic" extra-base hit under various provisions of Rules 5.05 and 5.06(b)(4).

FOR EXAMPLE: With the game tied in the bottom of the ninth, and the potential winning run at third, the batter hits the ball to the outfield and the ball bounces into the stands for a "ground-rule double."

Although the batter is entitled to credit for a two-base hit under ordinary circumstances, the comment to Rule 9.06(f) limits the batter to credit for a single because the runner who scored the winning run advanced only one base in order to do so.

WHAT IT MEANS: One could ponder why the authors of the rulebook choose to follow the policy of Rule 9.06(f) (strictly limiting the value of a game-ending hit to the number of bases advanced by the runner who scored the game winning run), as opposed to the policy manifest in 10.06(e) (where a batter's base hit is valued according to how many bases a batter is awarded as a result of a rules infraction committed by the defensive team), but little purpose is served in doing so.

The bottom line is that this portion of Rule 9.06(f)'s comment says what it means, and it means what it says. Any policy issues aside, the situations where it is applicable are relatively easy to recognize, and the rule is simple to apply.

VALUING BASE HITS WHERE THE GAME TECHNICALLY ENDS BEFORE THE BATTER-RUNNER RUNS OUT THE PLAY

Rule 9.06(f) Comment (continued): The official scorer shall credit the batter with a base touched in the natural course of play, even if the winning run has scored moments before on the same play.

For example, the score is tied in the bottom of the ninth inning with a runner on second base and the batter hits a ball to the outfield that falls for a base hit. The runner scores after the batter has touched first base and continued on to second base but shortly before the batter-runner reaches second base. If the batter-runner reaches second base, the official scorer shall credit the batter with a two-base hit.

Here's why this portion of Rule 9.06(f)'s comment was added by the rules committee as part of the 2007 revisions.

Playing Rule 7.01(g)(3) states (in salient part) that "If the home team scores the winning run in its half of the ninth inning (or its half of an extra inning after a tie), the game ends immediately when the winning run is scored." That being so, this portion of Rule 9.06(f)'s comment serves the purpose of making it clear that a batter—who would otherwise deserve credit for a game-ending extra base hit—is not deprived of credit for an extra-base hit based merely of the timing of the winning run scoring and the batter reaching the base at issue.

Valuing Game Ending "Home Runs"

Rule 9.06(g)   When the batter ends a game with a home run hit out of the playing field, the batter and any runners on base are entitled to score.

For example: On October 17, 1999, in the fifth game of that season's National League Championship Series between the Atlanta Braves and the New York Mets, Robin Ventura (batting for the Mets in the bottom of the 15th inning with the score tied 3–3) hit the ball over the fence in fair territory (with the bases loaded!) and the Mets won the game as a result.

Ventura was entitled to full credit for a home run (four-base hit), even though the runner who scored the run that gave New York the run necessary to win the game advanced only one base, but Ventura got credit for only a single! Why?

What it means: Rule 9.06(f) itself states that it is "subject to" Rule 9.06(g), and Rule 9.06(g) clearly recognizes that to apply Rule 9.06(f)'s restrictions to home runs hit over the fence would serve no legitimate purpose inasmuch as the reason for Rule 9.06(f)—the fact that the fielders for the losing team understandably give up on trying to put out a batter rounding the bases once he has touched first base safely and the game-winning run has scored—doesn't come into play when the batter has knocked the ball out of the park to win the game.

Ironically, as already noted, Ventura received credit only for a single, and not a home run, but that wasn't because Rule 9.06(f) limits a batter in a game-ending hit situation to credit for only as many bases as the runner who scored the winning run advanced to score the winning run. Rather, it was because Ventura was mobbed by his teammates after touching first base, and—to this day—he has yet to reach second base on that play, let alone score the run that he might have otherwise scored.

In other words, the denial of credit for anything more than a single came from the fact that Ventura didn't "run out" his hit for as many bases as he was entitled to, and the text of Rule 9.06(a) [set forth in the beginning of this section] mandates his doing so in order to receive credit for more than the one base he actually reached.

(Note also that the idea of a batter running out the bases he might be entitled to in order to get credit for those bases also appears in the final portion of Rule 9.06(f)'s text.)

In addition, it bears pointing out that Rule 9.06(g) only applies to "out-of-the-park" home runs—specifically, "a home run hit out of the playing field." In other words, if the ball stays in the park, it is virtually certain that a four-base hit on the part of the batter (in game-ending situations where the winning run is scored by a runner on base) would be the product of the defensive team simply giving up on getting the batter out after the winning run scored and the game officially ended. Therefore, an "inside-the-park" home run does not come under the purview of the exception to Rule 9.06(f) found in Rule 9.06(g).

To Catch a Thief
Rule 9.07

Rule 9.07—
Stolen Bases and Caught Stealing

NEGATION: A DEFINITION BY EXCLUSION
AND EXEMPTION—A STATEMENT OF
WHAT A THING IS NOT, FROM WHICH
ONE CAN INFER WHAT THAT SOMETHING IS

The official scorer shall credit a stolen base to a runner whenever the runner advances one base unaided by a hit, a putout, an error, a force-out, a fielder's choice, a passed ball, a wild pitch or a balk, subject to the following:

In scorekeeping, the scorer is obliged to attribute the advancement of every batter and runner from one base to the next to a specific statistical category. (See Rule 9.12(a)(7) Comment—"every base advanced by a runner must be accounted for.")

The primary text of Rule 9.07 sets out all the categories a scorer can choose from by specifically naming eight, and indicating that if the advancement is not attributable to any of those eight categories, the advancement is properly considered a "stolen base."

By doing so, Rule 9.07 defines a stolen base in a left-handed manner; it doesn't tell you what a stolen base is exactly but rather that it's advancement that cannot be categorized as any of the other eight categories.

There is no survey that I've seen to prove this, but my experience has been that there are few individuals involved in baseball at any level—let alone garden variety baseball fans—that conceive of or consider "stolen bases" to be advancement that can't be categorized in any other manner. Nevertheless, that is the bedrock definition of what constitutes a stolen base, and the premise on which all the provisions of Rule 9.07 are built.

In any case, as simple as the initial premise might seem, many aspects involved in the subject of stolen bases are among most complex in scorekeeping, as can be seen in the following.

The Interplay Between Stolen Bases and Wild Pitches and Passed Balls

Rule 9.07(a)   When a runner starts for the next base before the pitcher delivers the ball and the pitch results in what ordinarily is scored a wild pitch or passed ball, the official scorer shall credit the runner with a stolen base and shall not charge the misplay, unless, as a result of the misplay, the stealing runner advances an extra base, or another runner also advances, in which case the official scorer shall score the wild pitch or passed ball as well as the stolen base.

For example: With runners at first and third, the runner at first base takes off on the pitch.

The pitch is low, so low that it bounces off the ground a good five feet in front of the plate.

As a result, the ball eludes the catcher. Nevertheless, the catcher is able to retrieve the ball in time to deter the runner who had been at first base (but now is at second base) from advancing any further, but not in time to prevent the runner who had been at third base (who would have remained at third base but for the wild pitch) from capitalizing on the wild pitch to score a run.

Although the runner at first arguably benefited from the wild pitch, his advancement from first to second is not deemed as advancement on the wild pitch. Rather, because the runner at first didn't start for second base after seeing that the ball was going to get away from the catcher, but rather started running in an obvious attempt to steal second base regardless of whatever the quality of the pitch might turn out to be, that runner's advancement from first to second is properly categorized as a stolen base.

If that were all there was to it, no wild pitch would be scored at all. On the other hand, the runner at third scoring is properly attributed to the wild pitch, inasmuch as that advancement was precipitated by the wild pitch and would not have taken place but for the wild pitch, so the wild pitch goes "into the books" on that basis.

WHAT IT MEANS: The fundamental premise of Rule 9.07(a) is that you can't be sure that a runner would have been put out in an attempt to steal a base if the pitch on which the runner was attempting to steal had not eluded the catcher, either because it was a wild pitch (meaning that the catcher's failure to catch or otherwise stop the ball was the fault of the pitcher) or it was a passed ball (meaning that the fault was that of the catcher). Therefore, the rulebook chooses to afford the runner the benefit of the doubt in those instances, and the runner receives credit for a stolen base.

Note that this approach makes what might otherwise be a judgment call—deciding whether the runner would have been put out if the pitch hadn't been wild, or the catcher hadn't mishandled the pitch—an automatic determination on the part of the scorer, thereby advancing the fundamental policy of limiting discretion in scorekeeping calls and making scorekeeping more consistent.

At the same time, although charging the pitcher with a wild pitch, or charging the catcher with a passed ball, is overlooked in the strict context of the stolen base issue, a wild pitch or a passed ball is nevertheless charged in those situations if the runner who stole a base on the pitch ends up getting to yet another base, because that additional advancement is the product of the wild pitch or passed ball. Moreover, as in the example given above, if another runner on base capitalizes on the wild pitch or passed ball, the wild pitch or passed ball is counted in that context, even though it is overlooked in the limited context of the stolen base.

In addition, note that Rule 9.07(a) uses the word "misplay" instead of "error" in referring to the pitch getting away from the catcher: That is because wild pitches and passed balls are not considered official fielding errors, as stated in Rule 9.12(f).

GIVING A RUNNER CREDIT FOR A STOLEN BASE REGARDLESS OF A WILD THROW MADE BY THE CATCHER IN AN ATTEMPT TO PREVENT THE BASE BEING STOLEN

Rule 9.07(b)   When a runner is attempting to steal, and the catcher, after receiving the pitch, makes a wild throw trying to prevent the stolen base, the official scorer shall credit the runner with a stolen base. The official scorer shall not charge an error unless the wild throw permits the stealing runner to advance one or more extra bases, or permits another runner to advance, in which case the official scorer shall credit the runner with the stolen base and charge one error to the catcher.

For example: With runners at first and third, the runner at first base takes off on the pitch. The pitch is well outside the strike zone, but the catcher is able to catch the ball cleanly.

The catcher's subsequent throw to second base, made in attempt to put out the runner trying to steal second base, is well off the mark. In fact, it sails into the outfield, and the runner coming from first base gets to second base easily.

Fortunately (for the defensive team) the center fielder is able to retrieve the catcher's errant throw in time to keep the runner who stole second base at second base. However, the runner at third takes off when he sees that the catcher's throw is wild, and he scores a run.

The runner who was at first base is properly credited with a stolen base, and no error is charged to the catcher on the bad throw to second base (as far as the bad throw having to some extent facilitated the runner stealing second base). However, the catcher is charged with an error because the bad throw gave rise to the runner at third base advancing to home plate to score a run.

What it means: Although any bad throw made by any fielder in an attempt to put out a runner trying to steal a base is not considered an error, as stated in Rule 9.12(a)(5), Rule 9.07(b) focuses on the catcher—the fielder who makes throws to prevent stolen bases more than any other fielder, and it specifically exempts the catcher from being charged with an error in those instances. At the same time, as was the case in Rule 9.07(a), Rule 9.07(b) gives the runner attempting to steal a base the benefit of the doubt by awarding the runner credit for a stolen base regardless of the quality of the throw made in the attempt to prevent the runner from stealing the base in question.

After all, who is to say (at least in most cases) whether a runner attempting to steal a base would certainly have been put out if the catcher's throw had not been "wild."

At the same time, as was the case in Rule 9.07(a), any advancement over and above the stolen base by the runner, or any advancement by another runner on base arising from the wild throw, is looked upon as a result of the wild throw, and—in the context of Rule 9.07(b)—the catcher is charged with an error attendant to that "additional advancement."

Note also that Rule 9.07(b) speaks to the catcher being charged with only "one error" in these circumstances. Even if more than one runner advances on the wild throw (above and beyond the stolen base), and/or the advancement linked to the bad throw is more than a single base, the catcher is nonetheless charged with only one error.

(It's not unlike a waiter dropping a tray of dishes. Whether there was only one dish on the tray, or two or five or 50, it was still only one mistake on the part of the clumsy waiter, not two or five or 50.)

Runners Caught in Run-Down Plays

Rule 9.07(c) When a runner, attempting to steal, or after being picked off base, evades being put out in a run-down play and advances to the next base without the aid of an error, the official scorer shall credit the runner with a stolen base.

For example: Although the pitcher has made more than a few throws to first base to keep the runner at first from taking too big of a lead, the runner breaks for second base the moment he thinks the pitcher has committed himself to delivering the next pitch.

Exhibiting cunning worthy of a jungle cat, the pitcher—without committing a balk—delivers the ball to the shortstop, who has come from his customary position on the field to cover second base.

With the runner now "trapped" between first base and second base, a "run-down play" ensues, with the runner being chased back and forth, multiple fielders throwing the ball, catching the ball, and chasing the trapped runner in the process.

Ultimately, the runner manages to survive the ordeal and ends up safe at second, even though no fielding error was committed during the course of the run-down play that the runner managed to survive.

The runner is properly credited with a stolen base, just as though he had made it directly from first base to second base without deviation.

What it means: A stolen base doesn't have to be "clean."

The bottom line here is that the runner advanced in a manner that cannot be fairly categorized in any of the eight ways enumerated in the initial text of Rule 9.07. Therefore, the advancement is considered—if for no other reason, by default—as a stolen base.

All that Rule 9.07(c) adds to the concept already stated in Rule 9.07 is to make clear that just because a runner may find himself "in a pickle," that does not necessarily disqualify the runner from being credited with a stolen base.

The most intriguing aspect of Rule 9.07(c) is that it also applies to a runner who may not have intended to steal a base at all, inasmuch as the rule can apply to a runner who was simply "picked off," survived an errorless run-down play and ended up having advanced a base.

All that said, it is important to remember that the run-down play has to be without error. If an error is committed during the course of a run-down that leads to the runner advancing, the advancement cannot be fairly considered as having been on a stolen base. Rather, it is properly considered as advancement on the error.

At the same time, it should also be noted that Rule 9.12(a)(5) states that a wild throw made to prevent a stolen base is not to be deemed an error. Therefore, care and caution should be given to run-down plays inasmuch as a wild throw made to prevent a runner in a run-down play from advancing (ultimately stealing a base) is not properly looked upon as an error by the rulebook, and a blown run-down play in that case is properly considered as being "errorless."

A Runner on Base Advances While Another Runner on Base Gets Caught Up in a Run-Down Play: Part 1

Rule 9.07(c)—continued   If another runner also advances on the play, the official scorer shall credit both runners with stolen bases.

For example: With runners at first and third, the runner at first base gets caught in a run-down play between first and second. Whether it's a result of the runner at first base attempting to steal second base, or the runner being picked off, is of no consequence because this portion of Rule 9.07(a) applies to either situation.

The runner at first base survives the run-down without an error being committed by the defensive team during the course of the run-down play, and ends up safe at second base.

While that was unfolding, the runner at third advanced to home plate to score a run.

The runner who advanced from first to second is properly considered as having stolen a base (as per the first sentence of Rule 9.07(c)). At the same time, the runner who advanced from third to home plate also gets credit for a stolen base.

What it means: One might guess that the advancement of the runner at third base to home plate in this case could be attributable to a fielder's choice. After all, that runner advanced while the defensive team was (as per the definition of a fielder's choice in the rulebook) "attempting to put out another runner." However, this second sentence of Rule 9.07(c) expressly overrides that notion.

Moreover, the definition of a "fielder's choice" found in Rule 9.02 states that runner advancement on what might otherwise be considered as being made on a fielder's choice is not properly considered advancement on a fielder's choice if the advancement is made "by stolen base or error."

The bottom line is that a runner who advances while another runner is caught in a run-down play is considered as having stolen a base (along with the runner caught in a run-down play) if the runner caught in the run-down play survives the run-down (without the commission of an error by the defensive team) and makes it safely to the next base. However, if the runner who was caught in the run-down play was put out (or would have been put out but for the commission of an error), or advanced by virtue of a fielding error, the other runner's advancement is counted as advancement on a fielder's choice.

At the same time, if the runner who was caught in the run-down play survived the run-down play (without an error having been committed) by ending up back at the base that he started from, the next portion of Rule 9.07(c) applies.

A Runner on Base Advances While Another Runner on Base Gets Caught Up in a Run-Down Play: Part 2

Rule 9.07(c)—continued   If a runner advances while another runner, attempting to steal, evades being put out in a run-down play and returns safely, without the aid of an error, to the base he originally occupied, the official scorer shall credit a stolen base to the runner who advances.

A Summary of Rule 9.07(c)

Rule 9.07(c) crams a lot into one paragraph, and it can sometimes be daunting to sort it all out. Therefore, here is a summary of Rule 9.07(c)'s provisions to help you navigate the waters.

If a runner gets caught up in a run-down play, and advances to the next base without the benefit of an error, that runner is properly credited with a stolen base.

If that runner is put out, he's put out, but if he advances due to the commission of an error, the advancement is counted as being made on the error.

(Once again, bear in mind that Rule 9.12(a)(5) states that "The official scorer shall charge an error against any fielder … whose wild throw permits a runner to reach a base safely, when in the scorer's judgment a good throw would have put out the runner, unless such wild throw is made attempting to prevent a stolen base.")

If a runner on base advances while another runner on base gets caught up in a run-down play and advances to the next base without the benefit of an error, then both runners get credit for a stolen base. But if the runner is put out in the context of the run-down play, or advances aided by an error, the other runner's reaching the next base is properly scored as progress made on a fielder's choice.

Lastly, if a runner on base advances while another runner on base gets caught up in a run-down play and the runner in the run-down play gets back to the base that he was at prior to the run-down play (without the benefit of an error), then the runner who advances gets credit for a stolen base. However, if the runner in the run-down play is put out, or he gets back safely to his original base aided by an error, the other runner's advancement is (as before) properly deemed advancement on a fielder's choice.

Double-Steals and Triple-Steals

Rule 9.07(d)   When a double or triple-steal is attempted and one runner is thrown out before reaching and holding the base such runner is attempting to steal, no other runner shall be credited with a stolen base.

Rule 9.07(d) is straightforward and simple, and therefore requires little comment. Note the words "and holding." They refer to the concept dealt with in Rule 9.06(c), as well as the following Rule 9.07(e), and touched upon in Rule 9.07(h)(3), that when a runner is put out trying to get back to a base that the runner has lost safe contact with by virtue of oversliding, that runner is not to be credited with having reached (held) that base. On the other hand, if the safe contact was lost by way of the runner overrunning the base, credit is nonetheless given to the runner for having reached (held) that base.

Oversliding (and Overrunning) a Base

Rule 9.07(e)   When a runner is tagged out after oversliding a base, while attempting either to return to that base or to advance to the next base, the official scorer shall not credit such runner with a stolen base.

For example: The runner at first base slides into second base in a classic attempt to steal second base.

The catcher has made a decent throw, but the runner arrives at second base before the ball does, and the ball temporarily gets away from the fielder covering second base.

Unfortunately (for the runner), the force of the slide carries him well past second base, and the ball is retrieved in time to tag out the runner before he can scramble back to second or (alternatively) try for third base.

Although at least for a moment the runner reached second base safely on his steal attempt, the runner is nevertheless not credited with a stolen base.

WHAT IT MEANS: It's really quite simple, but note that if the runner in the example given above had been put out in the same manner after having overrun second base, credit for a stolen base would be in order.

As far as the thinking behind the differentiation between a runner being put out after overrunning a base—as opposed to oversliding a base—is concerned, reference can be made to the discussion set out following Rule 9.06(c) and following the comment attached to Rule 9.06(c).

THE RAMIFICATIONS OF A MUFFED CATCH IN THE CONTEXT OF STOLEN BASE ATTEMPTS

Rule 9.07(f) **When in the scorer's judgment a runner attempting to steal is safe because of a muffed throw, the official scorer shall not credit a stolen base. The official scorer shall credit an assist to the fielder who made the throw, charge an error to the fielder who muffed the throw and charge the runner with "caught stealing."**

FOR EXAMPLE: The runner at first base breaks for second base on the pitch.

The catcher handles the pitch cleanly and fires the ball to second base. The catcher's throw is dead on target, and the ball arrives at second base well before the runner, but the shortstop (covering second) inexplicably drops the ball, and as a direct result of that "muff" on the part of the shortstop, the runner is safe.

Because the runner would clearly have been put out but for the shortstop's failure to field the catcher's throw in a competent manner, the shortstop is charged with an error. At the same time, although the runner was not put out, the catcher is credited with an assist and the runner is charged with having been "caught stealing," just as though the runner had actually been put out.

WHAT IT MEANS: Here is a prime example of the rulebook instructing the scorer to do something that the scorer is often obliged to do: consider something as having happened that didn't really happen because of the commission of a fielding error.

The logic is sound, and the results are fair to all concerned.

The shortstop messed up, so his fielding statistics are adversely affected. At the same time, the catcher's competence is rewarded (with credit for an assist). In addition, the runner is denied credit for something that he does not deserve (credit for a stolen base) and charged with something that he does deserve (caught stealing).

Defensive Indifference: You Can't Steal Something That Someone Gives You, but Then Again, Maybe You Can

Rule 9.07(g)   The official scorer shall not score a stolen base when a runner advances solely because of the defensive team's indifference to the runner's advance. The official scorer shall score such a play as a fielder's choice.

Fair enough.

Rule 9.07(g) Comment: The scorer shall consider, in judging whether the defensive team has been indifferent to a runner's advance, the totality of the circumstances, including the inning and score of the game, whether the defensive team had held the runner on base, whether the pitcher had made any pickoff attempts on that runner before the runner's advance, whether the fielder ordinarily expected to cover the base to which the runner advanced made a move to cover such base, whether the defensive team had a legitimate strategic motive to not contest the runner's advance or whether the defensive team might be trying impermissibly to deny the runner credit for a stolen base.

So far, so good.

For example, with runners on first and third bases, the official scorer should ordinarily credit a stolen base when the runner on first advances to second, if, in the scorer's judgment, the defensive team had a legitimate strategic motive—namely, preventing the runner on third base from scoring on the throw to second base—not to contest the runner's advance to second base.

Come again? The runner gets credit for a stolen base when the defensive team doesn't contest the runner's advancement?

The official scorer may conclude that the defensive team is impermissibly trying to deny a runner credit for a stolen base if, for example, the defensive team fails to defend the advance of a runner approaching a league or career record or a league statistical title.

And therefore (one would tacitly assume), the official scorer should properly give the runner in question credit for a stolen base.

◆ ◆ ◆

Rule 9.07(g) itself is fairly forthright and understandable. However, its "comment" (which comment is entirely the product of the 2007 Rule 9 revisions) is baffling in the example that it gives.

All the verbiage in the comment about considering "the totality of the circumstances" is useful and helpful (although it seems to assume that an official scorer would not necessarily do so unless told to, and therefore is somewhat condescending). However, the problem lies in the fact that the term "legitimate strategic motive" is not defined, and the example given seems to be one where the defensive team conceded second base to the runner, and therefore it's hard to understand why the rulebook would consider the base in question as having been "stolen" when the defensive team acquiesced to the runner's intention of advancing without the aid of a hit, putout, error, force-out, fielder's choice, passed ball, wild pitch or balk.

That said, on the whole, it would seem (under Rule 9.07(g)'s comment) that whenever a defensive team decides that it is better off not trying to prevent a runner from stealing a base than doing something about it, that runner gets credit for a stolen base if that runner advances as a result, and perhaps the only time a runner is to be denied credit for a stolen base in these situations is when the defensive team just doesn't care whether the runner advances or not.

(By the way, what might be an illegitimate strategic motive?)

In any case, Rule 9.07(g) says what it says, and when all is said and done, it's up to the individual scorer to decide—after considering the totality of the circumstances—whether to credit a runner with a stolen base when no play is attempted to prevent or otherwise interfere with the runner's advancement, which advancement was unaided by a hit, a putout, an error, a force-out, a fielder's choice, a passed ball, a wild pitch or a balk.

(Note that one unquestionably praiseworthy aspect of Rule 9.07(g)'s comment is its final portion, which clearly and unequivocally allows the official scorer to thwart a team's attempt to sabotage a player's stolen base statistics by exhibiting indifference to that runner's advancement, thereby putting fair play and common sense ahead of strict adherence to the "letter of the law," at least in this case.)

THE CONCEPT OF "CAUGHT STEALING"

Rule 9.07(h)   The official scorer shall charge a runner as "caught stealing" if such runner is put out, or would have been put out by errorless play, when such runner

(1) tries to steal;

(2) is picked off a base and tries to advance (any move toward the next base shall be considered an attempt to advance); or

(3) overslides while stealing.

FOR EXAMPLE: A runner at first base takes off for second base on a pitch but is put out before he can get to second base.

WHAT IT MEANS: The runner is properly charged with a caught stealing; he tried to steal a base, but failed and was put out. It's as simple as that.

FOR EXAMPLE: The pitcher throws the ball to first, and the runner at first base realizes (having taken too large a lead off first) that he'll be put out if he attempts to return to the safety of first base. Consequently, the runner starts for second, but he is put out.

WHAT IT MEANS: The runner is properly charged with a caught stealing, even though his attempt to advance was far more an attempt to avoid being put out than his carrying out an intention to advance.

(Note also that Rule 9.07(h) clearly states that "any move toward the next base shall be considered an attempt to advance." Therefore, if this runner had taken only a single step toward second base, or had made "any move" in that direction, and then attempted to return to the safety of first base only to be put out, he would nevertheless be properly considered as having been caught stealing.)

FOR EXAMPLE: In his attempt to steal third base, a runner overslides third and (although he beat the throw made to put him out at third) he is put out when he fails to remain in contact with the bag after sliding.

WHAT IT MEANS: The runner is properly considered as having been caught stealing (in conformity with Rule 9.07(e)).

FOR EXAMPLE: In his attempt to steal third base, a runner overruns third and (although he beat out the throw made to put him out at third) he is put out due to his failure to remain in contact with the bag after touching third base.

WHAT IT MEANS: The runner cannot be fairly charged with a caught stealing (in conformity with what is implicit in Rule 9.07(e), i.e., that a runner who is put out after oversliding a base is not considered as having "held" the base, but a runner who is put out after overrunning base is considered as having "held" the base in question).

FOR EXAMPLE: The catcher throws to second in an attempt to put out a runner attempting to steal second base. Although the throw is good, the infielder covering second base botches the play and the runner is declared safe at second base.

WHAT IT MEANS: The runner was deemed caught stealing, even though he was safe, because were it not for the error committed by the fielder the ball was thrown to, the runner would have been put out. [See Rule 9.07/(f)]

FOR EXAMPLE: The catcher throws to third in an attempt to put out a runner attempting to steal third base. The throw is so bad that the ball sails into left field. However, the left fielder is able to retrieve the ball in time to dissuade the runner from advancing any further.

WHAT IT MEANS: The runner is not properly considered as having been caught stealing because the bad throw that allowed him to reach third base safely cannot be considered an error under Rule 9.12(d)(1), as well as under Rule 9.12(a)(5).

FOR EXAMPLE: The catcher throws to third in an attempt to put out a runner attempting to steal third base. The throw is so bad that the ball sails into left field. Fortunately (for the runner), the left fielder is unable to retrieve the ball in time to do anything about the runner advancing even further, and the runner scores.

WHAT IT MEANS: The runner is again not properly considered as having been caught stealing, even though the catcher's wild throw is scored an error. That is because the wild throw helping the runner to reach third base safely is not deemed an error by the rulebook (as in the preceding situation), but it is an error in allowing the runner's advancement beyond the stolen base.

PASSED BALLS AND WILD PITCHES

Rule 9.07(h) Comment: In those instances where a pitched ball eludes the catcher and the runner is put out trying to advance, the official scorer shall not charge any "caught stealing."

FOR EXAMPLE: With a runner on first, the pitcher delivers a pitch that gets away from the catcher. (Whether it's considered a passed ball, constituting a misplay on the part of the catcher, or a wild pitch, with the pitcher to blame, is of no consequence because the outcome will be the same in either case.)

Seeing the ball "elude" the catcher, the runner takes off for second base, but the catcher is able to get to the ball and deliver it to second base in time to put out the runner.

The putout of the runner at second does not fairly constitute a caught stealing, and no passed ball or wild pitch is properly charged.

WHAT IT MEANS: Simply put, the runner was not attempting to steal a base at all. Rather, the runner was attempting to advance on a "misplay" (a potential passed ball or wild pitch, which would have been scored as such if the runner had not been put out). Consequently, it's logical not to consider the runner as having been caught stealing.

Dealing with a Runner Who's Attempting to Steal a Base, but Ends Up Being Awarded the Base on an Obstruction Call, or Called Out Due to Batter Interference

Rule 9.07(h) Comment—continued: The official scorer shall not charge any caught stealing when a runner is awarded a base due to obstruction or when a runner is called out due to interference by the batter.

For example:
Situation #1: The runner at first breaks for second in an attempt to steal second base, and it's obvious that the runner will be put out at second base on the steal attempt. Nevertheless, the second baseman intentionally trips the runner between first and second.

Invoking Playing Rule 6.01, the umpire awards the runner second base.

As far as scorekeeping is concerned, the runner cannot be considered as having been caught stealing, although that most likely would have been the case but for the interference call.

Situation #2: The runner at third breaks for home on a pitch in an attempt to steal home plate. Unfortunately (for the runner), the batter "hinders the catcher's play at home base."

The action of the batter gives rise to the runner being called out under Rule 5.09.

Although the runner was "put out" because of the batter's actions on his attempt to steal home plate, he is nonetheless not considered as having been caught stealing.

What it means: In both instances, the runner may have been put out—caught stealing—in the ordinary course of things, but then again, who can fairly say that it would have been the case absent the interference of the fielder in the first case, or the obstruction by the batter in the second case? Whatever the reason may be, the rulebook chooses to forego having the scorer speculate what might have happened in the absence of interference or obstruction in situations such as these, and foregoes charging the runner with having been caught stealing in both cases.

A Repetitious Coda

Rule 9.07(h) Comment—continued: The official scorer shall not charge a runner with a caught stealing if such runner would not have been credited with a stolen base had such runner been safe (for example, when a catcher throws the runner out after such runner tries to advance after a ball that had eluded the catcher on a pitch).

This portion of Rule 9.07(h)'s comment fails to specify that it applies to runners that are put out, or would have been put out but for the commission of an error, but nevertheless that is clearly what it is intended to do.

At the same time, this final sentence of Rule 9.07(h)'s comment (that was added as part of the 2007 revisions) is really nothing more than a reiteration of the first part of Rule 9.07(h)'s comment (discussed above), only expanded from the narrow parameters of potential wild pitches and passed balls.

In sum, and as stated earlier, if a runner wasn't trying to advance unaided by a hit, a putout, an error, a force-out, a fielder's choice, a passed ball, a wild pitch or a balk, that runner can't be considered as having been caught stealing if that runner was put out during the course of whatever it was that he was doing.

♦ 9 ♦

God Said to Abraham, Kill Me a Son

Rule 9.08

Rule 9.08—Sacrifices

"Football has Clipping, Spearing, Piling On, Personal Fouls, Late Hitting and Unnecessary Roughness. Baseball has ... the Sacrifice!"—George Carlin.

Sacrifice Bunts (a/k/a Sacrifice Hits): The Starting Premise

Rule 9.08(a)   The official scorer shall ... score a sacrifice bunt when, before two are out, the batter advances one or more runners with a bunt and is put out at first base, or would have been put out except for a fielding error, unless, in the judgment of the official scorer, the batter was bunting exclusively for a base hit and not sacrificing his own chance of reaching first base for the purpose of advancing a runner or runners, in which case the official scorer shall charge the batter with a time at bat.

For example: With a runner at first, and less than two outs, the batter bunts the ball to the area of the playing field somewhere between home plate and the pitcher's mound in fair territory.

The pitcher has no trouble fielding the ball and delivering it to first base in time to retire the batter, but the play on the batter allows the runner at first base to advance to second base.

Unless it is judged that the batter was "exclusively" trying for a "bunt single," the batter is credited with a sacrifice (bunt), and the runner's advancement is properly attributed to the play made to put out the batter at first base.

WHAT IT MEANS: Rule 9.08(a) is a recognition of the fact that a common strategy employed in baseball is to have a batter intentionally allow the defensive team to put him out at first base in exchange for advancing a runner, or runners, on base.

Although the wisdom of this strategy is questionable (and some statistical studies discredit the practice of giving up an out for a somewhat marginal advantage, e.g., putting a runner into a better position to score a run when the next batter comes to the plate), the employment of the tactic is nonetheless longstanding, widespread, and certainly not without proponents.

It would be a great injustice to consider a batter who purposely invites/ allows the defensive team to retire him for the perceived "greater good" to be treated (from a statistical standpoint) in the same manner as someone who tries bunting for a base hit, but fails.

Consequently, we have the sacrifice, and crediting a batter with a sacrifice benefits the batter in the sense that if the batter's plate appearance is considered a sacrifice, that plate appearance—although it ends in the batter being put out or reaching base on an error—is not counted against the batter in terms of the batter's batting average, slugging average or on-base percentage, because it is not counted as an official at-bat.

(In this regard, reference may be made to Rule 9.21 where the formulas for computing the aforementioned statistics are laid out.)

In any case, to qualify for a sacrifice bunt, the batter must fulfill a list of specific criteria, and if—and only if—they are all met, it's a sacrifice for the batter.

First, there can only be one out or no outs when the batter comes to the plate. That is because—logically—if there were two outs, it would be nonsensical for a batter to purposely give the defensive team an opportunity to make the third out that would end the inning and therefore nullify any runner advancement that may have otherwise occurred.

Second, if no runner advances on the attempted sacrifice bunt, it's not a sacrifice bunt, because the paramount objective of a sacrifice bunt—advancing one or more runners—is not achieved.

(Note that there are no exceptions to this requirement: even if there was a runner on base who could have advanced on the batter's sacrifice bunt, but didn't—for whatever reason—a sacrifice cannot be scored.)

Third, the batter must bunt the ball.

Specifically, the batter cannot swing (in any sense of the word) at the pitch. The ball must be "intentionally met with the bat and tapped slowly into the infield," as set out in the rulebook's definition of a bunt.

Fourth, the batter must be put out at first base, or if not, the batter's safe arrival at first base must be the product of a fielding error. Otherwise, if the batter makes first base safely—without an error having been committed—the batter would then qualify for a base hit (which, from a statistical standpoint, and in all other respects, is far better than a sacrifice bunt).

(Note that the possibility of the batter reaching base on a fielder's choice is dealt with in Rule 9.08(b) and Rule 9.08(c).)

Lastly, the batter must try to execute the sacrifice bunt intentionally, and do so "exclusively" for the purpose of advancing a runner or runners at the expense of being put out at first base. That is to say, if the batter is judged to have bunted the ball with the notion of getting on base, the batter cannot be properly credited with a sacrifice bunt, even if all the other criteria for awarding a sacrifice are met.

Some guidance in terms of deciding whether a batter laid down a bunt to advance a runners or runners and be put out at first base in the process, as opposed to bunting for a base hit, is provided in the comment to Rule 9.08(a) that follows.

When in Doubt (Vis-À-Vis a Batter's Intentions), Score a Sacrifice Bunt

Rule 9.08(a) Comment: In determining whether the batter had been sacrificing his own chance of reaching first base for the purpose of advancing a runner, the official scorer shall give the batter the benefit of the doubt. The official scorer shall consider the totality of the circumstances of the at-bat, including the inning, the number of outs and the score.

This appendage to Rule 9.08(a) is a part of the 2007 revisions, and it serves a useful purpose: it instructs the official scorer to withhold credit for a sacrifice bunt from a batter in cases where the batter might have been attempting a "bunt single," as opposed to a sacrifice bunt, but only if there is no doubt whatsoever that a bunt single was what the batter was trying for. In every other case, a sacrifice bunt is properly scored (as long as all the other criteria for doing so are met, of course).

The Defensive Team Chooses to Try to Put Out a Runner on Base Instead of the Batter, and the Runner Is Not Put Out

Rule 9.08(b)   The official scorer shall ... score a sacrifice bunt when, before two are out, the fielders handle a bunted ball without error in an

unsuccessful attempt to put out a preceding runner advancing one base, unless an attempt to turn a bunt into a putout of a preceding runner fails, and in the judgment of the official scorer ordinary effort would not have put out the batter at first base, in which case the batter shall be credited with a one-base hit and not a sacrifice.

FOR EXAMPLE: With a runner on first, and less than two outs, the batter lays down a bunt in an obvious and overt attempt to advance the runner by way of the defensive team putting him (the batter) out at first base.

The ball is fielded cleanly, but rather that attempting to put out the batter at first base, the defensive team chooses to try to put out (at second base) the runner already on base.

If the batter reaches first base, and the runner on base is put out at second (or would have been put out but for an error), the batter is properly considered as having reached base on a fielder's choice: no runner advancement or no runner advancement but for an error means no sacrifice.

If the defensive team fails to put out the runner on base at second base (without the commission of an error), and the batter reaches first, the batter may be awarded a base hit, or the batter may be considered as having reached base on a sacrifice bunt, depending on the judgment of the scorer.

WHAT IT MEANS: Rule 9.08(b) crams a lot into one long sentence. Therefore, what Rule 9.08(b) attempts to convey can be somewhat hard to understand and apply, but broken down into its component parts, Rule 9.08(b) isn't difficult to understand or apply in game situations.

Simply put, when the defensive team chooses to try to put out a runner on base instead of the batter, the results are scored as follows:

(1) If the attempt to put out the runner on base was successful, the batter cannot be fairly credited with a sacrifice. Rather, the batter (if he makes it safely to first base) is properly considered as having reached base on a fielder's choice. (Note that in this case, and in all cases where Rule 9.08(b) applies, the runner must be attempting to advance only one base when put out. If that's not the case, Rule 9.08(b) does not apply, and the same is true when it comes to Rule 9.08(c) as well.)

(2) If the attempt to put out the runner on base fails by virtue of an error by the defensive team, the batter (if he reaches first base in the process) is rightly considered as having reached base on a fielder's choice.

(3) If the runner on base is not put out, the failure to put out the runner is not attributable to an error, and the batter reaches first base, the scorer must

judge if the batter would have reached base if the defensive team had made a play on the batter instead of the runner on base, and the scorer is obliged to score the batter's attainment of first base in the following manner:

(A)   If the batter would have been put out at first base but for the play having been made on the runner, it's a sacrifice bunt for the batter, not a fielder's choice.

(B)   If the batter would have reached base even if the defensive team had chosen to try to put out the batter instead of the runner on base, the batter is properly credited with a base hit.

The Defensive Team Chooses to Try to Put Out a Runner on Base Instead of the Batter, and the Runner Is Put Out

Rule 9.08(c)   The official scorer shall ... not score a sacrifice bunt when any runner is put out attempting to advance one base on a bunt, or would have been put out, except for a fielding error, in which case the official scorer shall charge the batter with a time at bat.

For example: With runners at first and third, and less than two outs, the batter lays down a bunt in an obvious and overt attempt to advance the runner at first to second in exchange for the defensive team putting him (the batter) out at first base.

The bunt is perfect in terms of accomplishing what the batter seeks to accomplish—advance the runner at first to second base—but the runner at third base foolishly tries to advance to home plate on the bunt as well, and ends up being put out as a result.

In the meantime, the batter reaches first base safely (although he would have been put out if a play had been made on him, absent an error of course) and the runner at first gets to second base as well.

Although the batter met the criteria required for a sacrifice, the batter in nonetheless properly denied credit for a sacrifice because the runner at third base was put out, and the batter's attainment of first base is therefore considered as being made on a fielder's choice.

What it means: It doesn't matter if a runner on base was simply reckless or imprudent in trying to advance on what might otherwise have been a bona fide sacrifice bunt. Rule 9.08(c) is as cut and dried as any dictum can be, and consequently a batter is denied credit for a sacrifice in situations such as this.

Granted, the batter cannot be fairly considered as the author of his own fate in cases like this: After all, the batter did everything "by the book" to warrant being awarded credit for a sacrifice bunt. Nevertheless, the rulebook chooses to draw a clear line and deny the batter a sacrifice if any runner is put out on what might otherwise be considered a sacrifice bunt, and in doing so, the rulebook once again promotes the policy of ensuring consistency in scorekeeping as much as possible, even if it comes at the cost of fairness from time to time.

Note however that the runner in question must have been trying to advance only one base for Rule 9.08(c) to apply, as is the case under Rule 9.08(b) as well, and if that isn't so, the batter can still be properly awarded credit for a sacrifice bunt even though a runner on base was put out (by trying to advance more than one base).

SACRIFICE FLIES

Rule 9.08(d)   The official scorer shall ... score a sacrifice fly when, before two are out, the batter hits a ball in flight handled by an outfielder or an infielder running in the outfield in fair or foul territory that

(1) is caught, and a runner scores after the catch, or

(2) is dropped, and a runner scores, if in the scorer's judgment the runner could have scored after the catch had the fly been caught.

FOR EXAMPLE: With a runner at third base, and less than two outs, the batter hits a fly ball to the outfield.

If the fly ball is caught to put out the batter, but the runner on base scores on the play, the batter's plate appearance is properly counted as a sacrifice fly.

If the fly ball isn't caught (by virtue of an error on the part of a fielder), and the runner scores on the play, the batter is entitled to credit for a sacrifice fly nevertheless if the scorer judges that the runner would have scored even if the ball had been caught to put out the batter.

In addition, note that in this second case, an error is charged to the fielder who botched the play in the outfield, but the batter—although he reached base because of the error—is not considered (in terms of the batter's batting statistics) as having reached base on an error. Rather, the sacrifice fly supercedes the fact that the batter reached base because of the error.

WHAT IT MEANS: This policy (of absolving a batter from the statistical negative of having his plate appearance considered and counted as an ordinary failed turn at bat if the batter hits the ball far enough that although it is caught for a put out, a run scores) has been around for many years, and it is easily understood and readily accepted by even the most casual followers of baseball. However, the way in which Rule 9.08(d) is worded leaves much to be desired.

For starters, the phrase "an infielder running in the outfield" sounds dated and bizarre, and it leads one to ask: what if the ball was caught by an infielder in the outfield who wasn't running (however one may care to define that)?

More significantly, the way Rule 9.08(d) is phrased can lead to results that do not jibe with the commonly held notion of what constitutes a sacrifice fly.

By way of illustration, assume that there's a runner at third, with no outs, and the batter hits a fly ball to the center fielder. Assume further that the center fielder catches the ball on the fly to put out the batter and the runner at third tags up to score on the play, in a classic sacrifice fly scenario. Then assume that the center fielder's throw to home plate is perfect, arriving at home plate well ahead of the runner, but the catcher muffs the thrown ball and (entirely because of the catcher's error) the runner scores.

Common sense would lead one to the conclusion that this is not a sacrifice fly for the batter because it was the catcher's error that gave rise to the run scoring, not the batter's having hit the ball to the outfield, but if you look at how the rule is worded, the batter has legitimate grounds to argue that he is nevertheless entitled to credit for a sacrifice fly.

After all, the batter hit the ball to the outfield with less than two outs. The ball was caught to put the batter out, and a run scored.

End of story.

In other words, Rule 9.08(d) does not expressly require that the run that scored must have scored unaided by an error. What's more, Rule 9.08(d) does not even say that the runner who scores must do so starting from third base. Therefore, you could have a runner scoring from second base, or even first base, perhaps aided by one or more errors after a batter hits the ball to the outfield for what ought to be a simple fly out with no runner advancement, but the batter gets credit for a sacrifice fly even though the reason that one or more runs scored was not what the batter did. Rather, it was what the fielders did.

So what does a scorer do in cases like that, given the way in which Rule 9.08(d) is written?

The answer would seem to be the same as when (according to baseball legend) the first commissioner of baseball—Judge Kenesaw Mountain Landis—sentenced a very old man to a very long term in prison, a term that would far exceed the convicted criminal's life span. The old man asked the judge how he could possibly serve out such a long sentence, given his advanced age. In reply, Judge Landis reportedly said, "Just do the best that you can."

In plain English, you either have to go with a strict reading of the rule's text or justify a lack of strict adherence to the text by superimposing "common sense," and either approach is arguably correct.

In any case, the idea of awarding batters sacrifice flies comes from the same line of thought that's the basis for awarding sacrifice bunts: in both cases, the fact that the batter's otherwise failed plate appearance nonetheless led to something beneficial for the batter's team is recognized and rewarded. However, there is a fundamental difference between sacrifice bunts and sacrifice flies.

Specifically, in order for a batter to be credited with a sacrifice bunt, the scorer must judge that the batter intended to execute a sacrifice bunt: Even if all the objective criteria for awarding a batter with a sacrifice bunt are met, the scorer may nevertheless withhold credit for a sacrifice bunt if it is judged that the batter did not specifically (exclusively) try to execute a sacrifice bunt. However, the same is not true when it comes to sacrifice flies: If all the criteria are met, the scorer is required to award the batter with a sacrifice fly regardless of what the batter may or may not have had in mind when he put the ball into play.

Why the difference?

Simply put, it's because when a batter hits a pitch to the outfield on a full swing, it's impossible to judge whether the batter was going for a base hit, as opposed to simply giving a teammate on base a chance to score. However, when a batter lays down a bunt, the intentions of the batter can be fairly ascertained in almost every case.

Getting Credit for a Sacrifice Fly While Reaching Base on a Fielder's Choice

Rule 9.08(d) Comment: The official scorer shall score a sacrifice fly in accordance with Rule 9.08(d)(2) even though another runner is forced out by reason of the batter becoming a runner.

For example: With runners at first and third, and less than two outs, the batter hits a fly ball to right field.

At the same time, the runner at third base tags up, and confident that the ball will certainly be caught, the runner at first takes only a short lead off first base. As soon as the ball touches the right fielder's glove, the runner at third takes off for home plate.

Inexplicably, the right fielder muffs the catch.

Unfortunately (for the runner at first), the right fielder's misplay is not immediately apparent, causing the runner at first base to hesitate on the base path. Consequently, the right fielder is able to retrieve the ball and deliver it to second base in time to retire the runner forced to advance to second base because of the right fielder's failure to catch the fly ball. Moreover, the runner at third scores, and even if the right fielder had caught the ball, the right fielder would not have been able to put out the runner advancing from third base (absent a remarkable play).

In the meantime, the batter reaches first base safely.

Although the batter reached base on what would otherwise be considered a fielder's choice, the batter is nonetheless credited with a sacrifice fly—as per Rule 9.08(d)'s comment—and the right fielder avoids being charged with an error as well.

WHAT IT MEANS: Note that under Rule 9.12(d)(4), "The official scorer shall not charge an error against ... any fielder when, after fumbling a ground ball or dropping a batted ball that is in flight or a thrown ball, the fielder recovers the ball in time to force out a runner at any base." Therefore, the right fielder does not get an error in this case.

At the same time, the runner at third would have scored on the batter's fly ball regardless of whether or not the right fielder had caught the ball, and the fact that the batter would otherwise be considered as having reached first base on a fielder's choice does not override that fact. Therefore, a sacrifice fly is fairly credited to the batter.

The bottom line is that a batter can reach base by way of an error or a fielder's choice, or be put out on a fly out and not reach base at all, but if the batter hit the ball with less than two outs to the outfield deep enough to allow a runner on base to score a run, and that runner does in fact score a run, the adverse statistical consequences of reaching base on an error or on a fielder's choice, or being put out on a fly out, are avoided by the batter.

♦ 10 ♦

Playing the Field
Rules 9.09–9.11

Rule 9.09—Putouts

A putout is a statistic credited to a fielder whose action causes the out of a batter-runner or runner, as set forth in this Rule 9.09.

Rule 9.09 begins simply enough, and one might even think that the entire topic might be covered by Rule 9.09's initial sentence—ending at the comma—with no further elucidation necessary. In fact, the provisions of Rule 9.09(a) seem to confirm that it's really all fairly cut and dried. However, the subsections of Rule 9.09 that follow (beginning with Rule 9.09(b)) evidence the fact that properly crediting putouts to fielders is not always as simple as it might appear at first glance.

Rule 9.09(a)(1)   The official scorer shall credit a putout to each fielder who … catches a ball that is in flight, whether fair or foul.

Although not stated, Rule 9.08(a)(1) clearly implies that the ball that the fielder catches "in flight" must be a batted ball, and that the catch—as defined in the rulebook's Definition of Terms—must result in the batter being called out, in order for the fielder in question to be credited with a putout.

Rule 9.09(a)(2)   The official scorer shall credit a putout to each fielder who … catches a batted or thrown ball and tags a base to put out a batter or runner.

In other words, any fielder who puts out a batter or a runner by tagging a base gets credit for the putout of the batter or runner in question (just like those fielders who caught "a ball in flight" to accomplish the same result under the provisions of Rule 9.09(a)(1)).

Rule 9.09(a)(2) Comment: The official scorer shall credit a fielder with a putout if such fielder catches a thrown ball and tags a base to record an out on an appeal play.

In plain English, if a batter or runner is put out on an appeal play, the putout is looked upon the same as if it were made in the ordinary course as far as the statistical records of the game are concerned.

(Note that this common sense approach to the issue was routinely followed by official scorers even prior to Rule 9.09(a)(2)'s comment being added to the rulebook as part of the 2007 revisions.)

Rule 9.09(a)(3)   The official scorer shall credit a putout to each fielder who … tags a runner when the runner is off the base to which the runner is entitled.

In other words, once again, a fielder who puts out a runner gets credit for the putout (that being the sum total of what Rule 9.09(a)(1), Rule 9.09(a)(2) and Rule 9.09(a)(3) represent).

"Automatic" Putouts: Starting with the Catcher

It can be noted that up to this point, Rule 9.09 has dealt with the obvious: Putouts made by fielders catching fly balls, or tagging bases, batters or runners, are ascribed to those fielders who actually put out the batter or runner in question. But at this juncture, Rule 9.09 turns its focus to putouts where a batter or runner is called out, but exactly which fielder is properly credited with the putout is not obvious because the putout arose from a "technicality"—a rule infraction on the part of a batter or runner—an "automatic" putout.

In addressing the issue of which fielder is properly credited with the putout that arises from an automatic putout, Rule 9.09 starts by listing a number of situations where the catcher is credited with putouts arising from automatic putouts, inasmuch as the catcher is the prime beneficiary of automatic putouts (as one can see from the following).

Rule 9.09(b)(1)   The official scorer shall credit an automatic putout to the catcher when a … batter is called out on strikes.

Note that this verbiage was added to Rule 9 as part of the 2007 revisions. Previously, official scorers would routinely credit catchers with putouts when a batter was called out for having struck out, even though no specific provision mandated doing so: it simply made sense to score it that way.

Now, with Rule 9.09(b)(1) being part of the rulebook, custom has become decree.

Rule 9.09(b)(2)   The official scorer shall credit an automatic putout to the catcher when a ... batter is called out for an illegally batted ball.

For example: In the top of the ninth inning in the game between the New York Yankees and the Kansas City Royals played at Yankee Stadium on July 24, 1983, George Brett hit a pitch over the outfield fence in fair territory for what appeared to be a home run, but the legitimacy of the apparent home run was challenged by Billy Martin (the Yankees' manager).

Although Brett's home run was later reinstated, he was originally called out for hitting an illegally batted ball—specifically, for having had pine tar extending too far up the handle of his bat.

Had the "pine tar putout" not been set aside, the Yankees' catcher (Rick Cerone) would have been credited with the putout.

What it means: Storied baseball history aside, there are a number of ways in which a batter can be called out for "an illegally batted ball." An example (far more common than the "pine tar incident") is when a batter hits a pitch with either one foot, or both feet, completely outside the batter's box, in violation of Playing Rule 5.09. In those instances, the catcher is properly credited with the putout, even though the catcher didn't really do anything to put out the batter, as is the case whenever a batter is called out for "an illegally batted ball."

Rule 9.09(b)(3)   The official scorer shall credit an automatic putout to the catcher when a ... batter is called out for bunting foul for his third strike.

Rule 9.09(b)(3) Comment: Note the exception in Rule 9.15(a)(4).

Taken together with its comment, Rule 9.09(b)(3) simply comes down to this.

Under Playing Rule 5.09, a batter is called out if he bunts a pitch foul on a two-strike count and the ball is not caught in flight. When that happens, the catcher is credited with the putout. However, if the two-strike bunt is caught (whether in foul territory or fair territory), the batter is considered as having been put out by the ball being caught in flight, and the fielder who caught the ball—be it the catcher or anyone else—gets credit for the putout in that case.

(Note that Rule 9.15(a)(4) deems an out arising from a pitch bunted foul on a two-strike count—that goes uncaught—as being a strikeout, but if a ball bunted on a two-strike count is caught, either in fair or foul territory, the resultant putout is considered as having been made by a batted ball being caught in flight, like any pop-up or fly ball, and not a strikeout.)

Rule 9.09(b)(4)   The official scorer shall credit an automatic putout to the catcher when a ... batter is called out for being touched by his own batted ball.

Rule 9.09(b)(5)   The official scorer shall credit an automatic putout to the catcher when a ... batter is called out for interfering with the catcher.

Rule 9.09(b)(6)   The official scorer shall credit an automatic putout to the catcher when a ... batter is called out for failing to bat in his proper turn.

Rule 9.09(b)(6) Comment: See Rule 9.03(d).
Note that Rule 9.03(d) specifically addresses how the official scorer is to deal with batters being called out for failure to bat in proper turn.

Rule 9.09(b)(7)   The official scorer shall credit an automatic putout to the catcher when a ... batter is called out for refusing to touch first base after receiving a base on balls, after being hit by a pitch or after a catcher's interference.

Rule 9.09(b)(8)   The official scorer shall credit an automatic putout to the catcher when a ... runner is called out for refusing to advance from third base to home plate.
Note that prior to the 2007 revisions, this provision was oddly limited to runners at third base refusing to advance to home plate "with the winning run."

"Automatic" Putouts: Not for Catchers Only

Rule 9.09(c)   The official scorer shall credit automatic putouts as follows (and shall credit no assists on these plays except as specified).
Rule 9.09(c) turns the spotlight away from the catcher and lists a number of situations where various fielders may get credit for a putout when a batter or a runner is called out on a technicality—an "automatic" putout.

Rule 9.09(c)(1)   When the batter is called out on an Infield Fly that is not caught, the official scorer shall credit the putout to the fielder who the scorer believes could have made the catch.
The salient portions of the rulebook's definition of an infield fly are as follows.

An **INFIELD FLY** is a fair fly ball (not including a line drive nor an attempted bunt) which can be caught by an infielder with ordinary effort, when first and second, or first, second and third bases are occupied, before two are out.

When it seems apparent that a batted ball will be an Infield Fly, the umpire shall immediately declare "Infield Fly" for the benefit of the runners.

In addition, Playing Rule 5.09(a)(5) states "**A batter is out when ... an Infield Fly is declared.**"

Therefore, a batter can be "put out" by being called out on an infield fly, even though the batter's "fair fly ball" isn't actually caught "in flight," and Rule 9.09(c)(1) simply sets out the logical choice when it comes to deciding which fielder is properly given credit for the putout in those instances.

Rule 9.09(c)(2)   When a runner is called out for being touched by a fair ball (including an Infield Fly), the official scorer shall credit the putout to the fielder nearest the ball.

There isn't any better candidate.

Rule 9.09(c)(3)   When a runner is called out for running out of line to avoid being tagged, the official scorer shall credit the putout to the fielder whom the runner avoided.

Reference may be made to Playing Rule 6.01 in this case.

In addition, note that an assist may be credited to a fielder in this situation under Rule 9.10(a)(2).

Rule 9.09(c)(4)   When a runner is called out for passing another runner, the official scorer shall credit the putout to the fielder nearest the point of passing.

Reference may be made to Playing Rule 5.09 in this case.

Rule 9.09(c)(5)   When a runner is called out for running the bases in reverse order, the official scorer shall credit the putout to the fielder covering the base the runner left in starting his reverse run.

Reference may be made to Playing Rule 5.09 in this case.

An "Automatic" Putout by Way of Interference Committed by a Runner Who's Called Out

Rule 9.09(c)(6)   When a runner is called out for having interfered with a fielder, the official scorer shall credit the putout to the fielder with whom the runner interfered, unless the fielder was in the act of throwing the ball when the interference occurred, in which case the official scorer shall credit the putout to the fielder for whom the throw was intended and shall credit an assist to the fielder whose throw was interfered with.

FOR EXAMPLE: The batter hits an easy "comebacker" to the pitcher. The pitcher fields the ball and runs toward the batter to tag him out.

Before the pitcher can tag out the batter, the batter intentionally knocks the ball out of the pitcher's glove, and he (the batter) is consequently called out for interference.

Logically, the pitcher is credited with the putout in this case, even though the pitcher did not actually tag out the batter.

In the same situation, assume that the pitcher was in the act of throwing the ball to the first baseman to force out the batter at first base when the batter interfered with the pitcher.

In that case, the pitcher (logically) is credited with an assist and the first baseman is credited with the putout, just as though the aborted "1–3" putout had actually been made.

AN "AUTOMATIC" PUTOUT BY WAY OF INTERFERENCE COMMITTED BY A PRECEDING RUNNER

Rule 9.09(c)(7)   When the batter-runner is called out because of interference by a preceding runner, as provided in Rule 6.01(a)(5), the official scorer shall credit the putout to the first baseman. If the fielder interfered with was in the act of throwing the ball, the official scorer shall credit such fielder with an assist but shall credit only one assist on any one play under the provisions of Rule 9.09(c)(6) and 9.09(c)(7).

FOR EXAMPLE: With less than two outs, and a runner on first, the batter hits a ground ball to the second baseman.

As one would expect, the second baseman delivers the ball to the shortstop covering second base in an attempt to force out the runner coming from first base—the lead runner.

The shortstop catches the ball and steps on second base to put out the approaching runner well before the runner reaches second base, and he steps away from the base in order to avoid a collision with the runner sliding into second base.

Nevertheless, the runner slides well wide of second base, directly at the shortstop, purposely and deliberately knocking the shortstop to the ground.

Obviously, the runner coming from first base was put out when the shortstop tagged second base, but the batter is also called out by virtue of the actions of the runner on base.

If the shortstop was in the act of throwing the ball to first base to put out the batter, the shortstop is properly credited with an assist in the context of the batter having been "automatically" put out due to the runner's overly aggressive base running.

If the shortstop wasn't in the act of throwing the ball, no assist is in order.

In either case, the first baseman is credited with having "put out" the batter.

As regards the prohibition against awarding multiple assists, reference may be made to the following chapter.

♦ ♦ ♦

Rule 9.10—Assists

An assist is a statistic credited to a fielder whose action contributes to a batter-runner or runner being put out, as set forth in this Rule 9.10.

As was the case in Rule 9.09, Rule 9.10 begins simply enough, and one might even think that nothing more need be said about the topic.

However, just as it was in Rule 9.09, the finer points can be tricky, and therefore they require more than the broad declaration found in Rule 9.10's opening text in order to be dealt with properly.

The Initial Premise, Plus a Significant Ancillary Concept

Rule 9.10(a)(1)   The official scorer shall credit an assist to each fielder who … throws or deflects a batted or thrown ball in such a way that a putout results, or would have resulted except for a subsequent error by any fielder.

Over and above Rule 9.10(a)(1)'s pronouncement of what a fielder must do in order to be credited with an assist (which is more or less just a restatement of Rule 9.10's introductory text), note that a significant additional concept is set out as well: that a fielder may be credited with an assist even though no putout was actually made.

In other words, if a fielder does everything right—does everything that ought to lead to a putout—the fact that another fielder commits an error ought not deprive the competent fielder from the statistical good that comes from being credited with an assist, even though it may seem a bit odd to credit a fielder for helping to achieve something that wasn't achieved.

Odd or not, as far as the rulebook is concerned, there is no legitimate justification not to credit fielders with assists in cases where a play is blown after the fielder in question did all that the fielder could be expected to do in a competent fashion.

In addition, crediting fielders with assists in some cases where a putout is not ultimately made leads to fielding statistics being more accurate than they would otherwise be if those assists were erased by errors. (In other words, overlooking a fielder's "good play" just because of another fielder's "bad play" distorts an accurate tally of "good plays.")

Consequently, if (for example) the third baseman fields a ground ball and delivers it to first base cleanly and in time to put out the batter who put the ball in play, but the batter is safe because the first baseman mishandles the third baseman's good throw, the third baseman nevertheless properly gets credit for an assist on the play that should have been made: a garden variety, routine "5–3" ground out.

ASSISTS IN THE CONTEXT OF RUN-DOWN PLAYS

Rule 9.10(a)(1)—continued   Only one assist and no more shall be credited to each fielder who throws or deflects the ball in a run-down play that results in a putout, or would have resulted in a putout, except for a subsequent error.

FOR EXAMPLE: With a runner on first, the pitcher delivers the ball to the first baseman covering first.

The runner, finding himself trapped in a run-down play, is chased back and forth between second base and first.

During the course of this, the ball (after being delivered to the first baseman by the pitcher) goes from the first baseman to the second baseman, from the second baseman to the pitcher, from the pitcher to the shortstop, from the shortstop to the first baseman, from the first baseman to the second baseman, and from the second baseman back to the pitcher covering first base when the runner dives back into first.

If the runner was ultimately put out at first base (or would have been put out but for a muff of the final throw by the second baseman to the pitcher), one might credit the pitcher with two assists, the first baseman with two assists, the second baseman with two assists, the shortstop with one assist, and the pitcher with the putout (or error if the final throw had been mishandled by him), because the pitcher, the first baseman and the second baseman each threw the ball twice in this scenario "in such a way that a putout results" (or would have resulted but for an error), while the shortstop did so only once. However, Rule 9.10(a)(1) prevents the potential inflation of the fielding averages of fielders in cases like this by imposing a "one play, one assist" standard, and each of the four fielders involved in the run-down play receives credit for only one assist (and "no more," as somewhat redundantly stated in the text of Rule 9.10(a)(1)).

(In passing, note the irony of the fact that under Rule 9.10(a)(1), if the pitcher in the example given had muffed the final throw, allowing the runner to return to first base safely, all the fielders involved in the run-down play would nevertheless be credited with assists—including the pitcher—while the pitcher would also be charged with an error on the same play.)

WHAT IT MEANS: Rule 9.10(a)(1) recognizes the fact that a fielder might handle the ball in the context of run-down plays more than once, and thereby might be considered as qualifying for more than one assist on one play. However, the thinking behind Rule 9.10(a)(1) is that handing out multiple assists on one play would skew fielding statistics (statistics designed to reflect—as fairly as possible—the true fielding prowess of any given fielder). Therefore, Rule 9.10(a)(1) cuts off fielders in situations like this from getting what might be considered "cheap assists" that would debase (at least to some degree) fielding statistics.

THE MEANING OF "DEFLECT": GIVING CREDIT TO A FIELDER FOR AN ASSIST WITHOUT THE FIELDER HAVING DELIVERED THE BALL TO ANOTHER FIELDER TO PUT OUT A BATTER OR RUNNER

Rule 9.10(a)(1) Comment: Mere ineffective contact with the ball shall not be considered an assist. "Deflect" shall mean to slow down or change the direction of the ball and thereby effectively assist in putting out a batter or runner.

FOR EXAMPLE: In the first instance, the batter hits a ground ball in the direction of the second baseman.

The pitcher reaches out to the ball on its way to the second baseman, and it ticks off the edge of the pitcher's glove.

Regardless, the ball gets to the second baseman in time for the second baseman to field it and deliver it to the first baseman to put out the batter (as would have been the case even if the ball had not come into contact with the pitcher's glove).

In this case, the pitcher is not entitled to an assist on the play.

In the second instance, the batter hits a solid line drive straight back at the pitcher.

Unable to react in time to field the ball, the pitcher can only turn away and hope that the ball doesn't hit him somewhere that will result in serious physical injury.

Sure enough, the ball smacks into the pitcher squarely, but it ricochets off the pitcher to the shortstop, who in turn is able to deliver the ball to first base in time to put out the batter.

Had the ball not come into contact with the pitcher, the ball would certainly have traveled to center field for a base hit.

In this case, the pitcher is credited with an assist.

WHAT IT MEANS: Simply put, a fielder does not necessarily have to "field" or throw the ball to another fielder to be credited with an assist. "Deflection" is enough if that deflection contributes in a genuine and material manner to a putout being made (or to a putout that would have been made absent an error).

In addition, note that there is no requirement whatsoever that the fielder do anything intentionally to garner credit for an assist: if the fielder "slow(s) down" or "change(s) the direction of the ball" so as to be considered as having assisted in getting a putout (or in setting up a putout that was ultimately spoiled by the commission of an error), the fielder's intentions are then irrelevant.

ASSISTS ON APPEAL PLAYS

Rule 9.10(a)(1) Comment—continued: If a putout results from an appeal play within the natural course of play, the official scorer shall give assists to each fielder, except the fielder making the putout, whose action led to the putout. If a putout results from an appeal play initiated by the pitcher throwing to a fielder after the previous play has ended, the official scorer shall credit the pitcher, and only the pitcher, with an assist.

For example: With less than two outs, and runners at first base and third base, the batter hits a fly ball to deep left field.

The left fielder manages to catch the ball in flight to put out the batter, and the runner at third base advances to home plate on the putout. The runner at first base stays put.

Situation #1: The ball is returned to the infield, just as it would be if the defensive team had conceded the run having scored. However, after the ball is returned to the pitcher, the pitcher throws the ball to the third baseman on an appeal play, claiming that the runner at third base left third base before the ball was caught by the left fielder.

The umpire grants the appeal, and the runner is called out.

In this case, the pitcher receives credit for an assist, and the third baseman—receiving the throw from the pitcher at third base—gets credit for the putout, but no assist is properly credited to the left fielder.

Situation #2: After catching the fly ball, the left fielder throws the ball to the shortstop at second base to ensure that the runner at first does not advance on the putout of the batter. Thereupon, the shortstop delivers the ball to the third baseman at third base, and—as before—the runner who had been at third base is called out on the "appeal play."

In this case, the left fielder and the shortstop are credited with assists, while—as in the first instance—the third baseman gets credit for the putout of the runner who had been at third base.

(Note that if—by virtue of some twisted turn of events—the third baseman had handled the ball prior to the appeal play at third base, the third baseman should not be credited with an assist because Rule 9.10(a)(1)'s comment specifically denies credit for an assist to the fielder who makes the putout in appeal plays.)

What it means: This portion of Rule 9.10(a)(1)'s comment was part of the 2007 revisions, and it is a simple effort to clarify who is entitled to credit for assists—and who is not—on appeal plays, and thereby remove any guessing on the part of the official scorer.

In sum, once the ball is returned to the pitcher (as the ball would be for the purpose of dealing with the next batter), only the pitcher can be properly credited with an assist on an ensuing appeal play. Otherwise, any and all fielders who cause the ball to be delivered to a base for a putout on an appeal play are credited with assists (with the exception of the fielder who ultimately makes the put out on the appeal play).

Assists Arising from "Technical" Putouts

Rule 9.10(a)(2)   The official scorer shall credit an assist to each fielder who ... throws or deflects the ball during a play that results in a runner being called out for interference or for running out of line.

For example: With a runner at second base, the batter hits a ground ball to the second baseman.

The second baseman fields the ball cleanly, but rather than throw the ball to first base to force out the batter, he—seeing that the runner at second is attempting to advance to third base—throws the ball to the third baseman.

After catching the second baseman's throw, the third baseman begins to chase the runner to tag him out, but although the runner is never actually tagged by the third baseman, the runner is nonetheless called out because he ran "more than three feet away from a direct line between bases to avoid being tagged," in violation of Rule 5.09.

In this situation, the second baseman is properly credited with an assist (as would also be the case if the runner had been called out for interference).

What it means: The sum total of Rule 9.10(a)(2) is that a fielder gets credit for an assist on a putout if the putout arises from a "technical" putout—a putout that is called by an umpire—in the same manner as a fielder would be entitled to credit for an assist on a putout that had been made in an ordinary manner.

Assists on Strikeouts

Rule 9.10(b)(1)   The official scorer shall not credit an assist to ... the pitcher on a strikeout, unless the pitcher fields an uncaught third strike and makes a throw that results in a putout.

For example: On a 0–2 count, the pitcher blows the ball past the batter and the batter is called out for having struck out.

Although the pitcher "contributed" to the batter being put out, and the catcher (under Rule 9.09(b)(1)) is entitled to a putout, the pitcher is not entitled to an assist.

If, however, the "strike three" pitch got away from the catcher, the batter was entitled to try for first base (as would be the case if first base was unoccupied by a runner, or if there were two outs), and the pitcher—instead of the catcher, or any other fielder—retrieved the ball in time to deliver it to first base to retire the batter at first base, the pitcher is credited with an assist and the fielder covering first base gets the putout.

WHAT IT MEANS: If pitchers were credited with an assist each and every time a batter was put out on a strikeout, the fielding averages of pitchers would be inflated to preposterous proportions. Consequently, Rule 9.10(b)(1) circumscribes the somewhat broad definition of what constitutes an assist when it comes to pitchers and strikeouts.

Note that this policy of limiting potential assists for the pitcher is carried over and extended in Rule 9.10(b)(2).

ASSISTS ON CATCHERS' PICK-OFF PLAYS

Rule 9.10(b)(2)   The official scorer shall not credit an assist to … the pitcher when, as the result of a legal pitch received by the catcher, a runner is put out, as when the catcher picks a runner off base, throws out a runner trying to steal or tags a runner trying to score.

FOR EXAMPLE: After fielding a legal pitch for a called strike, the catcher throws the ball to first base and successfully puts out the runner at first (who was taking a foolishly big lead when the pitch was delivered and couldn't get back to first base ahead of the catcher's "snap throw" to first base).

Although the pitcher (in a sense) contributed to the runner at first base being put out, the pitcher is nonetheless denied credit for an assist in this case (pursuant to Rule 9.10(b)(2)), as well as in similar situations.

WHAT IT MEANS: Once again, the rulebook seeks to limit the number of assists that pitchers might otherwise be entitled to, in recognition of the fact that the pitch made in cases like this was not a throw designed or otherwise intended to facilitate a runner on base being put out, and therefore the pitch was not a throw made to "assist" (per se) another fielder in putting out a runner.

(That said, if the pitch was a "pitchout," this line of thought does not hold up too well, but Rule 9.10(b)(2) does not take that into consideration.)

Note, however, that if a pitcher throws directly to a base to pick off a runner, and that runner is put out (or would have been put out but for a subsequent error), the pitcher can be properly credited with an assist. It is only after a catcher receives a "legal pitch" that the pitcher is eliminated from consideration for an assist in cases like those covered by Rule 9.10(b)(2).

MISPLAYS AND ERRORS DISQUALIFY A FIELDER FROM CONSIDERATION FOR AN ASSIST, EVEN IF A RUNNER IS NEVERTHELESS SUBSEQUENTLY PUT OUT

Rule 9.10(b)(3)   The official scorer shall not credit an assist to … a fielder whose wild throw permits a runner to advance, even though the runner

subsequently is put out as a result of continuous play. A play that follows a misplay (whether or not the misplay is an error) is a new play, and the fielder making any misplay shall not be credited with an assist unless such fielder takes part in the new play.

FOR EXAMPLE: The pitcher attempts to pick off the runner at first, but the throw is wild. Consequently, the ball gets away from the first baseman.

Fortunately (for the defensive team), the first baseman is nevertheless able to retrieve the ball and deliver it to second base in time to retire the runner who had been at first base and who attempted to advance on the pitcher's errant throw.

Although the pitcher's throw to first base started the sequence of events that ultimately led to the runner being put out, the pitcher is not entitled to an assist in this case.

WHAT IT MEANS: There is nothing fair or logical in awarding any statistical credit to a fielder who messed up, even if the mess-up was "redeemed" by another fielder or fielders and subsequently resulted in a putout.

That being so, Rule 9.10(b)(3) draws a line: Although a fielder arguably contributed to a putout by making a bad throw, that bad throw (whether it constitutes an official fielding error on the part of that fielder, or merely a misplay) terminates the play being attempted, and any play that follows the bad throw is looked upon as a new play that began after the bad throw.

The same holds true for a bad catch (be it an error or only a misplay): any play attempted thereafter is a new play.

By following this policy, a blunder cannot be transformed into a statistical plus (in the form of an assist) for the fielder who committed the gaffe, whether that gaffe constituted an official error or not.

At the same time, note that the fielder in issue may nevertheless receive credit for an assist (or putout) if the fielder competently participates in the play that follows the fielder's misplay or error, inasmuch as there is nothing illogical or unfair in doing so.

♦ ♦ ♦

Rule 9.11—
Double and Triple Plays

The official scorer shall credit participation in a double play or triple play to each fielder who earns a putout or an assist when two or three players are put out between the time a pitch is delivered and the time the ball next becomes dead or is next in possession of the pitcher in a pitching position, unless an error or misplay intervenes between putouts.

FOR EXAMPLE:

Situation #1: With a runner at first and less than two outs, the batter hits a ground ball to the shortstop.

The shortstop fields the ball and delivers it to the second baseman covering second base, and the runner forced to advance from first base by virtue of the ball being put into play is put out. In turn, the second baseman throws the ball to first base, where the batter is retired by the first baseman.

Because two players were "put out between the time the pitch was delivered and the ball next became dead or (was) next in possession of the pitcher in a pitching position," the shortstop, the second baseman and the first baseman are each credited with having participated in a double play.

Situation #2: With a runner at first, less than two outs, and a two-strike count on the batter, the runner at first breaks for second base on the pitch.

The batter strikes out, and as soon as the ball reaches the catcher, the catcher delivers the ball to second base where the runner on base is put out on his steal attempt by the shortstop covering the base.

Because the batter and the runner on base were both "put out between the time the pitch was delivered and the ball next became dead or (was) next in possession of the pitcher in a pitching position," the catcher and the shortstop are each credited with having participated in a double play.

At the same time, note that the pitcher is not considered as having participated in the double play because, under Rule 9.10(b)(1), a pitcher does not get credit for an assist on a strikeout, nor does the pitcher get credit for an assist when the catcher—after having received a legal pitch—throws out a runner attempting to steal a base (pursuant to Rule 9.10(b)(2)), and Rule 9.11 states that only fielders who "earn a putout or an assist when two or three players are put out..." can be credited with having participated in a double or triple play.

Situation #3: With a runner at first, and less than two outs, the batter hits a line drive to the right fielder that is caught in flight to retire the batter.

The runner at first does not advance.

Before the next batter comes to bat, the umpire calls "time," and the ball is considered "dead," as per the rulebook's Definition of Terms.

As soon as the pitcher gets back on the pitcher's rubber for the purpose of delivering the next pitch (i.e., the first pitch to the next batter), the pitcher throws the ball to first base to successfully pick off and retire the runner at first base.

Although two outs were made in succession, they do not constitute a double play because the ball was dead between the time the two putouts were made. In addition, and independent of that fact, the ball was "next in possession of the pitcher in a pitching position" between the time the two putouts were logged, and therefore the two outs do not constitute a double play.

(This situation is distinct, separate from, and not to be confused with situations addressed in the comment to Rule 9.11, which applies to outs made on appeal plays.)

Situation #4: With runners at first and second, and no outs, the batter hits a ground ball to the third baseman.

The third baseman fields the ball and steps on third base to force out the runner who is forced to advance from second base to third base by virtue of the ball being put into play.

Thereupon, the third baseman throws the ball to first base in an attempt to retire the batter, but the third baseman's throw is well off the mark and (consequently) the first baseman cannot catch the ball cleanly to retire the batter.

With this, the runner who had been at first base when the play began, and who advanced to second base on the ground ball, tries for third base.

Unfortunately (for the runner trying to advance to third base), the first baseman manages to retrieve the ball and get it to third base in time for the third baseman to tag out that runner.

Although two outs were made in succession, they do not constitute a double play because there was a intervening misplay, i.e., the bad throw made by the third baseman which precipitated the runner (who was ultimately tagged out for the second out) attempting to advance further than second base.

Note that the third baseman's throw is properly considered a misplay in this scenario, and not an error, because under Rule 9.12(d)(3), a bad throw made in an attempt to complete a double play is not (in and of itself) properly considered an error. On the other hand, if the third baseman's throw had been a good one, and the first baseman had muffed the throw—allowing the batter to reach base safely—that would be considered an error on the part of the first baseman, pursuant to Rule 9.12(d)(3)'s comment. Nevertheless, in either case, the result would be the same: the two putouts at third base would not constitute a double play.

WHAT IT MEANS: Double plays are achievements on the part of a defensive team that warrant recognition, and triple plays even more so. However, always bestowing that recognition to the fielders involved whenever two or three outs are logged—one right after the other—would serve to make a "legitimate" double play or triple play less special, and Rule 9.11's somewhat circumscribed definition of what is required is based, at least in part, on that.

APPEAL PLAYS

Rule 9.11 Comment: The official scorer shall credit a double play or triple play also if an appeal play after the ball is in possession of the pitcher results in an additional putout.

FOR EXAMPLE: With a runner on third, and less than two outs, the batter hits a fly ball to the outfield that is caught to retire the batter.

The runner on third "tags up" and advances to home plate on the play, and the ball is returned to the infield.

The umpire calls "time" (so as to allow the defensive team, and the player coming to bat, to get set for the game to continue).

When play is officially resumed, and the pitcher has the ball on the mound, ready to pitch to the next batter, an appeal play is promptly made at third base (inasmuch as the defensive team believes that the runner who had been at third base left third base on the preceding play before the outfielder who caught the batter's fly ball touched the ball).

The appeal is successful.

Pursuant to the provisions of Rule 9.11's comment, the two putouts are considered a double play, even though the ball "became dead" and was "in possession of the pitcher in a pitching position" between the time the first and the second putouts were made.

WHAT IT MEANS: Rule 9.11's comment's intention is to state that the official scorer should not consider a potential double play (or triple play) as not constituting a valid double play (or triple play) merely because one (or more) of the outs arose from a successful appeal play, and it supersedes the main text of Rule 9.11.

Granted, that could be stated more clearly by the rulebook. Regardless, that is how this provision of Rule 9.11 is applied by MLB, and doing so is consistent with the intent of Rule 9.11's comment.

To Err Is Human

Rule 9.12

Rule 9.12—Errors

An error is a statistic charged against a fielder whose action has assisted the team on offense, as set forth in this Rule 9.12.

Without a doubt, the Queen Mother of all scorekeeping decisions is whether or not to charge a fielder with an error on any given play where that's an issue.

Although there are many other aspects of scorekeeping that an official scorer must deal with—everything in this book that precedes this section, and all that follows—declaring errors, or declining to do so, is the fundamental part of an official scorer's job.

In fact, it is the "be all and end all" duty and function of an official scorer in the minds of many.

Simply put, aside from the decisions made by umpires on the field of play, scoring a hit versus an error is the ultimate "judgment call" in baseball, and it affects the statistics of baseball profoundly. Consequently, the rulebook devotes a good deal of verbiage to the issue.

At the heart of the matter is a fundamental turn of phrase, one that permeates virtually the entire topic of when to ascribe fielders with errors, and when not to do so, i.e., "ordinary effort." That being the case, a close look at what ordinary effort means is needed before any practical understanding of this aspect of scorekeeping can be had.

Ordinary Effort: It Really Isn't About Effort, When All Is Said and Done

The notion of ordinary effort is (and has been for a long, long time) a central concept used to determine whether a play should/could have been made by a fielder, and it's a term that is at the core of countless scoring controversies. However, despite its prominent place in the lexicon of scorekeeping, the term was undefined until the 2007 revisions.

At the same time, it is ironic that this significant portion of the 2007 revisions of Rule 9 is found in the rulebook's Definition of Terms.

In any case, for better or worse, it's defined as follows.

ORDINARY EFFORT is the effort that a fielder of average skill at a position in that league or classification of leagues should exhibit on a play, with due consideration given to the condition of the field and weather conditions.

(Ordinary Effort) Comment: This standard, called for several times in the Official Scoring Rules (e.g., Rules 9.05(a)(3), 9.05(a)(4), 9.05(a)(6), 9.05 (b)(3) [Base Hits]; 9.08(b) [Sacrifices]; 9.12(a)(1) Comment, 9.12(d)(2) [Errors]; and 9.13(a), 9.13(b) [Wild Pitches and Passed Balls]) and in the Official Baseball Rules (e.g., Definition of Terms [Infield Fly]), is an objective standard in regard to any particular fielder. In other words, even if a fielder makes his best effort, if that effort falls short of what an average fielder at that position in that league would have made in a situation, the official scorer should charge that fielder with an error.

It is laudable that the rulebook would—at long last—set out a definition of a term that is so central to scorekeeping. However, the official definition of ordinary effort is not altogether satisfactory.

For starters, the definition is somewhat of a tautology: a repetition of the same meaning in different words or phrases—ordinary effort is effort that is ordinary.

Moreover, the standard isn't about "effort" at all. It's about competence versus incompetence. It's not about how hard one tries. It's about messing up versus not messing up, regardless of the effort employed.

This can be seen by looking at how the phrase is used in the rulebook.

Rule 9.05(a)(3) **The official scorer shall credit a batter with a base hit when … the batter reaches first base safely on a fair ball that takes an unnatural bounce so that a fielder cannot handle it** *with ordinary effort,* **or that**

touches the pitcher's plate or any base (including home plate) before being touched by a fielder and bounces so that a fielder cannot handle the ball *with ordinary effort.*

Rule 9.05(a)(4)   The official scorer shall credit a batter with a base hit when ... the batter reaches first base safely on a fair ball that has not been touched by a fielder and that is in fair territory when the ball reaches the outfield, unless in the scorer's judgment the ball could have been handled *with ordinary effort.*

Rule 9.05(a)(6)   The official scorer shall credit a batter with a base hit when ... a fielder unsuccessfully attempts to put out a preceding runner and, in the official scorer's judgment, the batter-runner would not have been put out at first base *by ordinary effort.*

Rule 9.05(b)(3)   The official scorer shall not credit a base hit when a ... pitcher, the catcher or any infielder handles a batted ball and puts out a preceding runner who is attempting to advance one base or to return to his original base, or would have put out such runner *with ordinary effort* except for a fielding error.

Rule 9.08(b)   Score a sacrifice bunt when, before two are out, the fielders handle a bunted ball without error in an unsuccessful attempt to put out a preceding runner advancing one base, unless, an attempt to turn a bunt into a putout of a preceding runner fails, and in the judgment of the official scorer *ordinary effort* would not have put out the batter at first base, in which case the batter shall be credited with a one-base hit and not a sacrifice.

9.12(a)(1) Comment: If a ground ball goes through a fielder's legs or a fly ball falls untouched and, in the scorer's judgment, the fielder could have handled the ball with ordinary effort, the official scorer shall charge such fielder with an error. For example, the official scorer shall charge an infielder with an error when a ground ball passes to either side of such infielder if, in the official scorer's judgment, a fielder at that position making ordinary effort would have fielded such ground ball and retired a runner. The official scorer shall charge an outfielder with an error if such outfielder allows a fly ball to drop to the ground if, in the official scorer's judgment, an outfielder at that position making ordinary effort would have caught such fly ball.

Rule 9.12(d)(2)   The official scorer shall not charge an error against ... any fielder who makes a wild throw if in the scorer's judgment the runner would not have been put out *with ordinary effort* by a good throw, unless such wild throw permits any runner to advance beyond the base he would have reached had the throw not been wild.

Rule 9.13(a)   The official scorer shall charge a pitcher with a wild pitch when a legally delivered ball is so high, so wide or so low that the catcher does not stop and control the ball *by ordinary effort*, thereby permitting a runner or runners to advance.

Rule 9.13(b)   The official scorer shall charge a catcher with a passed ball when the catcher fails to hold or to control a legally pitched ball that should have been held or controlled *with ordinary effort*, thereby permitting a runner or runners to advance.

> Definition of Terms   An INFIELD FLY is a fair fly ball (not including a line drive nor an attempted bunt) which can be caught by an infielder *with ordinary effort*, when first and second, or first, second and third bases are occupied, before two are out.

So what is ordinary effort if how hard a fielder tries to make a play isn't the ultimate issue?

The answer is that the standard is better stated in terms of competence.

In other words, if, for instance, a fielder fails to catch a batted ball in flight that would put out a batter, it's a base hit for the batter if (allowing for any adverse playing conditions) another average fielder (in the league in question), exhibiting average (ordinary) athletic competence would not have caught the ball. Or, stated in the reverse, it's an error for the fielder if (allowing for adverse playing conditions) another average fielder (in the league in question), exhibiting average (ordinary) athletic competence would have caught the ball.

As far as the idea of ordinary effort (or any alternative phrase used to label the standard) being "objective"—as the rulebook's definition claims that it is—it's well to wish that it were so, but in reality, that's nonsense.

Consider the following.

A week is seven days. Consequently, six days constitutes less than a week. Eight days constitutes more than a week.

That's objective.

However, judging (for example) if a third baseman could/should have fielded a sharply hit ground ball cleanly and made a good throw to first base to put out a speedy batter is not—and can never be—wholly objective. It is inherently subjective because it is something that cannot be gauged undetached from the perception of the individual called upon to judge it, regardless of what the official definition of ordinary effort claims.

Simply put, there is no perfect or precise yardstick with which to measure something like ordinary effort—the exhibition of average (ordinary) athletic competence. There is only the judgment of the scorer, and as circumspect, as grounded in logic, experience and impartiality as it may be, a scorekeeper's call of base hit versus error can never be more than what it always and ultimately is: an opinion.

THE MEAT OF THE MATTER

Rule 9.12(a)(1)   The official scorer shall charge an error against any fielder ... whose misplay (fumble, muff or wild throw) prolongs the time at bat of a batter, prolongs the presence on the bases of a runner or permits a runner to advance one or more bases, unless, in the judgment of the official scorer, such fielder deliberately permits a foul fly to fall safe with a runner on third base before two are out in order that the runner on third shall not score after the catch.

All errors are misplays, but not all misplays are errors.

In other words, it is not enough for a fielder to "fumble" (fail to field a batted ball cleanly that could/should have been fielded cleanly), "muff" (fail to catch a thrown or batted ball that could/should have been caught), or make a "wild throw" (make a throw that cannot be caught "with ordinary effort" by the fielder for whom the thrown was intended). Rather, the fumble, muff or wild throw must give rise to a least one of two things: either (1) blowing an opportunity to put out a batter or a runner, or (2) allowing a runner or runners to advance along the base paths when—but for the misplay—the advancement would not have occurred.

FOR EXAMPLE: In the first instance, the batter hits an easy grounder back to the pitcher, who fields the ball cleanly. However, the pitcher proceeds to throw the ball a good seven feet over the first baseman's head at first base and into the stands.

As a result, the batter avoids being put out. Moreover, the umpires award the batter second base as well.

Because the pitcher's bad throw ruined the opportunity to put out the batter, an error is properly charged to the pitcher. At the same time, the fact that the pitcher's bad throw also allowed the batter to advance beyond first base constitutes additional independent grounds for charging the pitcher with an error (a "two-base error") in this case.

In the second instance, the batter hits a grounder back to the pitcher, who fields the ball cleanly, and (as before) the pitcher proceeds to make a bad throw to first base. However, this time the ball was hit in such a manner that the pitcher could not get to the ball in time to field it and deliver it to first base ahead of the batter. Moreover, the right fielder was able to back up the pitcher's poor throw and thereby keep the batter at first base.

In this case, no error is properly charged to the pitcher because (1) even if the pitcher's throw had been on the mark, the batter would have been safe at first base anyway, and (2) although the throw was bad, it did not lead to the batter advancing beyond first base.

A Short Postscript: Deliberately Committing an "Error"

As far as the final portion of Rule 9.12(a)(1) is concerned—the part that addresses a fielder deliberately choosing to allow a fly ball in foul territory to go uncaught—consider the following.

In Game 6 of the 1975 World Series between the Cincinnati Reds and the Boston Red Sox, the score was tied in the bottom of the ninth inning, with the bases loaded and no outs, when Boston's center fielder, Fred Lynn, came to bat.

He hit a fly ball into foul territory to the left of the left field foul line.

The Red Sox's second baseman, Denny Doyle, tagged up at third base and attempted to score after the Cincinnati left fielder, George Foster, caught Lynn's foul fly ball.

Had Doyle scored, the game would have been over right there, but Foster was able to catch the ball and deliver it to the Cincinnati catcher, Johnny Bench, and Doyle was put out on a 7/7–2 double play.

(Note that—as many baseball fans are well aware—the game went into extra innings, but the Red Sox ended up winning the game anyway on Carlton Fisk's dramatic solo home run in the bottom of the 12th inning. However, despite all the drama attendant to this game, Cincinnati—the "Big Red Machine"—went on to win Game 7 and the Series).

In any case, if Foster had deliberately let Fred Lynn's foul fly ball drop uncaught, it would have "prolonged the time at bat of a batter" (Lynn), and therefore that might be deemed an error on the part of Foster. However, if Foster had chosen to do so to avoid the possibility of Doyle tagging up on the catch to score the game-winning run, Foster could not have been properly charged with an error on the play because of Rule 9.12(a)(1)'s specific exception, and simple logic would lead one to the same conclusion as well.

Note that the "comment" to Rule 9.12(a)(1) consists of 435 words, while Rule 9.12(a)(1) itself consists of only 85 words.

The irony of that aside, Rule 9.12(a)(1)'s comment is key, inasmuch as it sets out numerous scorekeeping principles and precepts, all of which are very important when it comes to the official scorer's functions in the context of judging errors.

Given its proportions and complexity, the myriad portions of Rule 9.12(a)(1) will be dealt with separately, and in turn.

Rule 9.12(a)(1) Comment: Slow handling of the ball that does not involve mechanical misplay shall not be construed as an error. For example, the official scorer shall not charge a fielder with an error if such fielder fields a ground ball cleanly but does not throw to first base in time to retire the batter.

FOR EXAMPLE: The batter bunts the ball roughly halfway to the pitcher's mound.

The catcher trudges out from behind home plate to field the ball.

He does nothing wrong; his actions in fielding the ball and delivering it to first base are altogether competent, but everything he does on the play is as deliberate and methodical as one could ever imagine, and that—coupled with the fact that the batter is extraordinarily fast on his feet—results in the batter reaching first base safely.

Given the first portion of Rule 9.12(a)(1)'s comment, the catcher is not properly charged with an error, and the batter is fairly credited with a base hit.

By the same token, if the catcher had realized (once he had fielded the ball) that he couldn't deliver the ball to first base in time to retire the batter, and therefore made no throw at all, the batter would likewise be entitled to a base hit, and no error ought to be charged to the catcher.

If, however, the catcher had—for example—dropped the ball after first picking it up, and therefore had to "field" the ball a second time to make his throw, and it was judged that but for the catcher dropping the ball the batter would/should have been put out at first base, the catcher is properly charged with an error and the batter is fairly considered as having reached base on the error.

It is not necessary that the fielder touch the ball to be charged with an error. If a ground ball goes through a fielder's legs or a fly ball falls untouched and, in the scorer's judgment, the fielder could have handled the ball with ordinary effort, the official scorer shall charge such fielder with an error. For example, the official scorer shall charge an infielder with an error when a ground ball passes to either side of such infielder if, in the official scorer's judgment, a fielder at that position making ordinary effort would have fielded such ground ball and retired a runner. The official scorer shall charge an outfielder with an error if such outfielder allows a fly ball to drop to the ground if, in the official scorer's judgment, an outfielder at that position making ordinary effort would have caught such fly ball.

One of the great fallacies in scorekeeping, and one that is among the most repeated, is that a fielder must touch the ball in order to be charged with an error.

Certainly, this portion of Rule 9.12(a)(1)'s comment should make it crystal clear to everyone that that isn't the case.

No better example exists than one of the most infamous errors in baseball's history, the ground ball hit by Mookie Wilson of the New York Mets in Game 6 of the 1986 World Series between the Mets and the Boston Red Sox that passed through the legs of Boston's first baseman, Bill Buckner, leading to the Mets winning the game on the run that scored as a result.

Buckner didn't touch the ball, but it was an error nonetheless.

In sum, although a fielder's proximity to the ball is a factor to be considered in deciding whether or not the fielder could/should have made any given play, touching or not touching the ball is far from an absolute criterion in making the decision to charge an error or not.

If a throw is low, wide or high, or strikes the ground, and a runner reaches base who otherwise would have been put out by such throw, the official scorer shall charge the player making the throw with an error.

This portion of Rule 9.12(a)(1)'s comment was added as part of the 2007 revisions, and—at first blush—it appears to be straightforward and simple. However, there is a problem: it does not jibe with Rule 9.12(7), which reads as follows. **"The official scorer shall charge an error against any fielder … whose throw takes an unnatural bounce … thereby permitting any runner to advance."**

In short, Rule 9.12(7) plainly implies that a throw that does not take an "unnatural bounce"—that takes a "natural bounce" and can be readily caught by the fielder for whom the throw is intended—is not an error for the fielder who made the throw if the fielder receiving the throw muffs the catch, and therefore a throw can be "bounced" (strike the ground) and still be considered a good throw.

That said, this apparent conflict might be reconciled by reading into this portion of Rule 9.12(a)(1)'s comment's text that the throw at issue must be—in addition to being "low, wide or high" or one that "strikes the ground"—a throw that is also not capable of being caught with "ordinary effort" by the fielder for whom the throw was intended.

The official scorer shall not score mental mistakes or misjudgments as errors unless a specific rule prescribes otherwise.

Here's the source of another often repeated scorekeeping cliché and fallacy: that mental errors are never, ever scored as official fielding errors.

A perfunctory reading of this portion of Rule 9.12(a)(1)'s comment could certainly lead one to assume that that is the case, but what is often overlooked is that specific reference is made to other rules where a mental mistake or misjudgment can lead to a fielder being charged with an error, and therefore some (albeit limited) mental mistakes or misjudgments are in fact properly scored as official fielding errors.

In that regard, see Rule 9.12(a)(3), Rule 9.12(a)(4) and Rule 9.12(a)(8), as well as the next portion of Rule 9.12(a)(1)'s comment.

A fielder's mental mistake that leads to a physical misplay—such as throwing the ball into the stands or rolling the ball to the pitcher's mound, mistakenly believing there to be three outs, and thereby allowing a runner or runners to advance—shall not be considered a mental mistake for purposes of this rule and the official scorer shall charge a fielder committing such a mistake with an error.

Of all the provisions added to Rule 9 as part of the 2007 revisions, this is among the most welcome, and here's why.

Sometimes fielders lose track of how many outs there are in an inning, and, as a result, behave as if the second (or even the first) out of an inning was the third out when it was not. That being so, scorers have been faced with a quandary when that happens: the fielder's mistaken belief "assisted the team on offense" by way of runner advancement brought on by a fielder's inattention, but mental mistakes are not to be deemed or considered fielding errors unless a specific provision directs the scorer to do so, and no specific provision—until the 2007 revisions—addressed this set of circumstances.

As a result, scorers have struggled to conjure up justifications (sometimes quite convoluted) to charge an error to the clueless fielder in cases like this, perhaps relying on Rule 9.01(b)(1) wherein the official scorer is given authority to rule on any point not specifically covered "in these rules."

But that was then, and this is now, and a reoccurring scorekeeping headache has been addressed in a reasonably straightforward and satisfactory manner by the 2007 revisions.

The official scorer shall not charge an error if the pitcher fails to cover first base on a play, thereby allowing a batter-runner to reach first base safely.

FOR EXAMPLE: The batter hits a ground ball to the area between second base and first base, but close enough to the first baseman so that the first baseman can dive and stop the ball from leaving the infield.

Unfortunately (for the defensive team), the first baseman can't get back up and run with the ball to first base to put out the batter before the batter can get there. However, more than sufficient time exists for the first baseman to toss the ball to someone covering first base and force out the batter.

Notwithstanding, the pitcher—whose universally understood responsibility it is to cover first base whenever there's even a chance that the first baseman may have to leave the proximity of first base to field a batted ball—inexplicably remains on the pitcher's mound, and (as a result) the batter reaches first base easily.

It's a base hit for the batter, and no error is charged.

WHAT IT MEANS: As was the case in the previous provision of Rule 9.12(a)(1)'s comment, here is a situation that was not directly addressed by the rulebook before the 2007 revisions.

Before the 2007 revisions, not charging the pitcher in cases like this with an error would have been appropriate inasmuch as the pitcher's mistake in failing to cover first base was a mental mistake (which generally are not properly considered official fielding errors), and this mental mistake was not one of the few mental mistakes that qualify as fielding errors. Be that as it may, this new portion of Rule 9.12(a)(1)'s comment serves the purpose of making it explicitly clear that not charging an error is appropriate (although it gives credit to a batter for a base hit that isn't altogether deserved).

The official scorer shall not charge an error to a fielder who incorrectly throws to the wrong base on a play.

FOR EXAMPLE: In the motion picture *A League of Their Own*, the right fielder for the Rockford Peaches had a ball hit to her in the top of the sixth inning, when her team was in the lead. Because there was a runner on base, she chose (foolishly) to throw the ball to home plate instead of the "cutoff woman." This allowed the potential tying run for the opposing team (in the person of the batter who hit the ball to the outfield) to reach scoring position (i.e., second base), and that, in turn, led to the score subsequently being tied by the visiting team in that inning.

On her way back to the dugout, the right fielder (Evelyn) is "admonished" by the Peaches' manager (played by Tom Hanks), which leads to Evelyn bursting into tears and the resultant famous—and endlessly repeated—declaration that "there's no crying in baseball."

The point is that what Rockford's right fielder did was a mistake in terms of baseball strategy: throwing the ball to the "wrong base," so to speak. However, what she did is not properly considered an error pursuant to this portion of Rule 9.12(a)(1)'s comment, and the advancement of the batter from first base to second base in this situation is simply considered as having been made on a fielder's choice.

WHAT IT MEANS: This provision of Rule 9.12(a)(1)'s comment is nothing more than another manifestation of the general policy of not elevating mental miscues ("errors" in judgment only) to official fielding errors, inasmuch as it would be unfair to the players, and quite onerous for scorekeepers if they were called upon to second-guess the choices made by players actually engaged in the game (with all its pressures) while sitting in the press box (where it's quite easy to play the game in one's head flawlessly).

The official scorer shall charge an error to a fielder who causes another fielder to misplay a ball—for example, by knocking the ball out of the other fielder's glove. On such a play, when the official scorer charges an error to the interfering fielder, the official scorer shall not charge an error to the fielder with whom the other fielder interfered.

FOR EXAMPLE: A high fly ball is hit into left-center field.

The center fielder gets to the spot where the ball will come down, well before the left fielder does. Moreover, the center fielder "calls off" the left fielder quite clearly, both verbally and with broadly animated physical gestures.

On top of that, it is understood throughout the world of baseball that the center fielder is generally the "captain" of the outfield, and therefore entitled to deference by the other fielders on his team.

Regardless, in attempting to catch the ball, the left fielder crashes into the center fielder just at the moment the center fielder is about to catch the ball to put out the batter. Consequently, the ball goes uncaught and the batter reaches base safely.

Although the left fielder could have caught the ball if the center fielder had not attempted to make the catch himself, the left fielder is nonetheless properly charged with an error in this case.

WHAT IT MEANS: Granted, situations where this portion of Rule 9.12 (a)(1)'s comment might apply are rarely as cut and dried as the one set forth above, and deciding which fielder is going to be the goat is usually far more difficult than it is in the example given. Nonetheless, here is another portion of the rulebook that was added as part of the 2007 revisions to make certain situations—where the proper scoring is not altogether obvious—much easier to deal with.

INDELIBLE ERRORS

Rule 9.12(a)(2)   The official scorer shall charge an error against any fielder ... when such fielder muffs a foul fly to prolong the time at bat of a batter, whether the batter subsequently reaches first base or is put out.

FOR EXAMPLE: The batter hits a lazy fly ball that is destined to come down a few yards to the left of third base in foul territory. A can of corn.

The third baseman casually drifts over to make the easy catch, but the ball bounces off the heel of his glove, uncaught.

If the batter then goes on to reach base, charging the third baseman with an error on the blown catch is a no-brainer because the batter would not have reached base but for the third baseman's failure to put out the batter when the opportunity presented itself.

However, even if the batter goes on to be put out without reaching base, and therefore the third baseman's failure to put out the batter when he had the chance would have no real consequence, the third baseman is nevertheless properly charged with an error.

WHAT IT MEANS: Fielding averages—calculated as the number of assists and putouts made divided by the total of assists, putouts and errors committed—are far from being altogether accurate measurements of fielding abilities, for a great many reasons.

The methodology is crude, especially when contrasted with the ability of modern computer-driven baseball analysis to generate numbers reflecting and measuring fielding abilities and achievements that go far beyond the superficiality of simple fielding averages.

Be that as it may, to turn a blind eye to a fielder's bad play, to ignore it just because the fielder's poor performance was—in a sense—erased by further play, would certainly not enhance the accuracy of fielding statistics. In fact, it would serve to distort them.

Consequently, an error is an error in this case, and there's no getting away from it in situations such as those covered by Rule 9.12(a)(2). However, there are cases when what would appear at first to be an error ends up not being scored as an error, as is the case in situations addressed under Rule 9.12(d)(4).

A Mental Mistake That Constitutes a Fielding Error

Rule 9.12(a)(3)   The official scorer shall charge an error against any fielder … when such fielder catches a thrown ball or a ground ball in time to put out the batter-runner and fails to tag first base or the batter-runner.

FOR EXAMPLE: With a runner at third, and less than two outs, the batter hits a ground ball to the first baseman.

The first baseman fields the ball easily and begins to take a few steps toward first base, where he can simply step on the bag in advance of the batter and thereby force out the batter. However, although the runner at third makes no move that might indicate that he has any notion of advancing on the play, the first baseman focuses his attention on the runner at third to the point that he fails to tag first base in time to put out the batter (although there was ample opportunity to do so without any risk of the runner at third advancing).

When the dust clears, the runner at third base is still at third base and the batter is a runner at first base.

By virtue of Rule 9.12(a)(3), the first baseman is properly charged with an error in this case, and the batter is considered as having reached base on the first baseman's error.

WHAT IT MEANS: The first baseman in this case did not "fumble," "muff," or make a "wild throw." Nonetheless, the first baseman is considered as having committed an error, even though it was essentially a mental lapse on his part and not an act of athletic/physical incompetence.

Essentially, the rulebook relaxes its general ban on charging errors that are really only mental mistakes in cases like this because blunders like these are obvious. There is no second-guessing the fielder's thought processes: they're bonehead plays with no legitimate excuse or justification.

Another Mental Mistake That Constitutes a Fielding Error

Rule 9.12(a)(4)   The official scorer shall charge an error against any fielder … when such fielder catches a thrown ball or a ground ball in time to put out any runner on a force play and fails to tag the base or the runner.

All that Rule 9.12(a)(4) does is simply take the idea behind Rule 9.12(a)(3) and extend its application from blown plays on batters headed for first base to blown plays that are made on any runners who are forced to advance when a ball is put into play.

In that regard, care should be taken not to go too far and apply Rule 9.12(a)(4) to runners who are not forced to advance.

For example: With a runner at second base, the batter pounds the ball into the ground in the direction of the shortstop.

The ball bounces high into the air, a classic "Baltimore chop."

Once the ball is fielded by the shortstop, there is little chance that he can deliver the ball to first base to force out the batter. At the same time, the runner at second is only a step or two from the shortstop when the ball finally reaches the shortstop's glove and—with little effort—the shortstop could tag out the runner between second and third.

Nonetheless, the shortstop ignores the runner and instead makes a heroic throw to first base, but because the ball had such incredible "hang time," the batter beats out the shortstop's throw.

In the meantime, the runner at second skips into third base standing up.

Even though the shortstop caught "a ground ball in time to put out a runner," his failure to put out the runner (who was at second base) is not counted as an error because the runner he failed to put out was not forced to advance.

What it means: Rule 9.12(a)(3) and Rule 9.12(a)(4) take the attitude that a fielder's failure to tag first base or the "batter-runner" before the batter-runner reaches first base to put out a batter, or a runner who is forced to advance (when the fielder had the opportunity to do so) is such an inexcusable lapse on the part of the fielder that an error ought to be charged even though the "error" was committed not so much on the field of play as it was committed in the space between the offending fielder's ears.

On the other hand, tagging out a runner who isn't forced to advance is—more often that not—not as simple a thing to do. Therefore, a wider berth is afforded fielders in that case, and an error is not properly charged.

A Restatement of Rule 9.12's Basic Premise, with a Significant Caveat Regarding Runners Attempting to Steal a Base

Rule 9.12(a)(5)   The official scorer shall charge an error against any fielder ... whose wild throw permits a runner to reach a base safely, when

in the scorer's judgment a good throw would have put out the runner, unless such wild throw is made attempting to prevent a stolen base.

FOR EXAMPLE: With a runner at second base, and the pitcher on the mound—ready to make the next pitch—the runner breaks for third.

As a result, the pitcher fires the ball to third base, but his throw is "wild" and gets away from the third baseman as the runner is sliding into third.

Seeking to capitalize on this turn of events, the runner gets up and sprints toward home plate.

While that's going on, the third baseman retrieves the ball in time to throw the ball to home plate ahead of the runner, but the third baseman's throw is just as "wild" as the pitcher's throw was, and the runner scores a run.

In this case, no error is charged to the pitcher. Nonetheless, the third baseman is properly charged with an error.

WHAT IT MEANS: The pitcher's throw was made in an attempt "to prevent a stolen base," and under Rule 9.12(a)(5), charging the pitcher with an error is not appropriate. On the other hand, the third baseman's throw was not made to prevent the runner from stealing home plate. Rather, the throw was made to prevent the runner from advancing beyond third base on the pitcher's bad throw.

In addition, it should be noted that if the runner in this case would have scored even if the third baseman's throw had not been wild, the third baseman would not be charged with an error under Rule 9.12(a)(5). Moreover, the pitcher would be charged with an error [pursuant to Rule 9.12(a)(6)], not because the pitcher's wild throw allowed the runner to steal third base, but because the pitcher's wild throw (and not the third baseman's wild throw) allowed the runner to advance and score a run.

Rule 9.12(a)(6)   The official scorer shall charge an error against any fielder ... whose wild throw in attempting to prevent a runner's advance permits that runner or any other runner to advance one or more bases beyond the base such runner would have reached had the throw not been wild.

FOR EXAMPLE: The batter hits a line drive down the right field line for a solid, standup double.

In returning the ball to the infield, the right fielder throws the ball far out of the reach of the cutoff man, and the ball rolls a good distance before any fielder can get to it. Watching the events unfold, the batter capitalizes on the opportunity and advances to third base.

The right fielder is properly charged with an error on the throw in this case.

WHAT IT MEANS: Note that the right fielder's throw was not made to put out the batter. Rather, the idea was simply to get the ball back to the infield in an orderly manner so as to keep the batter from advancing any further than he already had on the two-base hit.

Nevertheless, simply put, but for the right fielder's errant throw, the batter would not have advanced to third. That being so, the batter's advancement from second to third is logically attributable to the bad throw, and charging the fielder who made the bad throw is therefore logical as well.

In addition, note that if a runner other than the runner a play is being made on advances on a wild throw, charging an error is also appropriate.

FOR EXAMPLE: With a runner at first, the batter drives the ball off the left field wall.

The runner who had been on first goes to third base and stops. At the same time, the left fielder fields the ball and fires it to second base in hopes of putting out the batter who hit the line drive.

The throw to second base is late, but more significantly, it's wild and gets away from the fielder covering second base.

As soon as that happens, the runner who had been at first base but is now at third, races home to score, but the batter chooses to stay at second base for fear of being put out attempting to advance any further.

WHAT IT MEANS: In this case, the left fielder is properly charged with an error even though the left fielder's wild throw did not "permit" the runner (batter-runner) that the left fielder was trying to put out to advance: the advancement by the "other runner" is enough to qualify the left fielder for an error under Rule 9.12(a)(6).

WHEN A GOOD THROW MIGHT NONETHELESS CONSTITUTE AN ERROR

Rule 9.12(a)(7)   The official scorer shall charge an error against any fielder ... whose throw takes an unnatural bounce, touches a base or the pitcher's plate, or touches a runner, a fielder or an umpire, thereby permitting any runner to advance.

Rule 9.12(a)(7) Comment: The official scorer shall apply this rule even when it appears to be an injustice to a fielder whose throw was accurate. For example, the official scorer shall charge an error to an outfielder whose accurate throw to second base hits the base and caroms back into the outfield, thereby permitting a runner or runners to advance, because every base advanced by a runner must be accounted for.

Rule 9.12(a)(7), together with its comment, speaks for itself. It even gives an example of what it's talking about (which example was added as part of the 2007 rule revisions).

In addition, Rule 9.12(a)(7) is unique in that it acknowledges that its application can lead to results that are unquestionably unfair.

That said, perhaps the most significant aspect of Rule 9.12(a)(7) is buried in the final words of its comment, and—that being so—it is a shame that more emphasis is not given to it: "every base advanced by a runner must be accounted for."

Those ten words are key to proper scorekeeping. They sum up what it's all about and constitute a de facto creed for every conscientious scorer.

Do so, and you can't go wrong. Don't, and sooner or latter you'll wish you had.

ANOTHER MENTAL MISTAKE THAT CONSTITUTES A FIELDING ERROR

Rule 9.12(a)(8)   The official scorer shall charge an error against any fielder ... whose failure to stop, or try to stop, an accurately thrown ball permits a runner to advance, so long as there was occasion for the throw. If such throw was made to second base, the official scorer shall determine whether it was the duty of the second baseman or the shortstop to stop the ball and shall charge an error to the negligent fielder.

FOR EXAMPLE: A pitch is made and caught by the catcher. At the same time, the runner at first base breaks for second base on a steal attempt.

The catcher throws the ball to second base quite competently, but no one covers second base. As a result, the ball ends up in the outfield and the runner ends up at third base.

Having made a good throw, for a good reason, and with the intention of preventing a stolen base, the catcher in this case cannot be properly charged with an error. However, if a fielder had covered second base and had competently fielded the catcher's throw, the runner would not have been able to advance to third base. Consequently, that additional advancement is properly attributed to an error on the part of the fielder who should have fielded the catcher's throw, but didn't.

WHAT IT MEANS: Here we have another example of a "mental mistake" that is an exception to the general rule that mistakes that are not a "fumble," a "muff" or a "wild throw" are not considered official fielding errors.

As far as judging which fielder ought to be charged with an error under Rule 9.12(a)(8) when more than one fielder might be looked upon as having failed to do his job (that is, the shortstop or the second baseman in terms of fielding throws made to second base), no guidance is given by the rulebook. Common sense would dictate that the scorer should consider which fielder was closer to the base in question, whether the batter was batting from the left side or the right side of the plate, and any other aspects of the situation that might be relevant.

In addition, note that in order for Rule 9.12(a)(8) to apply, the ball must be thrown "accurately." In other words, if the catcher's throw in the example given had been a wild throw that could not have been caught or stopped even if someone had covered second base, Rule 9.12(a)(8) does not apply, and an error is properly charged to the catcher (in terms of the runner's additional advancement, but not in terms of the runner's getting to second base, because a wild throw made to prevent a stolen base is not considered an error, as per Rule 9.12(a)(5) and Rule 9.12(d)(1)).

Rule 9.12(a)(8) Comment: If, in the official scorer's judgment, there was no occasion for the throw, the official scorer shall charge an error to the fielder who threw the ball.

FOR EXAMPLE: With a speedy runner at second base and third base open, the catcher is acutely anxious about the possibility that the runner on second base might try to steal third (so much so that it seriously clouds the catcher's thinking).

On the next pitch, the runner at second makes no move that would indicate an intention to steal third, but the catcher—as soon as he catches the pitch—unwisely rockets the ball to third base anyway.

Inasmuch as the third baseman (along with everyone else on the field of play for that matter) didn't anticipate the catcher's throw to third base, the ball sails well into left field, and the runner takes off from second base, rounds third and scores easily.

The runner's advancement from second base to home plate is properly considered as having been made on an error, and the error is properly charged to the catcher, even if there would have been no runner advancement if the third baseman had covered third base.

WHAT IT MEANS: The term "occasion for the throw" is not defined.

Therefore, knowing when to apply Rule 9.12(a)(8)'s comment, and when not to, can sometimes be a bit tricky. Be that as it may, the comment is really nothing more than the flip side of Rule 9.12(a)(8)'s main text, and it is the rulebook's final example of when a fielder's mental mistake is properly considered an official fielding error.

Multiple Base Errors

Rule 9.12(b)   The official scorer shall charge only one error on any wild throw, regardless of the number of bases advanced by one or more runners.

For example: With the bases loaded, the catcher makes a snap throw to first base in hopes of putting out the runner at first base (who's taken a big lead and does not seem to be paying too much attention to what's going on).

Although the first baseman alertly covers first base, the catcher's throw is appalling, and there is no way that the first baseman can come close to catching the throw, or even knocking it down.

As a result, once the ball is retrieved and returned to the infield from right field, the runner at third has advanced one base to score, the runner at second has advanced two bases to score, and the runner at first has advanced two bases to end up at third.

Although a total of five bases were advanced by three runners, the catcher's error is counted as a single error, just the same as if only one runner had advanced only one base.

What it means: While some errors lead to the advancement of a single base by a single runner (or more than one runner), and some errors lead to multiple base advancement by a runner (or more than one runner), the rulebook chooses to keeps things simple by calling upon the official scorer to charge an offending fielder with only one error regardless of how limited, or how catastrophic, the consequences of the error might be.

In short, it's the action of the fielder that is counted, not the ramifications that arose from that action. To do otherwise would open a Pandora's box of complexity.

An Error That Isn't Always an Error

Rule 9.12(c)   When an umpire awards the batter or any runner or runners one or more bases because of interference or obstruction, the official scorer shall charge the fielder who committed the interference or obstruction with one error, no matter how many bases the batter, or runner or runners, may advance.

Rule 9.12(c) Comment: The official scorer shall not charge an error if obstruction does not change the play, in the opinion of the scorer.

FOR EXAMPLE: A runner is caught in a rundown play between second base and third base.

As the runner is about to drop down to slide into third base ahead of the throw being made to try to put him out at third base, the shortstop (not in possession of the ball or in the act of fielding the ball) sticks his foot out and trips the runner.

As a result, the runner is awarded third base by virtue of the shortstop's obstruction.

If the scorer judges that the runner would have been put out at third base but for the obstruction call, the shortstop is properly charged with an error. On the other hand, if the scorer's opinion is that the runner would have been safe at third regardless of the shortstop's malfeasance, no error is properly scored.

WHAT IT MEANS: Rule 9.12(c) and its comment carry forward several of the main themes that precede them in Rule 9.12.

For starters, Rule 9.12(c) echoes the "only one error charged regardless of how many ramifications" notion contained in Rule 9.12(b).

In addition, Rule 9.12(c) is another manifestation of the idea that the advancement of each runner from base to base must be accounted for, and in this case, if a runner or runners would not have advanced but for a fielder's act of obstruction or defensive interference, the advancement is ascribed to the fielder in the form of an error.

At the same time, if the advancement would have occurred anyway— even if an umpire had not called obstruction or defensive interference—there is no good reason to saddle the offending fielder with an error. It isn't as though the advancement would not have occurred but for the obstruction or defensive interference; the advancement would have been made nonetheless.

A SHORT NOTE ON NOMENCLATURE

The terms "obstruction" and "interference" are often confused and therefore misapplied, for a number of reasons. That being the case, here are the official definitions of those terms (in salient part), as they appear in the MLB rulebook.

OBSTRUCTION is the act of a fielder who, while not in possession of the ball and not in the act of fielding the ball, impedes the progress of any runner.

INTERFERENCE (a) Offensive interference is an act by the team at bat which interferes with, obstructs, impedes, hinders or confuses any fielder attempting to make a play. (b) Defensive interference is an act by a fielder which hinders or prevents a batter from hitting a pitch.

In short, when a member of the defensive team messes with a runner in violation of the rules, it's obstruction.

When a member of the team at bat messes with a fielder in violation of the rules, it's interference.

When a member of the defensive team (the catcher, usually) messes with a batter in violation of the rules, it's defensive interference.

The Beginning of the Portions of Rule 9.12 That Address When Not to Score an Error, and the First of Two Redundant Provisions

Rule 9.12(d)(1)   The official scorer shall not charge an error against … the catcher when the catcher, after receiving the pitch, makes a wild throw attempting to prevent a stolen base, unless the wild throw permits the stealing runner to advance one or more extra bases or permits any other runner to advance one or more bases.

What is now Rule 9.12 was Rule 9.13 and 9.14 before the 2007 rulebook revisions, with Rule 9.13 representing (generally) instances where a scorer ought to charge an error, and Rule 9.14 concerned (generally) with when not to score an error.

In any case, Rule 9.12(d)(1) is the first in a series of the "thou shalt not score an error" subsections of the "new" Rule 9.12, and it is nothing more than a reiteration of Rule 9.12(a)(5), discussed previously.

The Second of Two Redundant Provisions

Rule 9.12(d)(2)   The official scorer shall not charge an error against … any fielder who makes a wild throw if in the scorer's judgment the runner would not have been put out with ordinary effort by a good throw, unless such wild throw permits any runner to advance beyond the base he would have reached had the throw not been wild.

Rule 9.12(d)(2) is nothing more than a reiteration of Rule 9.12(a)(6), discussed previously.

The Basis of the Old, Often Repeated, but Not Altogether Accurate Adage— "You Can't Assume a Double Play"

Rule 9.12(d)(3) The official scorer shall not charge an error against … any fielder who makes a wild throw in attempting to complete a double play or triple play, unless such wild throw enables any runner to advance beyond the base such runner would have reached had the throw not been wild.

For example: In classic fashion, with a runner at first and less than two outs, the batter hits a ground ball to the second baseman.

The second baseman fields the ground ball cleanly and flips it to the shortstop at second base, thereby putting out the runner coming from first base on a force out.

After making the putout at second base, the shortstop has ample time to deliver the ball to first base and force out the batter, but makes a terrible throw to first base, and the batter escapes being put out on what could/should have been a double play.

Under Rule 9.12(d)(3), the shortstop is absolved of any liability for failing to make a good throw to first base to complete the potential double play, no matter how easy doing so might have appeared to be, because it was a throw made in an attempt to complete a double play.

What it means: One can assume that this policy of the rulebook comes from an appreciation of the fact that logging two putouts, back-to-back, is inherently difficult in many cases. After all, in the example given, the shortstop first had to position himself at second base, then field the throw from the second baseman (which may not have been altogether perfect), tag second base (or come as close as the umpires might require for a putout), and make a throw to first base that is both accurate and timely (all the while avoiding contact with a base runner intent on "breaking up" the double play) so as to force out the batter.

Consequently, it is fairly easy to see why it would be unfair to hold fielders to such a high standard: a standard where every potential double play that is not turned exposes the fielder—who had to do the lion's share of the work—to being charged with an error.

However, note that the latitude extended in this case is not unlimited, inasmuch as if the wild throw made to complete the double play is so poor that it not only allows the runner who could have been the second out in the potential double play to reach base he was headed for safely, but also allows that runner—or one or more other runners—to advance further along the base paths than would have been the case had the throw not been wild, the fielder making the wild throw is charged with an error (so as to account for the additional advancement arising from the wild throw).

In addition, it should be noted that Rule 9.12(d)(3) is where the maxim "you can't assume a double play" comes from.

No doubt, the adage is well known and often repeated in scorekeeping, and it is valid—but only to a limited degree, given the following "comment."

THE REASON WHY YOU CAN "ASSUME" A DOUBLE PLAY—SOMETIMES

Rule 9.12(d) Comment: When a fielder muffs a thrown ball that, if held, would have completed a double play or triple play, the official scorer shall charge an error to the fielder who drops the ball and credit an assist to the fielder who made the throw.

FOR EXAMPLE: In exactly the same situation as before, the shortstop makes a perfectly good throw to first base, well ahead of the batter, but the first baseman muffs the throw and the batter is safe.

In this case, an error is charged in connection with the blown double play, and it is charged to the first baseman.

At the same time, although the batter was not put out, the shortstop is properly credited with an assist (in accordance with Rule 9.10(a)(1)).

WHAT IT MEANS: When a bad throw results in a blown potential double play, one can rarely be 100 percent certain that a good throw would have definitely completed the double play.

Doubtless, that fact constitutes at least some of the thinking behind not charging an error to a fielder who makes a wild throw to complete a potential double play (as long as there is no additional runner advancement on the wild throw).

However, if a potential double play is ruined by a muff of a good throw, there's no guess work: it's as plain as day that but for the failure to catch the good throw, a double play would have been turned.

Therefore, we have the comment to Rule 9.12(d) (somewhat mislabeled because it actually applies only to Rule 9.12(d)(3)). Unfortunately, this provision is often over-looked because the main provision of Rule 9.12(d)—which is the basis of the old maxim "you can't assume a double play"—has a pleasing ring to it and sounds like it's the final word on the subject.

Sometimes an Error Can Be Erased

Rule 9.12(d)(4) **The official scorer shall not charge an error against ... any fielder when, after fumbling a ground ball or dropping a batted ball that is in flight or a thrown ball, the fielder recovers the ball in time to force out a runner at any base.**

For example: With a runner at first and less than two outs, the batter hits a fly ball to shallow right field that can be easily caught by the right fielder, but the right fielder fails to make the catch. Nevertheless, the right fielder is able to pick up the ball and deliver it to second base in time to force out the runner at first who was forced to advance when the batter put the ball into play and the right fielder failed to catch the ball in flight.

At the same time, the batter ends up safe at first base.

Although the right fielder's incompetence led to the failure to put out the batter on the batter's pop fly, no error is properly charged to the right fielder, and the batter is considered as having reached base on a fielder's choice.

What it means: Applying Rule 9.12(d)(4) to the situation described above is eminently fair. That is to say, the right fielder's "error" in not catching the batter's fly ball was of no consequence inasmuch as the end result was the same as if the right fielder had caught the ball.

In other words, if the ball had been caught, the defensive team would have logged one more out, and a runner would be at first base when the next batter came to bat. However (in this case), even though the batter's fly ball was not caught, the right fielder's delivering the ball to second base in time to put out the runner forced to advance from first base when the ball went uncaught, results in the same end product: one more out logged by the defensive team and a runner at first.

Granted, there are situations where a fielder misplays the ball (initially) and recovers in time to log a putout by way of a force-out, but the misplay has bad consequences.

For example, if there had been runners at first and second in the previous example, and the right fielder muffed the catch of the batter's fly ball but retrieved the ball in time to deliver it to second base to force out the runner coming from first base, the end result would have been runners at first and third with one more out logged, as opposed to—if the ball had been caught (as it should have been)—one more out, but runners (in all probability) at second and first instead of third and first (which, for a number of reasons, is preferable for the team at bat).

In any case, special note should be taken of the fact that Rule 9.12(d)(4) applies only if the putout following the "error" is made on a force-out. Therefore, if the fielder in question "recovers" the ball in time to put out a runner who was not forced to advance, automatic absolution from being charged with an error is not available to the fielder.

Be that as it may, Rule 9.12(d)(4) says what it says, and there is a very good argument to be made that uniform application of Rule 9.12(d)(4)—even if that application might sometimes lead to somewhat dubious results—is desirable because doing so fosters consistency in scorekeeping, and consistency enhances the credibility of the statistics that come from the data recorded and accumulated by official scorers.

Setting Apart Wild Pitches and Passed Balls from Fielding Errors

Rule 9.12(d)(5)   The official scorer shall not charge an error against … any fielder when a wild pitch or passed ball is scored.

Apparently, the rules committee (in putting together the 2007 revisions) decided that "less is more," inasmuch as Rule 9.12(d)(5) is a distillation of the former Rule 9.14(f), but a good deal was lost in the process.

The problem is that pitchers—and only pitchers—can be charged with wild pitches, while catchers—and only catchers—can be charged with passed balls. Therefore, the reference to "any fielder" in Rule 9.12(d)(5) is misleading.

In point of fact, the "old" Rule 9.14(f) stated the proposition that Rule 9.12(d)(5) stands for more clearly (although the old Rule 9.14(f) also has room for improvement in terms of precision in language).

"Because the pitcher and catcher handle the ball much more than other fielders, certain misplays on pitched balls are defined in Rule 9.15 (now Rule 9.13) **as wild pitches and passed balls. No error shall be charged when a wild pitch or passed ball is scored."**

In other words, there is a recognition of the fact that if wild pitches and passed balls were counted and categorized as errors, pitchers and catchers would have many more errors than other fielders simply because pitchers and catchers handle the ball over and over again throughout the course of a game, as opposed to their teammates whose direct involvement with the ball is comparatively sporadic.

That said, the thrust of Rule 9.12(d)(5) is simply that wild pitches and passed balls are not scored (counted) as errors, inasmuch as if they were, pitchers (in the case of wild pitches) and catchers (in the case of passed balls) would have skewed fielding statistics.

Also, when pitchers make pitches, and when catchers handle those pitches, they are not "fielding" the ball (as such) because it is only when a ball is put into play by a batter that the defensive team is (generally) called upon to "field." Consequently, it makes sense to treat wild pitches and passed balls as being in a category distinct and separate from ordinary fielding errors, and that is what Rule 9.12(d)(5) is really all about.

A Continuation of Rule 9.12(d)(5)

Rule 9.12(e)   The official scorer shall not charge an error when the batter is awarded first base on four called balls, when the batter is awarded first base when touched by a pitched ball, or when the batter reaches first base as the result of a wild pitch or passed ball.

Rule 9.12(e) Comment: See Rule 9.13 for additional scoring rules relating to wild pitches and passed balls.

As was the case in Rule 9.12(d)(5), Rule 9.12(e) once again dissociates "mistakes" made by pitchers and catchers in the course of pitching and handling pitches from fielding errors made by fielders once a ball has been put into play by a batter, for the same reasons as touched upon in the discussion of Rule 9.12(d)(5).

A Continuation of Rule 9.12(e)

Rule 9.12(f)   The official scorer shall not charge an error when a runner or runners advance as the result of a passed ball, a wild pitch or a balk.

Here, the delineation between the commission of official fielding errors by fielders after a batter has put the ball into play, and the commission of "lapses" committed by pitchers and catchers before a pitch is put into play, is once again set forth, this time in the context of runner advancement—as opposed to a batter reaching base on a wild pitch or a passed ball—and, once again, the underlying reasoning is along the same lines as it is in Rule 9.12 (d)(5) and Rule 9.12(e).

The Interplay Between Wild Pitches, Passed Balls and Walks

Rule 9.12(f)(1)   When the fourth called ball is a wild pitch or a passed ball and as a result (i) the batter-runner advances to a base beyond first base; (ii) any runner forced to advance by the base on balls advances more

than one base; or (iii) any runner, not forced to advance, advances one or more bases, the official scorer shall score the base on balls and also the wild pitch or passed ball, as the case may be.

For example: With runners on first and third, and a three-ball count on the batter, the pitcher makes a pitch that is well out of the strike zone.

Consequently, the batter doesn't swing at the pitch, the umpire declares "ball four," the batter thereby becomes entitled to advance to first base, and the runner at first advances to second base as well.

However, the pitch is so far out of the strike zone that the catcher has no chance to block the ball or even knock it down, let alone catch it. As a result, the batter is able to advance all the way to second base, the runner who had been at first advances to third base, and the runner who had been at third base comes home to score a run.

The batter's advancement to first base is properly ascribed to a base on balls, along with the runner's advancement from first base to second base. At the same time, the batter's advancement from first base to second base is fairly imputed to the "wild pitch," as well as the advancement of the runner on base from second to third and the advancement of the other runner from third base to home plate.

What it means: When all is said and done, Rule 9.12(f)(1) comes down to simply this: the advancement of each and every runner (and batter), base to base, must be accounted for and attributed to an appropriate statistical category.

In the example given (which covers all three of Rule 9.12(f)(1)'s "subcategories"), the advancement of the batter to first base and the advancement of the runner at first to second base are directly and fundamentally attributable to the batter having drawn a walk. However, the rest of the advancements made by the two players on base, as well as the additional advancement of the batter, would not have occurred but for the wild pitch. Therefore, all of the additional advancements are attributed to the wild pitch.

The Interplay Between Wild Pitches, Passed Balls, Strikeouts and Runner Advancement

Rule 9.12(f)(2)   When the catcher recovers the ball after a wild pitch or passed ball on the third strike, and throws out the batter-runner at first base, or tags out the batter-runner, but another runner or runners advance, the official scorer shall score the strikeout, the putout and assists, if any, and credit the advance of the other runner or runners on the play as a fielder's choice.

For example: With a runner at second base, less than two outs and a two-strike count on the batter, the pitcher throws his next pitch squarely in the middle of the strike zone.

Understandably, the batter swings at the pitch, but he misses the ball altogether. At the same time, the ball gets away from the catcher.

Inasmuch as the third strike on the batter was not caught, and there's no runner on first base, the batter is entitled to try to reach first base regardless of the "strikeout," which is exactly what the batter tries to do.

(Note that if first base had been occupied, the batter in this case could not have legitimately tried for first base, unless there had been two outs, as set forth in Rule 5.05.)

The catcher is able to retrieve the ball in time to put out the batter by making a good and timely throw to the first baseman covering first base.

Meanwhile, the runner at second base advances to third.

The pitcher is credited with a strikeout (pursuant to Rule 9.15), while the catcher gets credit for an assist and the first baseman gets credit for the putout.

At the same time, the runner's advancement to third base is considered as having been made on a fielder's choice, and no passed ball is charged.

What it means: Rule 9.12(f)(2) is a most useful rule: It solves an otherwise troublesome scorekeeping quandary.

One could argue that the advancement of the runner from second base to third base in this case was a result of the catcher's failure to catch the pitcher's "strike-three" pitch: but for the "passed ball" there would have been no advancement. However, one could also argue that it wasn't the catcher's failure to catch the pitch that led to the advancement of the runner. Rather, it was the catcher's putting out the batter at first base that ultimately gave the runner at second base the opportunity to advance to third base.

Regardless, Rule 9.12(f)(2) cuts the debate short by taking the position that the runner's advancement, in cases like this, is more a product of the runner having the opportunity to capitalize on the defensive team being "otherwise engaged" in putting out the batter than a product of the pitch getting away from the catcher.

Simply put, the runner is properly considered as having advanced on the putout.

Given the general policy of the rulebook not to charge errors unless doing so is necessary and appropriate, it's obvious that Rule 9.12(f)(2) was written in the manner it was with that general policy in mind.

Rule 9.12(f) Comment: See Rule 9.13 for additional scoring rules relating to wild pitches and passed balls.

This cross-reference is nothing more than a reiteration of "Rule 9.12(e) Comment."

♦ 12 ♦

Free Passes and Punched Tickets

Rules 9.13–9.15

Rule 9.13—
Wild Pitches and Passed Balls

A wild pitch is defined in the Definition of Terms (Wild Pitch). A passed ball is a statistic charged against a catcher whose action has caused a runner or runners to advance, as set forth in this Rule 9.13.

IN GENERAL

Note that the definition of a wild pitch in the rulebook ("a wild pitch is one so high, so low, or so wide of the plate that it cannot be handled with ordinary effort by the catcher") is basically the same as what follows in Rule 9.13(a).

At the same time, a passed ball is not defined in the Definition of Terms at all, but it is in Rule 9.13(b).

Go figure.

THE KEY INGREDIENT TO THE RECIPE

Rule 9.13(a)   The official scorer shall charge a pitcher with a wild pitch when a legally delivered ball is so high, so wide or so low that the catcher does not stop and control the ball by ordinary effort, thereby permitting a runner or runners to advance.

It is not enough for a pitch to be so far from the catcher's reach that the catcher can't catch, or "stop and control" the ball (exhibiting average and ordinary athletic competence) in order for a pitch to be considered a wild pitch:

there must also be advancement by a runner or runners, and/or "advancement" by a batter on a "strike three" wild pitch, that would not have occurred but for the pitch being "wild."

FOR EXAMPLE: With no runners on base and a 1–2 count on the batter, the pitcher makes a pitch that is not only outside the strike zone, but so "wild" that the catcher can do nothing more than turn around as the ball goes sailing by and wonder where the ball will ultimately go.

If a runner or runners were on base, there is no doubt that runner advancement would have taken place, and that advancement would be fairly ascribed to the wild pitch. However, with the bases empty, the pitch is tallied as just another "ball," the same as if it had been caught by the catcher but was nonetheless enough outside the strike zone for the umpire to declare the pitch a ball.

WHAT IT MEANS: The critical portion of Rule 9.13(a) is not so much the description of a wild pitch in terms of "high, wide or low." Rather, it's that a runner or runners (or a batter in a "third-strike not caught" situation) can advance as a result of the wild pitch.

Simply put, as it is in the case of errors, there must be a ramification or consequence that arises from the "misplay" in order for the misplay to be recorded and charged to the offending player.

AN AUTOMATIC WILD PITCH

Rule 9.13(a) (continued)   The official scorer shall charge a pitcher with a wild pitch when a legally delivered ball touches the ground or home plate before reaching the catcher and is not handled by the catcher, thereby permitting a runner or runners to advance.

FOR EXAMPLE: With a runner on first, and a 1–2 count on the batter, the catcher gives the pitcher the requisite target for a pitch that's low and a bit outside.

Dutifully, the pitcher gives the catcher what he wants, but the pitch is so low that it bounces off the ground before it reaches the catcher.

In the ordinary course of events, one would expect the catcher to "block" the pitch and thereby prevent the runner at first base from advancing, but the ball gets away from the catcher and the runner at first saunters to second base without any trouble.

Although one might argue that the reason the runner at first base advanced was far more a product of the catcher failing to block the ball (as catchers are expected to do) than the nature of the pitch in question, the pitcher is nonetheless properly charged with a wild pitch under Rule 9.13(a).

WHAT IT MEANS: Sometimes, a catcher is not able to handle a pitch because the ball makes contact with the ground before it reaches him and the ball takes a bounce that makes it extremely difficult—if not impossible—for the catcher to stop or block or otherwise catch the ball.

At the same time, sometimes a pitch "in the dirt" will get away from a catcher even though the catcher could/should have been able to "handle" the ball regardless.

Be that as it may, this portion of Rule 9.13(a) draws a bright line by declaring that any pitch that bounces before reaching the catcher, and which thereupon leads to a runner or runners on base advancing, and/or a batter getting to first base on a "strike-three" pitch, is always to be scored as a wild pitch, regardless of whether or not one might judge that the catcher could/should have blocked the ball and thereby prevented any adverse ramification for the catcher's team.

(Note that this is another of many manifestations of the rulebook's policy of keeping judgment calls to a minimum in scorekeeping, so as to make official scorekeeping more uniform and thereby eliminate—as much as possible—inconstancies in scorekeeping.)

GOOD NEWS, BAD NEWS: THE INTERPLAY BETWEEN WILD PITCHES AND STRIKEOUTS

Rule 9.13(a) (continued)   **When the third strike is a wild pitch, permitting the batter to reach first base, the official scorer shall score a strikeout and a wild pitch.**

FOR EXAMPLE: On an 0–2 count, no outs and the bases empty, the pitcher lets go with all he's got, with little or no regard to where the ball will go once it leaves his hand.

As one might expect, the ball is far from the strike zone: in fact, it's so far from the general vicinity of home plate that the catcher has no chance of getting his mitt on the ball at all.

Nevertheless, the batter is fooled and swings at the pitch.

Because "strike three" was not caught by the catcher, the batter is entitled to try to reach first base, and—inasmuch as the pitch was so "wild" that the catcher had absolutely no chance of catching the ball and ended up having to run a good distance just to retrieve the ball—the batter gets to first base easily.

The pitcher is properly credited with a strikeout, even though the batter reached base. At the same time, the pitcher is fairly charged with a wild pitch, inasmuch as but for the "strike three" pitch being a wild pitch, the batter would not have reached first base (absent a misplay or error).

WHAT IT MEANS: Here is a prime example of when credit and blame are simultaneously imputed to a player under baseball's scorekeeping rules.

On the one hand, the pitcher did what every pitcher strives to do: get three strikes on the batter. At the same time, the pitcher committed an egregious blunder; he allowed the batter to reach base.

The rulebook chooses not to judge the pitcher as having either succeeded or failed, one to the exclusion of the other. Rather, this portion of Rule 9.13(a) rewards the pitcher with credit for a strikeout (in conformity with Rule 9.15(a)(3)), but also charges the pitcher with a wild pitch (in conformity with the general principles that underlie Rule 9.13).

WHAT'S GOOD FOR THE GOOSE IS GOOD FOR THE GANDER: THE INTERPLAY BETWEEN PASSED BALLS AND STRIKEOUTS

Rule 9.13(b)   The official scorer shall charge a catcher with a passed ball when the catcher fails to hold or to control a legally pitched ball that should have been held or controlled with ordinary effort, thereby permitting a runner or runners to advance. When the third strike is a passed ball, permitting the batter to reach first base, the official scorer shall score a strikeout and a passed ball.

Rule 9.13(b) is nothing more than the "flip side" of Rule 9.13(a), with Rule 9.13(b) dealing with passed balls in virtually the same manner as Rule 9.10(a) deals with wild pitches.

In any case, all told, the main text of Rule 9.13 basically boils down to this: If a pitch gets away from the catcher, and that allows a runner or runners on base to advance, or a batter to reach first base in a "third strike not caught" situation, and the fault is judged to be that of the pitcher, it's scored as a wild pitch and charged to the pitcher. However, if the fault is judged to be that of the catcher, it's a passed ball charged to the catcher.

In either case, a strikeout may be scored at the same time as a wild pitch or a passed ball.

What Might Start Out Looking Like a Wild Pitch Or Passed Ball May Not Always End Up Being One, and Dealing with the Ramifications That May Arise from That

Rule 9.13 Comment: The official scorer shall not charge a wild pitch or passed ball if the defensive team makes an out before any runners advance. For example, if a pitch touches the ground and eludes the catcher with a runner on first base, but the catcher recovers the ball and throws to second base in time to retire the runner, the official scorer shall not charge the pitcher with a wild pitch. The official scorer shall credit the advancement of any other runner on the play as a fielder's choice. If a catcher drops a pitch, for example, with a runner on first base, but the catcher recovers the ball and throws to second base in time to retire the runner, the official scorer shall not charge the catcher with a passed ball. The official scorer shall credit the advancement of any other runner on the play as a fielder's choice.

See Rules 9.07(a), 9.12(e) and 9.12(f) for additional scoring rules relating to wild pitches and passed balls.

Rule 9.13's comment is fundamentally nothing more than a reiteration of a primary part of the concept behind wild pitches and passed balls: that it is not enough for a ball to "elude" the catcher for a wild pitch or a passed ball to be charged, there must also be a consequence adverse to the team in the field.

In that regard, take a look at the two examples given in the comment.

"For example, if a pitch touches the ground and eludes the catcher with a runner on first base, but the catcher recovers the ball and throws to second base in time to retire the runner, the official scorer shall not charge the pitcher with a wild pitch."

"If a catcher drops a pitch, for example, with a runner on first base, but the catcher recovers the ball and throws to second base in time to retire the runner, the official scorer shall not charge the catcher with a passed ball."

In both instances, you have a runner attempting to advance on a "potential misplay" on the part of the pitcher (in the first instance) or the catcher (in the second instance), but that advancement doesn't happen; the runner is put out. Therefore, logically, there is no reason to look upon the misplay as a misplay at all, and consequently, no wild pitch or passed ball is charged in either situation.

The same would be the case if (for example) with the bases empty, a batter tried to reach base on a "strike three" pitch that wasn't caught: if the batter is nonetheless put out before reaching base safely, there is no reason to charge a wild pitch to the pitcher or a passed ball to the catcher.

However, if you add to these situations, or any similar scenario, another runner or runners on base (or a batter attempting to reach base on a "strike three" pitch that isn't caught) who advances while the play that leads to the putout is being made, it gets tricky. That's because the advancement in question could arguably be looked upon as the result of a wild pitch or passed ball, even though a putout was logged in the bargain, and charging a wild pitch or passed ball would seem to be appropriate so as to account for the advancement of the "other" runner or runners, or the batter who reaches base in this sort of situation.

Luckily, the comment to Rule 9.13 (added as part of the 2007 revisions) cuts through whatever fog there might otherwise be in these circumstances and simply directs the scorer to attribute any such advancement as having been made on the putout—a fielder's choice—and forget about the ball eluding the catcher (inasmuch as a putout was made). Thereby, the scorer is spared from having to figure out how to score it, and at the same time, the goal of consistency in scorekeeping is served.

◆ ◆ ◆

Rule 9.14—Bases on Balls

A base on balls is defined in the Definition of Terms (Base on Balls).

In General

Note that the relevant text referred to above reads as follows:

"A base on balls is an award of first base granted to a batter who, during his time at bat, receives four pitches outside the strike zone."
It is well known that in common baseball parlance a base on balls is also referred to as a "walk," and the two terms are interchangeable.

A Statement of the Obvious, and the Not So Obvious

Rule 9.14(a)   The official scorer shall score a base on balls whenever a batter is awarded first base because of four balls having been pitched

outside the strike zone, but when the fourth such ball touches the batter it shall be scored as a "hit batter."

Rule 9.14(a) Comment: See Rule 9.16(h) for the procedure when more than one pitcher is involved in giving a base on balls. See also Rule 9.15, which addresses situations in which a substitute batter receives a base on balls.

The proposition that the official scorer is to charge a pitcher with issuing a base on balls, and that the scorer is to account for a batter's attainment of first base on a base on balls, is so obvious that there is little point in stating the proposition. However, dealing with a pitch that hits a batter and (in and of itself) entitles a batter to take first base, but which could also be considered as "ball four," is not quite so cut and dried.

FOR EXAMPLE: On a 3–0 count, the pitcher delivers a pitch that hits the batter squarely, and the umpire awards the batter first base.

Although the batter took four pitches outside the strike zone, his award of first base (in terms of the batter's statistics, as well as the pitcher's numbers) is not categorized as a base on balls. Rather, it's counted as a "hit batter" (a/k/a "hit by a pitched ball" under Rule 9.02(a)(1)(c) from the batter's perspective, and as a "batter hit by pitched ball" under Rule 9.02(c)(12) from the pitcher's perspective).

WHAT IT MEANS: In a sense, an umpire could award first base to a batter hit by a pitch outside the strike zone on a three-ball count because that pitch would constitute the fourth pitch (not swung at) delivered to the batter outside the strike zone.

(Note that if a batter is hit by a pitched ball in the strike zone, it's a strike under Rule 5.05. Consequently, a base on balls, or a "hit by pitched ball," could not be fairly declared by the umpire in that case. By the same token, if a pitch is swung on and missed, it's still considered a strike even if the pitch ultimately hits the batter—whether or not the pitch was in the strike zone—as per subsection (e) of the definition of a strike found in the rulebook.)

Inasmuch as being hit by a pitch outside the strike zone entitles a batter to first base regardless of the count, and inasmuch as (in the final analysis) it's simpler and makes more sense to do so, Rule 9.14(a) gives precedence to being hit by a pitch over considering a batter as having drawn a walk if a pitch that hits the batter would otherwise have been "ball four."

Note also that Rule 9.14(a)'s Comment cites the relevant portions of Rule 9 in terms of dealing with walks issued during the course of a plate appearance where there is either a change of pitchers or a change of batters.

IT'S ONLY THE LAST PITCH THROWN TO A BATTER THAT DETERMINES WHETHER A BASE ON BALLS IS "INTENTIONAL" OR NOT

Rule 9.14(b)   The official scorer shall score an intentional base on balls when the pitcher makes no attempt to throw the last pitch to the batter into the strike zone, but purposely throws the ball wide to the catcher outside the catcher's box.

Everyone well acquainted with how baseball is played knows that sometimes—for strategic reasons—a pitcher will intentionally allow a batter to reach first base on a base on balls, and it's almost always obvious from the get-go when that takes place. However, an intentional base on balls is not always carried out in an altogether straightforward manner, even though it is nevertheless properly scored as such.

FOR EXAMPLE: In the bottom of the ninth, with two outs and runners at second and third, and the scored tied, the batter coming to the plate is the "clean up" batter for his team.

He leads the league in hits, doubles, triples, home runs, runs batted in, slugging average, batting average, and every other measure of prowess that defines a "power hitter"; in short, he's someone to be feared and respected when he has a bat in his hands.

At the same time, he also leads the league in strikeouts.

Regardless of the batter's abilities, and in hopes that the batter's propensity for striking out will predominate, the pitcher decides to give the batter no quarter, so he gives the batter his "best stuff."

Nonetheless, the count goes to 3–0.

At this point, realizing that discretion is indeed the better part of valor, the pitcher intentionally throws his fourth and final pitch to the batter well outside the strike zone with the clear purpose of intentionally issuing a walk (because first base is empty, and a base on balls would give rise to far less "damage" than would most likely ensue from giving the batter a pitch that he can hit).

Consequently, the batter is awarded first base, and the base on balls is logged as being an intentional base on balls, even though it was only the last pitch delivered to the batter that was thrown intentionally outside of the strike zone.

WHAT IT MEANS: The great majority of intentional walks come from the pitcher throwing four pitches in succession that are far from where the batter would have any chance to hit the ball, with the catcher clearly indicating the pitcher's intentions by standing up well before each pitch is thrown and giving a "target" to the pitcher that is well off the plate. But, as Rule 9.14(b) clearly states, all of that is not necessary for the scorer to judge a base on balls as being an intentional walk.

It is only the last pitch that has to be an overtly premeditated "ball four" in order for an intentional base on balls to be scored, and everything that precedes that pitch is of no consequence in terms of whether any given walk is an intentional base on balls or not.

(Note that Rule 9.14(b) uses the term "outside the catcher's box" to define how far from the strike zone a "ball-four" pitch must be thrown in order for that pitch to give rise to an intentional base on balls, and that would seem to imply that a ball-four pitch that is caught by the catcher inside the catcher's box cannot be considered an intentional base on balls. However, it is hard to imagine any official scorer putting that fine an edge on the subject by considering an overt and manifest intention to put a batter on base by way of a walk as not providing more than adequate grounds for scoring an intentional base on balls just because the catcher caught the "ball-four" pitch while standing inside the catcher's box, and it's safe to say that the rulebook's intention is not to have that result.)

Rule 9.14(c)   If a batter awarded a base on balls is called out for refusing to advance to first base, the official scorer shall not credit the base on balls and shall charge a time at bat.

The situation that Rule 9.14(c) addresses is so rare (and altogether bizarre) that one might question why the rulebook even bothers to address it, but address it it does, nonetheless.

That said, note that because a batter refusing to advance to first base in cases like this is considered as having been "put out" as a result of his action, a fielder must be given credit for that putout in order for the final game tally of statistical data to "balance" (as per Rule 9.03(c)), and the putout in cases like this is properly credited to the catcher (under Rule 9.09(b)(7)).

♦ ♦ ♦

Rule 9.15—Strikeouts

A strikeout is a statistic credited to a pitcher and charged to a batter when the umpire calls three strikes on a batter, as set forth in this Rule 9.15.

In General

This introductory portion of Rule 9.15 seems as guileless as one could imagine, but an essential concept in discerning when to score strikeouts lies in what it doesn't say.

Specifically, this initial delineation of what constitutes a strikeout purposely does not indicate that a batter must be put out in order for a strikeout to be scored (inasmuch as the official scorer is sometimes obliged to score a strikeout even when a batter is not put out after "the umpire calls three strikes on a batter").

The Obvious

Rule 9.15(a)(1)   The official scorer shall score a strikeout whenever a batter ... is put out by a third strike caught by the catcher.

Here's the ground floor: the straight-ahead, easily understood and self-evident situation where a batter is considered as having struck out, and the pitcher is considered as having struck out a batter.

Still Fairly Obvious, If You Understand the Playing Rule in Issue

Rule 9.15(a)(2)   The official scorer shall score a strikeout whenever a batter ... is put out by a third strike not caught when there is a runner on first before two are out.

For example: On an 0–2 count, with less than two outs and a runner on first base, the pitcher delivers a pitch that the batter flails at like a blindfolded chimpanzee.

As one might guess, the batter fails to make any contact with the ball. However, the catcher fails to catch the ball.

Although, under Rule 5.09(a)(2), a strike-three pitch must be "legally caught" by the catcher in order for a batter to be called out on strikes, under Rule 5.09(a)(3) the batter is out even when the catcher doesn't catch a "strike-three" pitch if there are less than two outs and there's a runner at first base.

Consequently, the batter is this case is considered and counted as having struck out even though the catcher didn't catch the pitch to put out the batter. Rather, the batter was "put out" by application of Rule 5.09(a)(3).

(Note that if there had been two outs, even with a runner at first, or if first base had not been occupied by a runner, regardless of how many outs there may have been, the catcher's failure to catch the strike-three pitch would have allowed the batter to try for first base, even though the batter had three strikes called against him. Note also that if a batter has the right to try for first base after having been delivered three strikes, but he abandons any attempt to advance to first base and he is called out as a result of that abandonment, a strikeout is properly scored just as it would be in the example given above.)

WHAT IT MEANS: Rule 9.15(b) is really nothing more than an extension of Rule 9.15(a), inasmuch as Rule 9.15(b) and Rule 9.15(a), taken together, stand for the same fundamental proposition: If a batter has three strikes called on him, the batter is considered as having struck out.

It's as simple as that.

At the same time, the next sub-section of Rule 9.15 carries the central concept one step further by addressing situations where a batter has three strikes called against him but isn't put out.

NOT SO OBVIOUS AT ALL

Rule 9.15(a)(3)   The official scorer shall score a strikeout whenever a batter ... becomes a runner because a third strike is not caught.

FOR EXAMPLE: As in the preceding example, the catcher fails to catch "strike three," only this time there are two outs and/or first base is not occupied. Therefore, the batter tries for first base (as allowed by the playing rules) in hopes that the ball cannot be retrieved in time for the defensive team to put him out.

Whether or not the batter reaches first base, or if another runner on base is put out on whatever play follows the pitch getting away from the catcher, the batter is nevertheless considered as having struck out, and the pitcher is considered as having struck out the batter.

WHAT IT MEANS: There is an inherent irony at work here that comes from the fact that the term "strikeout" is somewhat a misnomer because a batter need not necessarily be put out in order to be considered as having struck out.

Simply put, if a pitcher gets three strikes on a batter, the pitcher is entitled to credit for a strikeout, regardless of whether the batter is put out or not. (After all, when that happens, the pitcher has accomplished something notable by getting three strikes on a batter, and there is no reason not to recognize it statistically.) At the same time, a batter who has three strikes delivered to him has failed—at least in one sense—by allowing the pitcher to do so, and therefore it makes sense to recognize the batter's failure (from a statistical point of view) and consider the batter as having struck out whether or not the batter was put out.

That said, there is nothing wrong with the time-honored custom of using the term "strikeout" even when a batter is not necessarily put out, as long as it is understood that the definition of a strikeout may go beyond situations where a batter is actually retired on three strikes.

At the same time, there's also a way for a batter to strike out without swinging at a pitch and failing to make contact with the ball, or by having "strike three" called by the umpire, and that's spelled out in the following subsection of Rule 9.15.

STRIKEOUTS ARISING FROM A BATTER PUTTING THE BALL INTO PLAY

Rule 9.15(a)(4)   The official scorer shall score a strikeout whenever a batter ... bunts foul on third strike, unless such bunt on third strike results in a foul fly caught by any fielder, in which case the official scorer shall not score a strikeout and shall credit the fielder who catches such foul fly with a putout.

FOR EXAMPLE: On a two-strike count, the batter bunts the ball into foul territory.

Although the ball is not caught on the fly, the batter is nevertheless called out under Rule 5.09(a)(4), which states that "A batter is out when ... he bunts foul on third strike," and under Rule 9.15(a)(4), the batter is considered as having "struck out."

WHAT IT MEANS: In the previous sub-sections of Rule 9.15, you have situations where a batter strikes out in the most literal sense, and situations where a batter strikes "out" without being put out. Here, in Rule 9.15(a)(4), you have a batter being put out on a strikeout, but it wasn't because the batter swung at a pitch on a two-strike count and missed, or because the umpire deemed a pitch that the batter didn't swing at as being the third strike delivered to the batter.

Given all that, it's clear that what constitutes a strikeout is not always so cut-and-dried as many people might think.

Special attention should be given to the fact that if a pitch made on a two-strike count is bunted, and it's caught on the fly (whether in fair or foul territory), there's no strikeout. Instead, the batter's plate appearance is considered as having ended on the putout that arises from the batted ball being caught in flight (as would be the case with any batted ball caught on the fly and in play), and credit for the putout goes—logically—to the fielder who caught the batted ball in flight.

(In passing, note that when a batter is called out under Rule 5.09(a)(4) for having bunted the ball into foul territory on a two-strike count that wasn't caught, the putout is credited to the catcher under the provisions of Rule 9.09(b)(3), regardless of where the ball may have traveled in foul territory.)

Dealing with Multiple Batters in the Course of a Single Plate Appearance

Rule 9.15(b)   When a batter leaves the game with two strikes against him, and the substitute batter completes a strikeout, the official scorer shall charge the strikeout and the time at bat to the first batter. If the substitute batter completes the turn at bat in any other manner, including a base on balls, the official scorer shall score the action as having been that of the substitute batter.

For example: Batter #1 swings at the first pitch delivered to him, and he misses it for strike one.

The second pitch leads to the same result, only this time the batter wrenches his back quite badly on the swing and therefore cannot continue to play. Consequently, another batter (Batter #2) comes to the plate to complete Batter #1's turn at bat.

Batter #2 swings at the first pitch he sees, misses, and the umpire declares Batter #2 out on strikes.

Although he didn't strike out himself, the strikeout is properly charged to Batter #1.

(Note that if Batter #2 had ended the plate appearance in any other fashion, the end result of the shared plate appearance would be charged to Batter #2. Moreover, if the count inherited by Batter #2 had been a one-strike count, or a no-strike count, the end result of the plate appearance would be charged or credited to Batter #2, even if a strikeout was the ultimate outcome of the plate appearance.)

What it means: The consequence of every turn at bat is charged to the batter who completes the turn at bat, with only one quite narrow and rare exception, and that is when: (1) the batter who completes a plate appearance is a batter substituting for another batter during the course of the time at bat;

(2) the substitute batter inherits a two-strike count; and (3) the plate appearance ends with a strikeout. It is then—and only then—that the outcome of the plate appearance (in the form of a strikeout) is charged to a batter who did not complete the plate appearance in question.

[In passing, note that the issues arising from multiple pitchers appearing during the course of a single batter's plate appearance are dealt with in Rule 9.16(h).]

♦ 13 ♦

You Get What You Deserve

Rule 9.16

Rule 9.16—
Earned Runs and Runs Allowed

An earned run is a run for which a pitcher is held accountable.

SEPARATING RUNS ATTRIBUTABLE TO PITCHING
FROM THOSE ATTRIBUTABLE TO FIELDING

Oddly, although Rule 9.16 constitutes the largest single portion of Rule 9, it dedicates only one terse sentence to explaining what an earned run is (and what—by implication—an unearned run is as well).

One might fairly assume that the idea of "earned runs" is so widely recognized and utilized in baseball, going as far back as the 1870s, that the authors of the rulebook apparently believe that nothing more need be said about what earned runs actually are, and that only the subject of how to determine which runs scored during the course of a game are earned runs needs to be addressed at any length.

Regardless, some analysis of what the term really means, and what role earned and unearned runs serve in baseball statistics, is worthwhile in terms of having a better understanding of the subject in general, and why the rules in regards to how to determine earned runs are the way they are.

♦ ♦ ♦

Essentially, unearned runs constitute those runs that would not have scored but for the commission of fielding errors or passed balls. Therefore,

189

those runs cannot be fairly considered as having come from—directly and without question—the actions of the pitcher in delivering pitches to batters (divorced from any errors or passed balls).

Conversely, earned runs are those runs that scored without the benefit of any fielding errors or passed balls, or runs that would have scored even if no fielding errors or passed balls had been committed. Therefore, those runs may be fairly considered as runs that arose from the actions of the pitcher in delivering pitches to batters.

(Note that passed balls must be referred to separately in this context inasmuch as—under Rule 9.12(f)—passed balls are deemed a category of misplays that is separate and distinct from ordinary fielding errors. At the same time, wild pitches are not included along with passed balls in determining earned runs because wild pitches are solely the responsibility of pitchers in the same way that the over-all quality of pitches is the responsibility of any given pitcher.)

FOR EXAMPLE: At the end of the game, the final score is 4 to 3 in favor of the home team.

Both teams used only one pitcher.

It could be said that the home team's pitcher did a better job of pitching than the visiting team's pitcher (to the extent that the home team's pitcher is properly credited with a "win" and the visiting team's pitcher is properly charged with a "loss" under Rule 9.17). However, in terms of earned runs, the opposite may be true.

WHAT IT MEANS: If, for instance, no errors or passed balls were committed by the home team in the field, the three runs scored by the visiting team and charged to the home team's pitcher would all be earned runs. However, if the four runs given up by the visiting team were all runs that would not have scored if the visiting team had not committed errors and/or passed balls, all four of the runs scored by the home team and charged to the visiting team's pitcher would be considered unearned runs.

Consequently, if that were the case, in a very real sense the visiting team's pitcher did a far better job of pitching because he "gave up" no earned runs. None of the four runs were attributable to how he pitched; the pitching was as good as can be expected. At the same time, the home team's pitcher "gave up" three runs that were all attributable to the quality—or lack thereof—of his pitching, and therefore his pitching could fairly be considered inferior to that of the visiting team's (losing) pitcher.

The Heart of the Matter: A Shadow Scorecard

Rule 9.16 (continued)   In determining earned runs, the official scorer shall reconstruct the inning without the errors (which exclude catcher's interference) and passed balls, giving the benefit of the doubt always to the pitcher in determining which bases would have been reached by runners had there been errorless play.

This portion of Rule 9.16 is singularly essential inasmuch as virtually everything else contained in the text of Rule 9.16 is to some degree an elaboration on it.

In sum, it calls upon the official scorer to draw up a second (shadow) scorecard for each inning in which one or more runs scored and one or more errors or passed balls were committed, so as to "reconstruct" that inning as if no errors or passed balls had been committed.

Any of the runs that "score" in the reconstructed inning are earned runs. Any runs that do not score in the reconstructed inning, but did score in the actual inning as played, are unearned runs.

(Note that if no runs score during the course of any given inning, the exercise is obviously not necessary, even if errors or passed balls occurred. At the same time, if no errors or passed balls were committed, it would also be unnecessary to reconstruct an inning because all runs scored would be considered earned runs.)

For example: Here is the scorecard from an inning in which two runs scored, but only one of the two runs was an earned run.

As you can see, in this inning, the #1 batter strikes out.

The #2 batter hits the ball to the first baseman, but the first baseman mishandles it, thereby allowing the batter to reach first base on an error (E3).

Next, the #3 batter draws a walk and the runner on first advances to second base as a result.

The #4 batter singles, advancing the runner at first base to second base, and allowing the runner at second base to score.

Subsequently, the #5 batter knocks out a double that advances the runner at first base to third base and drives in the runner at second for another run.

The #6 batter hits a line drive to the shortstop that is caught to retire the batter. That is immediately followed by the shortstop

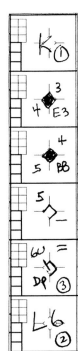

putting out the runner at second base, thereby ending the inning with a double play.

To determine whether one, none or both of the two runs were "earned" by the pitcher, the same sequence of events is "reconstructed" without the error.

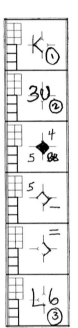

As in the "real" inning, the #1 batter strikes out, however the #2 batter is retired by the first baseman at first base.

With two outs, the #3 batter draws a walk, followed by the #4 batter hitting a single (which single advances the runner at first base to second base).

With runners at first and second, the #5 batter doubles. As a result, the runner at first advances to third base and the runner who had been at second base advances to home plate to score a run.

The #6 batter hits a line drive to the shortstop that is caught for the third and final out of the reconstructed inning.

In the reconstructed inning only one run scored, so that run (scored by the #3 batter) is counted as an earned run. The other run scored in the "real" inning (scored by the #2 batter) is properly considered an unearned run.

WHAT IT MEANS: Although the rulebook's directive to reconstruct innings does not say so in so many words, the obvious intent is to lay out a basic procedure and methodology to be employed to discern which runs are earned runs, and which runs are not, and it works.

However, as simple as that may seem to be, there are countless situations that can prove to be quite problematic when reconstructing innings. Therefore, you have (essentially) the balance of Rule 9.16 addressing those situations.

A QUICK NOTE ABOUT GIVING PITCHERS "THE BENEFIT OF THE DOUBT"

A polestar in the reconstruction of innings (and therefore a guiding principle in the area of assessing earned runs) is the concept that the pitcher is to be afforded "the benefit of the doubt."

In other words, only that advancement which the scorer is certain would have occurred if no errors or passed balls had been committed is assumed in the reconstructed inning.

FOR EXAMPLE: Here is a scorecard from an inning in which a run scores, but—applying the "benefit of the doubt" rule—does not score in the reconstructed inning, and therefore would not constitute an earned run for the pitcher.

As you can see, the #1 batter strikes out.

That is followed by the #2 batter reaching first base by virtue of being hit by a pitch.

While the #3 batter is at bat, the runner at first base advances to second base on a passed ball.

Ultimately, the #3 batter doubles and the runner at second advances to home plate to score a run as a result.

Thereafter, the #4 batter strikes out, and the #5 batter strikes out as well to end the inning.

If the pitcher is afforded "the benefit of the doubt" when the inning is reconstructed without the catcher's passed ball, the run scored in this inning would not score, and therefore that run would be counted as an unearned run.

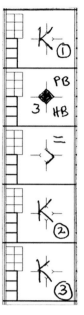

As in the "real" inning, the #1 batter strikes out, followed by the #2 batter getting hit by a pitch.

The #3 batter's double advances the runner at first base to third base.

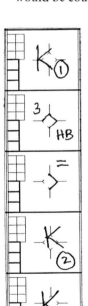

Then, with runners at second and third, the #4 batter strikes out, followed by the #5 batter striking out as well to end the inning and leave the two runners on base.

WHAT IT MEANS: The key here is that if, and only if, the scorer were certain that the #2 batter would have scored from first base on the #3 batter's double (first base being where the #2 batter would have been at the time of the #3 batter's double but for the passed ball), then, and only then, would the #2 batter score in the reconstructed inning, leading to the pitcher being charged with an earned run.

In other words, the run that scored in the actual inning would not have scored (without a doubt) if there had been no passed ball allowing the runner (the #2 batter) to advance to second base.

Perhaps the ultimate way to approach the "benefit of the doubt" issue is simply to reconstruct innings from the perspective of the pitcher (or the pitcher's agent, or parent, or anyone else with a vested interest in keeping the pitcher's earned run tally as low as possible without violating the rules governing scorekeeping in baseball).

In any case, it ultimately comes down to the idea that only runs that would have scored—without a doubt—if the inning had been errorless or otherwise devoid of any passed balls, are earned runs (because, after all, that's what it's all about: segregating runs that were without question the responsibility of the pitcher from those that weren't).

A Quick Note on "Which Exclude Catcher's Interference"

Before the 2007 revisions, this portion of the rulebook specifically stated that catcher's interference should be *included* with other errors in the reconstruction of innings, and that made sense inasmuch as the initial text of what is now Rule 9.12(c) instructs the official score to charge a fielder with an error when an umpire "awards the batter ... one or more bases because of interference."

However, that directive in regards to reconstructing innings was changed to the complete opposite (*exclude*) in 2007, with the official explanation that doing so was a "correction" based on "existing interpretation of treatment of catcher's interference."

Note that further discussion of the somewhat troublesome implications arising from this can be found in the analysis following Rule 9.16(a), as well as in the analysis of the "comments" that follow Rule 9.16(a).

Nobody Ever Said That Life Was Always Fair

Rule 9.16 (continued)   For the purpose of determining earned runs, an intentional base on balls, regardless of the circumstances, shall be construed in exactly the same manner as any other base on balls.

For example: The lead-off batter reaches second base on a two-base error (a terrible throw to first base that not only allowed the batter to reach first base safely, but also allowed him to advance easily to second base).

In order to create the possibility of force plays at second base and third base when the next batter comes to bat, the pitcher's manager orders the pitcher (over the pitcher's objections) to issue the next batter an intentional base on balls, which the pitcher does, reluctantly.

Now, with runners at first base and second base, the next batter hits a home run, scoring three runs.

The next three batters each strike out in succession to end the inning.

The run scored by the batter who reached second base on the error is not counted as an earned run because, when the inning is reconstructed without the error, that batter would not have reached base at all and therefore he would not have scored a run. However, the run scored by the batter who hit the home run, as well as the run that was scored by the batter who was issued an intentional walk, both go into the book as earned runs.

WHAT IT MEANS: The unfairness of charging a pitcher with an earned run on a run scored by a batter that was purposefully put on base for strategic purposes is obvious. After all, it's not as though it was poor pitching on the part of the pitcher (in situations like the one described above) that gave rise to the run being scored by the batter who was intentionally put on base. To the contrary, if the pitcher had been allowed the opportunity to do so, the pitcher may well have struck out the batter in question, or at least gotten the batter to make an out.

Regardless, the rulebook chooses to keep it simple and looks upon intentional walks just the same as "unintentional" walks for the purpose of reconstructing innings—no matter what—inasmuch as to do otherwise could create a good deal of undesirable vagaries and inconsistencies in the reconstruction of innings for the purpose of ascertaining earned versus unearned runs.

THE INITIAL TEXT OF RULE 9.16 STATED IN A DIFFERENT WAY, WITH A LITTLE EXTRA SOMETHING: "FIELDING CHANCES"

Rule 9.16(a)   The official scorer shall charge an earned run against a pitcher every time a runner reaches home base by the aid of safe hits, sacrifice bunts, a sacrifice fly, stolen bases, putouts, fielder's choices, bases on balls, hit batters, balks or wild pitches (including a wild pitch on third strike that permits a batter to reach first base) before fielding chances have been offered to put out the offensive team.

Fundamentally, the text of Rule 9.16(a) constitutes a reiteration of the provisions of Rule 9.16 that precede it. However, it does introduce another term—"fielding chances"—which term serves to flesh out the concept of earned runs.

FOR EXAMPLE: The first batter hits an easy ground ball to the third baseman, but the third baseman boots the ball and thereby allows the batter to reach first base.

The second batter hits an easy ground ball to the second baseman, which the second baseman flips to the shortstop covering second base to force out the runner coming from first base. However, although the second baseman's toss is good and arrives at second base well in advance of the approaching runner, the shortstop drops the ball and the runner coming from first base is consequently safe, as is the batter at first base.

The third batter hits a balloon to right field, but although there's no reason the right fielder should not catch the batter's lazy fly ball with ease, the catch goes unmade, leaving the bases loaded with no outs for the next batter.

At this point, any runs that may score in the remainder of the inning—runs that would be charged to the pitcher who faced the three batters in the example given—will be unearned runs.

WHAT IT MEANS: If one were to reconstruct this inning, it would be obvious that the defensive team could/should have put out the first three batters, and that the inning could/should have ended before the fourth batter even stepped into the batter's box. Therefore, in the reconstruction of this inning, no runs score—from the perspective of the pitcher in question—regardless of how many runs may actually score in the "real" inning as it continues.

In short, the defensive team had three "fielding chances ... offered to put out the offensive team": three opportunities to field the ball and log three putouts during the course of the first three batters' turns at bat. Once those three opportunities came and went, the pitcher—in a manner of speaking—gets a free ride in terms of being tagged with earned runs.

Although it is not difficult to conjure up scenarios where application of this particular scorekeeping tenet leads to somewhat absurd results (for instance, a pitcher giving up home run after home run after the magic three fielding chances and avoiding being charged with any earned runs), the principle is not subject to exceptions, even in the most extreme cases.

(Note however that the concept does bend a bit when it comes to dealing with relief pitchers, as discussed under Rule 9.16(i).)

AN INCONSISTENCY THAT COMES AS A RESULT OF THE CHANGE FROM INCLUDING CATCHER'S INTERFERENCE WITH OTHER FIELDING ERRORS AND PASSED BALLS, TO EXCLUDING CATCHER'S INTERFERENCE, IN THE CONTEXT OF RECONSTRUCTING INNINGS

Rule 9.16(a) (continued)   For the purpose of this rule, a defensive interference penalty shall be construed as a fielding chance.

As touched upon in the discussion of the language found in the initial text of Rule 9.16 involving catcher's interference, the 2007 revisions changed the pre-existing directive for official scorers to *include* calls of catcher's interference along with all other fielding errors and passed balls when reconstructing innings for the purpose of figuring out whether runs scored were earned runs. Specifically, scorers are now required to *exclude* catcher's interference when reconstructing innings.

In other words, under the "old" rule, a scorer would consider a batter who reached base on a call of catcher's interference as having been put out instead of reaching base when reconstructing innings, the same as other fielding errors and passed balls. Now, with the 2007 revisions, that is no longer the case.

(Note that an explanation of exactly how an award of first base to a batter on a catcher's interference call is to be dealt with is laid out in the context of Rule 9.16(a) Comments (3) and (4), as well as the preface to those sections.)

In any case, this portion of Rule 9.16(a), (left over from the old Rule 9.18(a)), still adheres to the now officially discarded idea of counting an act of catcher's interference as being a blown "chance," a lost opportunity to log a putout, and therefore constituting an out in the context of a reconstructed inning (but other acts of defensive interference are still to be considered blown chances, it would seem).

The bottom line is that this revision regarding the reconstruction of innings has unfortunately injected ambiguity into what was once unambiguous.

Rule 9.16(a) (continued)   A wild pitch is solely the pitcher's fault and shall contribute to an earned run just as a base on balls or a balk.

FOR EXAMPLE: With a runner on third base, a pitch gets away from the catcher and the runner at third base scores a run.

If the reason the pitch got away from the catcher was that the pitcher threw a wild pitch (as defined in Rule 9.13), the "wild pitch" is included in the reconstruction of the inning for the purpose of determining earned runs; it happens in the reconstructed inning in the same way it did in the "real" inning. However, if the reason the pitch eluded the catcher was the catcher failing to handle the pitch properly (as per the aforementioned Rule 9.13), the reconstructed inning treats the "passed ball" in the same manner as any other fielding error, and the result of the passed ball (i.e., the advancement of the runner from third base to home plate) is considered as not having happened in the reconstructed inning.

WHAT IT MEANS: This portion of Rule 9.16(a) is in line with the underlying principle that earned runs are those runs—and only those runs—that are ascribable solely to the pitcher's actions in the context of delivering pitchers to batters. Any runs attributable to anything else (specifically, bad fielding in the form of official fielding errors and passed balls) are unearned runs.

IT'S ALWAYS GOOD TO TEACH BY EXAMPLE

Rule 9.16(a) Comment: The following are examples of earned runs charged to a pitcher.

Despite any criticisms that might be made in regards to certain parts of Rule 9, the rulebook deserves some praise inasmuch as a number of concrete and serviceable examples of how portions of Rule 9.16 are to be applied are given, and they are helpful in understanding how it all works.

In passing, it may be noted that under the rules as they existed prior to the 2007 revisions, successive pitchers in examples like that ones that follow were referred to as "P1," "P2" and "P3." At the same time, batters were referred to as simply "A," "B," "C," and so forth. Now (for reasons unexplained), pitchers are "Peter" (which one would assume was chosen because name Peter begins with the letter P, just as the word pitcher does), then "Roger" (skipping the letter Q, for whatever reason), then "Sierra" (?), and batters are "Abel," "Baker," "Charlie," "Daniel," "Edward," "Frank," and finally "George."

(I cannot help but note that the choice of "Peter" for the initial pitcher in all the examples put forth in Rule 9.16 leads to the rather awkward phrasing of "Peter pitches," which brings to mind, at least for me, Peter Piper picking a peck of pickled peppers.)

All that aside, there certainly is nothing inherently wrong with this new nomenclature, although it is less clear and less precise than what it replaced. Regardless, it is mysterious why these particular names were chosen (aside from their alphabetical order) and why they vacillate between typical European first names and surnames, virtually all of them having a decidedly masculine slant (even though the rulebook has declared itself to be gender neutral in the final text of the Definition of Terms).

Rule 9.16(a) Comment (1): Peter pitches and retires Abel and Baker, the first two batters of an inning. Charlie reaches first base on an error charged to a fielder. Daniel hits a home run. Edward hits a home run. Peter retires Frank to end the inning. Three runs have scored, but no earned runs are charged to Peter, because Charlie should have been the third out of the inning, as reconstructed without the error.

In other words, the defensive team had three "fielding chances" before any runs scored. Therefore, the three runs are all unearned.

Rule 9.16(a) Comment (2): Peter pitches and retires Abel. Baker hits a triple. While pitching to Charlie, Peter throws a wild pitch, allowing Baker to score. Peter retires Daniel and Edward. One run has scored, charged as an earned run to Peter, because the wild pitch contributes to an earned run.

If you look at this example carefully, you'll realize that we're never told how the plate appearance of the third batter (Charlie) ended.

It can be safely assumed—given the balance of the example—that Charlie wasn't put out because Abel, Daniel, and Edward account for the requisite three outs. At the same time, it would seem that Charlie did not score either, because only one run (that of Baker) scores in the example.

In any case, this example simply reaffirms that wild pitches are not excluded in the reconstruction of innings because wild pitches are part and parcel of a pitcher delivering pitches to batters, as discussed earlier.

THE RULEBOOK'S ATTEMPT TO CLARIFY WHAT IT MEANS WHEN IT SAYS THAT CATCHER'S INTERFERENCE IS TO BE EXCLUDED IN THE RECONSTRUCTION OF INNINGS

In an inning in which a batter-runner reaches first base on a catcher's interference, such batter-runner shall not count as an earned run should he subsequently score. The official scorer shall not assume, however, that such batter would have made an out absent the catcher's interference (unlike, for example, situations in which a batter-runner reaches first base safely because of a fielder's misplay of a ball for an error). Because such batter never had a chance to complete his time at bat, it is unknown how such batter would have fared absent the catcher's interference. Compare the following examples:

Rule 9.16(a) Comment (3): With two out, Abel reaches first on an error by the shortstop in misplaying a ground ball. Baker hits a home run. Charlie strikes out. Two runs have scored, but none is earned, because Abel's at-bat should have been the third out of the inning, as reconstructed without the error.

Rule 9.16(a) Comment (4): With two out, Abel reaches first on a catcher's interference. Baker hits a home run. Charlie strikes out. Two runs have scored, but one (Baker's) is earned, because the official scorer cannot assume that Abel would have made an out to end the inning, absent the catcher's interference.

Inasmuch as the third and fourth examples of "earned runs charged to a pitcher" are given specifically to try to explain what is meant by Rule 9.16's directive vis-à-vis excluding catcher's interference from the things (errors and passed balls) that are excluded when reconstructing innings in order to ascertain earned runs, a rather extended preamble is given, the gist of which can be broken down into two basic notions.

First, any run scored by a batter who reaches base on a call of catcher's interference cannot be considered an earned run. That's simple enough, and, in fact, it comports with including catcher's interference with the other things that are excluded in the reconstruction of innings, just as was the case prior to the 2007 revisions.

Second, the act of interference is also not to be considered a blown chance to put out the batter (even though the opposite is stated in the next-to-last sentence in the main text of Rule 9.16(a)) and—when all is said and done—the scorer is to look upon a plate appearance that ends in an award of first base by virtue of catcher's interference as never having happened at all when reconstructing innings: it's a nullity because (according to the rulebook) one cannot be sure if the batter would have reached base, or would have been put out, if the interference had not occurred.

(In this regard, note that the preamble to examples 3 and 4 states that a batter who is awarded first base on catcher's interference "never had a chance to complete his time at bat," but in fact, the time at bat was completed by a call of catcher's interference. Go figure.)

All that said, one has to question—aside from the contradiction of Rule 9.16's instruction to "construe" a defensive interference penalty as a "fielding chance"—how this approach can be reconciled with the rulebook's pronouncement in the initial text of Rule 9.16 about "giving the benefit of the doubt always to the pitcher." After all, if a batter who reaches first base on an interference call might have been put out if interference had not been called, shouldn't the benefit of the doubt be given to the pitcher and it be assumed that the batter would have been put out but for the interference?

One can only hope that the issues caused by the decision to exclude catcher's interference from being included with errors and passed balls in the reconstruction of innings will someday be addressed.

Dealing with a Player Who Reaches Base After That Player Should Have Been Put Out

Rule 9.16(b)(1)   No run shall be earned when scored by a runner who reaches first base on a hit or otherwise after his time at bat is prolonged by a muffed foul fly.

For example: The leadoff batter swings at the first pitch he sees and sends the ball almost straight up into the air just behind home plate.

Although it's an easy, routine play to make, the catcher muffs the catch and the batter's turn at bat continues as a result.

On the next pitch, the batter crushes the ball and rockets it to the fence in right-center field for a standup double.

If the batter ends up scoring a run later in the inning, it's an unearned run.

What it means: On the one hand, the batter got on base in a most legitimate fashion: a bona fide base hit. On the other hand, he would not have had the opportunity to do so but for the catcher's error.

As before, if this inning is reconstructed without errors or passed balls, the batter doesn't reach base; his plate appearance goes into the book as a putout logged by the catcher. Therefore, any run that the batter may ultimately score is an unearned run.

In addition, as before, if you look at it from the pitcher's point of view, it makes sense to consider any run this batter might score in the inning as an unearned run. After all, the pitcher precipitated a good opportunity to put out the batter. That being the case, the pitcher ought not to be saddled with the consequences of the catcher's failure to field a batted ball properly by having an earned run charged to him.

Dealing with a Player Who Reaches Base on an Interference Or Obstruction Call

Rule 9.16(b)(2)   No run shall be earned when scored by a runner who reaches first base because of interference or obstruction.

Once again, you have a batter reaching base through no fault of the pitcher in process of the pitcher delivering pitches. Therefore, once again, the pitcher is absolved of blame in cases like this if the batter ends up scoring a run during the course of the inning.

Dealing with a Player Who Reaches Base on a Fielding Error

Rule 9.16(b)(3)   No run shall be earned when scored by a runner who reaches first base because of any fielding error.

As was the case in Rule 9.16(b)(1), in a reconstruction of the inning, the batter is considered as having been put out in cases like this. The batter cannot score a run in the context of the reconstructed inning, and consequently any run that the batter might score in the "real" inning must be considered and counted as an unearned run.

At the same time, any run scored by a batter who reaches base on an error would be a run that cannot be fairly attributable to the pitcher's efforts in delivering pitches to the batter in question. It's as "unearned" as any unearned run can be.

Dealing with a Run Scored by a Runner on Base Who Could Have Been Put Out While on Base

Rule 9.16(c)   No run shall be earned when scored by a runner whose presence on the bases is prolonged by an error, if such runner would have been put out by errorless play.

FOR EXAMPLE: With a runner on first taking a big lead, the pitcher adroitly delivers the ball to the first baseman, taking the runner completely by surprise.

Although the runner desperately dives back to first, it is certain that he'll be put out as long as the first baseman catches the pitcher's well-thrown ball, but the first baseman muffs the throw and the runner ends up safe at first base.

The pitcher is properly credited with an assist under Rule 9.10(a)(1) in this case, and the first baseman is properly charged with an error.

Moreover, any run subsequently scored by the runner at first—who survived the attempt to put him out that was botched by the first baseman— would be considered an unearned run.

WHAT IT MEANS: If the first baseman had not committed the error, the runner would have been put out. Consequently, if you reconstruct this inning without the error, the runner is put out. Therefore, the runner cannot score a run in the reconstructed inning. Accordingly, any run he might score in the "real" inning must be deemed an unearned run.

Dealing with Runner Advancement Aided by an Error, Passed Ball, Interference or Obstruction

Rule 9.16(d) No run shall be earned when the scoring runner's advance has been aided by an error, a passed ball or defensive interference or obstruction, if in the official scorer's judgment the run would not have scored without the aid of such misplay.

For example: With a runner at second base and one out, the catcher lets a pitch get away from him and it's judged a passed ball because the runner on second makes it to third base easily while the catcher is busy retrieving the ball he failed to catch or otherwise reasonably control.

But for the passed ball, the runner would not have advanced to third base as he did. Therefore, in the reconstruction of this inning, the runner stays at second base following the pitch that resulted in the passed ball.

Continuing Scenario #1: On the next pitch, the batter hits the ball between the first baseman and the second baseman.

Although the second baseman is able to dive and smother the ball to keep it from going into the outfield, there's no way that he can deliver the ball to home plate to put out the runner attempting to advance on the play. The second baseman is nonetheless able to get the ball to first base in time to put out the batter.

The next two batters strike out.

It is obvious that on the play made on the batter at first base, if the runner who scored had still been at second base, he would not have been able to score (absent a major malfunction on the part of the defensive team). Therefore, there's no question that the passed ball led to the run scoring. Consequently, the run is properly deemed an unearned run.

Continuing Scenario #2: Picking up the scenario again, just after the runner reached third base on the passed ball, the batter hits the next pitch for a solid triple, and the runner at third handily scores a run.

The next batter strikes out.

Obviously, even if there had been no passed ball, the runner (who would have been at second base but for the passed ball) would have scored on the triple. Therefore, the passed ball is really of no consequence; the run would have scored anyway. The run is fairly counted as an earned run.

What it means: Just because a run is scored by a runner who was "aided" by an error, passed ball, defensive interference or obstruction doesn't necessarily mean that the run will be an unearned run. It is only when a run scores that would not have scored but for an error, passed ball, defensive interference or obstruction that the run can be properly considered an unearned run.

This leads to a common situation in scorekeeping.

For instance, consider the following.

A run has scored, aided to some degree by one or more errors, passed balls, acts of defensive interference or obstruction.

Question: Is the run an earned run?

Answer: Maybe yes, maybe no.

Often, it is only when the inning has concluded that a scorer can judge whether any given run would or would have not scored without whatever errors, passed balls, acts of defensive interference or obstruction that aided the runner in question traveling around the bases. Only then can the scorer judge if the run (1) would have scored regardless of whatever "help" the defensive team may have provided (an earned run) or (2) if the run would not have scored but for that "help" (an unearned run).

DEALING WITH ERRORS COMMITTED BY PITCHERS

Rule 9.16(e)   An error by a pitcher is treated exactly the same as an error by any other fielder in computing earned runs.

FOR EXAMPLE: Bottom of the ninth. Bases loaded. Two outs and a full count on the batter.

Given the situation, the runners take off on the next pitch, but the batter hits the payoff pitch for a weak pop-up, and it's as plain as the day is long that the ball will gently come down like a parachute right to where the pitcher is standing in the middle of the infield for an easy catch that will send the game into extra innings.

The pitcher calls off all his fellow fielders and steadies himself for the play to come (with more than a fair amount of understandable confidence), but inexplicably, the pitcher muffs the catch.

The runner at third scores, the batter advances to first base safely and the other runners on base advance as well to seal the deal and win the game for the home team in dramatic fashion.

All else aside—as far as the scorekeeping issue in this case is concerned—the winning run is properly scored as a run "unearned" by the pitcher.

WHAT IT MEANS: Earned runs are the responsibility of the pitcher, but strictly within his role as a pitcher. That is to say, once a pitcher has delivered a pitch, the pitcher is no longer the pitcher, as such. Rather, the pitcher then becomes a fielder (just like the eight other defensive players on the field).

The key thing is that unearned runs are attributable to fielding issues, as is the run in the example given. Earned runs are those runs directly attributable to pitching.

From that perspective, the run in this case—as well as any run scored under similar circumstances—is without a doubt the responsibility of the pitcher in a broad sense, but the run is actually the responsibility of the pitcher in the context of the pitcher's actions as a fielder, divorced from pitching.

Consequently, it is the pitcher's fielding average that suffers under 9.16(e), and not the pitcher's earned run average in this and similar cases.

Giving the Pitcher the Benefit of the Doubt in Terms of Runner Advancement

Rule 9.16(f) **Whenever a fielding error occurs, the pitcher shall be given the benefit of the doubt in determining to which bases any runners would have advanced had the fielding of the defensive team been errorless.**

For example: With a runner at second base, the batter hits a ground ball past the pitcher that rolls into shallow center field.

It's clearly a base hit in any case, but the center fielder misplays the ball, and the batter capitalizes on that fact by taking second base.

While this is going on, the runner who had been at second base makes it all the way to home plate to score a run.

Granted, it is not unusual for a runner at second base to score on a single, but in this case it is far from clear whether the runner at second could have successfully made it all the way to home plate—or whether the runner would have even tried to do so—if the center fielder had not committed the error and had fielded the ball cleanly.

Given that doubt, when the inning is reconstructed without the center fielder's error, the runner at second base should be considered as having advanced no further than third base on the batter's hit.

What it means: Simply put, a central policy in reconstructing innings is to do so in a manner that is most favorable to the pitcher, because (as stated a number of times earlier in this analysis of Rule 9.16) a cornerstone of the rubric of principles governing earned runs is that only those runs that—without question—would have scored even if no fielding errors or passed balls were committed by the defensive team are properly considered and counted as earned runs.

Dealing with Relief Pitchers—
Part 1: Charging Runs (Earned and Unearned) to Relief Pitchers and Pitchers Relieved

Rule 9.16(g)   When pitchers are changed during an inning, the official scorer shall not charge the relief pitcher with any run (earned or unearned) scored by a runner who was on base at the time such relief pitcher entered the game, nor for runs scored by any runner who reaches base on a fielder's choice that puts out a runner left on base by any preceding pitcher.

Here, the rulebook turns its focus (for the balance of Rule 9.16) to situations where more than one pitcher faces a batter or batters during the course of an inning.

Note that this section of Rule 9.16, and the ones that follow, are among the most complex in the entire rulebook. That being so, a number of specific examples and illustrations are given by the rulebook that shed a good deal of light on the problems that can arise in this context.

Note also that this section of Rule 9.16 is not about earned versus unearned runs at all, despite how Rule 9.16 is labeled. Rather, it's about the threshold issue of how to assign runs properly (regardless of whether they are earned runs or not) when multiple pitchers come to the mound and face batters during the course of an inning.

That said, the primary premise—set forth in the initial text of Rule 9.16(g)—seems simple at first reading. However, as demonstrated in the examples given after Rule 9.16(g)'s comment, there is a lot of complexity that can arise.

An Amplification of the Initial Text

Rule 9.16(g) Comment: It is the intent of Rule 9.16(g) to charge each pitcher with the number of runners he put on base, rather than with the individual runners. When a pitcher puts runners on base and is relieved, such pitcher shall be charged with all runs subsequently scored up to and including the number of runners such pitcher left on base when such pitcher left the game, unless such runners are put out without action by the batter (i.e., caught stealing, picked off base or called out for interference when a batter-runner does not reach first base on the play).

Rule 9.16(g)'s comment is much more than a mere comment: it moves well beyond the rather narrow scope of the main text, and it is much more a continuation and elaboration of the rule that it "comments" on because it adds dimensions that are not in the text that precedes it.

Note that the first six of the seven examples conform to the instructions laid out in Rule 9.16(g) quite closely. However, that is not the case in the seventh example: it is in fact an exception to the precepts that make up Rule 9.16(g). Therefore, special attention should be given to the last of the seven examples that follow.

(Note also that the seven examples are each one long paragraph in the Official Rules of Baseball, as currently published. However, here—for the purpose of making the examples clearer—each sentence comprising each of the seven paragraphs is set forth separately.)

Rule 9.16 (g) Comment: (1) Peter is pitching.
Abel reaches first base on a base on balls.
Roger relieves Peter.
Baker grounds out, advancing Abel to second base.
Charlie flies out.
Daniel singles, scoring Abel.
Abel's run is charged to Peter.
Another way to look at this is to approach it in terms of considering the bases empty (as far as the relief pitcher is concerned) whenever a relief pitcher enters a game.

Applying that technique, no run is charged to Roger because none of the batters that Roger faced scored a run.

Rule 9.16(g) Comment: (2) Peter is pitching.
Abel reaches first base on a base on balls.
Roger relieves Peter.
Baker forces Abel at second bases (sic).
Charlie grounds out, advancing Baker to second base.
Daniel singles, scoring Baker.
Baker's run is charged to Peter.
Employing the alternative approach mentioned above, the result is just the same as in the preceding example: the run is charged to the pitcher that was relieved.

In plain English, the first batter that the relief pitcher (Roger) faced—in the person of Baker—was not put out, and he (Baker) scored the run in issue. However, if the bases had been empty when Roger came to the pitcher's mound in relief of Peter, Baker would not have reached base at all: he would have been put out.

Rule 9.16(g) Comment: (3)　Peter is pitching.
Abel reaches first base on a base on balls.
Roger relieves Peter.
Baker singles, advancing Abel to third base.
Charlie grounds to short, with Abel out at home plate and Baker advancing to second base.
Daniel flies out.
Edward singles, scoring Baker.
Baker's run is charged to Peter.

In sum, the run scored by Baker is not properly charged to Roger because Peter left a runner on base when he was relieved by Roger, and the run is charged to Peter even though Baker reached base on a single given up by Roger.

This result is a manifestation of the "intent" stated in the first paragraph of Rule 9.16(g)'s comment, that—generally—a pitcher who is relieved while an inning is in progress is to be charged with runs that subsequently score equal to "the number of runners he left on base," divorced from whether or not the runner who scored was a batter that the relieved pitcher actually faced.

Rule 9.16(g) Comment: (4)　Peter is pitching.
Abel reaches first base on a base on balls.
Roger relieves Peter.
Baker reaches on a base on balls.
Charlie flies out.
Abel is picked off second base.
Daniel doubles, scoring Baker from first base.
Baker's run is charged to Roger.

The stated exception to the general premise in Rule 9.16(g)'s comment is embodied in this example #4.

In other words, Peter left a runner on base for Roger, in the person of Abel. However, Abel was "put out without action of the batter" (as mentioned in the final part of Rule 9.16(g)'s comment); he (Abel) was "picked off base." Therefore, although Peter left a runner on base, the run that scored is not charged to him. Rather, it's charged to Roger.

(Note that the same result would come from Abel being put out on an attempt to steal a base, or if Abel had been called out for interference on a play where "a batter-runner does not reach first base on the play.")

Rule 9.16(g) Comment: (5)　Peter is pitching.
Abel reaches first base on a base on balls.

> *Roger relieves Peter.*
> *Baker reaches first base on a base on balls.*
> *Sierra relieves Roger.*
> *Charlie forces Abel at third base.*
> *Daniel forces Baker at third base.*
> *Edward hits a home run, scoring three runs.*
> *The official scorer shall charge one run to Peter, one run to Roger and one run to Sierra.*

In sum, none of the batters who reached base were put out "without action of the batter" (see above), Peter left one runner on base when he left the game, and Roger did the same. Therefore, both Peter and Roger each get charged with a run, even though neither of those runs was scored by a batter that either Peter or Roger faced, and (with Peter and Roger's "quota" satisfied) the additional run goes to Sierra.

(Note that the third run would be charged to Sierra in any case because it arose from a home run hit by a batter with whom neither Peter nor Roger had any connection.)

Rule 9.16(g) Comment: (6) Peter is pitching.
> *Abel reaches first base on a base on balls.*
> *Roger relieves Peter.*
> *Baker reaches first base on a base on balls.*
> *Charlie singles, filling the bases.*
> *Daniel forces Abel at home plate.*
> *Edward singles, scoring Baker and Charlie.*
> *The official scorer shall charge one run to Peter and one run to Roger.*

Once again, Peter is charged with a run scored by a batter he did not face because Peter left the game with a runner on base and none of the exceptions are applicable here to the basic premise (set forth in Rule 9.16(g)'s comment) that a pitcher is to be charged with runs commensurate with the number of runners the pitcher left on base when relieved.

Rule 9.16(g) Comment: (7) Peter is pitching.
> *Abel reaches first base on a base on balls.*
> *Roger relieves Peter.*
> *Baker singles, but Abel is out trying to reach third base and Baker advances to second base on the throw.*
> *Charlie singles, scoring Baker.*
> *Baker's run is charged to Roger.*

Before the 2007 revisions, the preface to these seven examples ended with the words "EXCEPTION: see example 7."

Inasmuch as charging the run to the relief pitcher in this case does not altogether comport with the principles laid out in Rule 9.16(g) and its comment (which principles are followed unwaveringly in the first six examples), it is difficult to surmise why the rules committee deleted the warning— "EXCEPTION: see example 7"—that the previous version of Rule 9 made a special point of highlighting.

In any case, what is at work here requires some explanation. Therefore, consider the following.

In this case, Peter left a runner on base when he was relieved by Roger. A run scored, and although the runner that Peter left on base for Roger was not put out trying to steal a base, by being picked off, or by virtue of an act of interference, and neither was that runner put out on a fielder's choice where—for all intents and purposes—the runner left on base was in a sense "substituted" for by another batter, the run is nevertheless charged to the relief pitcher, Roger.

That being the case, you have to figure out (without any explicit assistance from the rulebook itself) what this last of the seven examples means, as well as its logic and the reasoning behind it.

All in all, it appears to go back to the notion expressed in the observations made earlier about Rule 9.16's examples: that the principles of Rule 9.16 are tied to the idea that a relief pitcher ought to be viewed as having come into the game with the bases empty.

Following that line of thought, you have Roger (in a sense) allowing Baker to reach base, outright. (After all, Baker hit a single. It was not as though Baker reached base on a fielder's choice.)

That being so, the run that Baker scored can be looked upon—quite fairly—as being the responsibility of Roger, not Peter, even though Peter left a runner on base for Roger when Peter left the game.

The long and the short of it is that the general precepts of Rule 9.16(g) are not to be adhered to at the exclusion of a little common sense, and runs ought to be charged to the pitcher who was responsible for "allowing" (so to speak) the runner who scored the run to reach base, or to the pitcher who was responsible for a runner who scored a run, which runner would not have reached base if the relieved pitcher had not "allowed" (so to speak) that preceding runner to reach base.

In any case, to navigate these waters, it is quite helpful (as stated before) simply to imagine the bases being empty whenever a relief pitcher enters the game during the middle of an inning for the purpose of deciding how runs scored should be assigned to multiple pitchers. In doing so, the great majority of situations can be dealt with adequately. However, reference should never-theless always be made to the express provisions of Rule 9.16(g) so as to ensure that whatever decision is made in regards to assigning runs to multiple pitchers is made correctly.

Rule 9.16(h)   **A relief pitcher shall not be held accountable when the first batter to whom he pitches reaches first base on four called balls if such batter has a decided advantage in the ball and strike count when pitchers are changed.**

Dealing with Relief Pitchers— Part 2: Relievers Taking Over While a Batter's Plate Appearance Is Still in Progress

As was the case with Rule 9.16(g), the subject that Rule 9.16(h) deals with is not earned runs versus unearned runs. Rather, the question addressed here is as follows:

If a relief pitcher comes into the game during a batter's plate appearance (as opposed to coming into the game between innings or between the plate appearances of two batters), when is the pitcher who began the batter's plate appearance properly charged with the outcome of the batter's plate appear-ance, and when is the relief pitcher so charged?

Happily, the answer to the question is not phrased in terms that might require analysis or interpretation, and the term "decided advantage" does not go undefined. Rather, the rulebook lays it all out as clear as can be by simply listing all the various ball and strike counts that a relief pitcher might inherit and plainly stating which pitcher ("starter" or "reliever") is properly charged with the plate appearance in question.

Rule 9.16(h)(1)   **If, when pitchers are changed, the count is**
   2 balls, no strike,
   2 balls, 1 strike,
   3 balls, no strike,
   3 balls, 1 strike,
   3 balls, 2 strikes,
   and the batter gets a base on balls, the official scorer shall charge that

batter and the base on balls to the preceding pitcher, not to the relief pitcher.

Rule 9.16(h)(2)   Any other action by such batter, such as reaching base on a hit, an error, a fielder's choice, a force-out, or being touched by a pitched ball, shall cause such a batter to be charged to the relief pitcher.

(Why Rule 9.16(h)(2) isn't just an additional sentence in Rule 9.16(h)(1) is a complete mystery to me.)

Rule 9.16(h) Comment: The provisions of Rule 9.16(h)(2) shall not be construed as affecting or conflicting with the provisions of Rule 9.16(g).

(Note that the meaning and purpose of this rather terse and enigmatic aside is dealt with following Rule 9.16(h)(3).)

Rule 9.16(h)(3)   If, when pitchers are changed, the count is
2 balls, 2 strikes,
1 ball, 2 strikes,
1 ball, 1 strike,
1 ball, no strike,
no ball, 2 strikes,
no ball, 1 strike,
the official scorer shall charge that batter and the actions of that batter to the relief pitcher.

Although the majority of Rule 9.16(h) is as clear as clear can be, there is the rather mysterious digression tucked in between the cataloging of various ball and strike counts: Rule 9.16(h) comment.

As written, it can be a bit puzzling, but what it means can be fairly easily understood by considering the following.

FOR EXAMPLE: P1 begins the inning by issuing a walk to the first batter he faces.

Thereafter, P1 delivers three straight balls to the second batter.

At this point, P2 is brought into the game to relieve P1.

The first pitch delivered by P2 is grounded to the shortstop.

The shortstop fields the ball and steps on second base to force out the runner coming from first. At the same time, the batter gets to first base safely on a fielder's choice.

In terms of Rule 9.16(g)'s concerns, the runner at first base is not the responsibility of P2 as far as which of the two pitchers would be charged with the run that might eventually be scored by that runner. That's because that runner can be looked upon as the runner that P1 allowed to reach base on a base on balls before P2 came to the mound, and the new runner is nothing more than a substitute for the runner who was put out at second base.

At the same time, because P2 inherited a 3–0 count from P1, and the batter with the 3–0 count reached base on a fielder's choice, the plate appearance of that batter is charged to P2 under 9.16(h)(2).

WHAT IT MEANS: The bottom line is that a batter who reaches base may be looked upon as the responsibility of a relief pitcher under the provisions of Rule 9.16(h) [in terms of the batter's plate appearance being charged to the relief pitcher] but that same batter (batter-runner) may be looked upon as the responsibility of a pitcher who was relieved before that batter reached base under the provisions of Rule 9.16(g) [in terms of which pitcher might be charged with a run if that batter ultimately scores].

Apples and oranges, and Rule 9.16(h)'s comment could just say so, but it doesn't.

Perhaps it's a case of striving to be brief leading to being obscure.

Rule 9.16(i)   When pitchers are changed during an inning, the relief pitcher shall not have the benefit of previous chances for outs not accepted in determining earned runs.

Rule 9.16(i) Comment: It is the intent of Rule 9.16(i) to charge a relief pitcher with earned runs for which such relief pitcher is solely responsible. In some instances, runs charged as earned against the relief pitcher can be charged as unearned against the team.

DEALING WITH RELIEF PITCHERS—
PART 3: "PREVIOUS CHANCES" AND EARNED RUNS

In this final portion of Rule 9.16, the question of how to determine earned runs versus unearned runs from the perspective of relief pitchers is finally addressed, and—in a sense—all the salient provisions of Rule 9.16 that precede this final part of Rule 9.16 are brought together.

Luckily, the rulebook gives three examples that are most helpful in dealing with relief pitchers and earned runs. However, Rule 9.16(i) does not attempt to amplify or otherwise explain what is meant by "benefit of previous chances for outs not accepted." Therefore, a quick example of what that means would seem to be in order here.

Consider the following.

P1 strikes out the first two batters he faces, but the third batter P1 deals with reaches base on an error.

P2 relieves P1.

If P1 had continued to pitch, any and all runs scored while P1 was pitching would have been considered unearned runs because the third batter P1 faced should have been the final out of the inning. However, P2 can end up having runs score that will be counted as earned runs charged against him because—from P2's perspective—he came in to pitch with two outs in the inning (as is the case in reality) and not three outs (as is the case in the reconstruction of the inning without errors or passed balls).

Consequently, one can say (in a decidedly "old school" manner) that P2 will not get "the benefit of previous chances for outs not accepted in determining earned runs" in the case presented above.

For example:

(1) With two out and Peter pitching, Abel reaches first base on a base on balls.

Baker reaches first base on an error.

Roger relieves Peter.

Charlie hits a home run, scoring three runs.

The official scorer shall charge two unearned runs to Peter, one earned run to Roger and three unearned runs to the team (because the inning should have ended with the third out when Baker batted and an error was committed).

Note that the official scorer is not obliged to record and report runs as being earned or unearned by a team in the official scorer's report, but only in terms of individual pitchers. Therefore, it is puzzling why this example speaks to that. Nevertheless, the important point is made: Roger did not have the "benefit" of his team having failed to log the third out of the inning while Peter was still in the game in terms of earned and unearned runs.

(2) With two out, and Peter pitching, Abel and Baker each reach first base on a base on balls.

Roger relieves Peter.

Charlie reaches first base on an error.

Daniel hits a home run, scoring four runs.

The official scorer shall charge two unearned runs to Peter and two unearned runs to Roger (because the inning should have ended with the third out when Charlie batted and an error was committed).

In other words, here, what should have been the third out ending the inning was made while Roger was on the mound. Consequently, all the runs are unearned.

(3) With none out and Peter pitching, Abel reaches first base on a base on balls.
    Baker reaches first base on an error.
    Roger relieves Peter.
    Charlie hits a home run, scoring three runs.
    Daniel and Edward strike out.
    Frank reaches first base on an error.
    George hits a home run, scoring two runs.
    The official scorer shall charge two runs, one of them earned, to Peter, three runs, one of them earned, to Roger and five runs, two of them earned, to the team (because only Abel and Charlie would have scored in an inning reconstructed without the errors).

Again, for the rulebook to talk about charging runs as earned or unearned to a team is a bit dubious inasmuch as the official scorer (as stated before) is not obliged to do so in the official scorer's report. Be that as it may, the balance of this final example brings together neatly the essential concepts regarding earned runs and unearned runs in the context of multiple pitchers appearing in the same inning.

◆ 14 ◆

Winning Isn't Everything

Rules 9.17–9.18

Rule 9.17—
Winning and Losing Pitcher

(a) The official scorer shall credit as the winning pitcher that pitcher whose team assumes a lead while such pitcher is in the game, or during the inning on offense in which such pitcher is removed from the game, and does not relinquish such lead, unless
    (1) such pitcher is a starting pitcher and Rule 9.17(b) applies; or
    (2) Rule 9.17(c) applies.

THE INITIAL PREMISE

If both teams used only one pitcher throughout the course of a game, deciding which pitcher is the winning pitcher and which is the losing pitcher would be as simple as deciding who's the winning jockey and the losing jockey in a two-horse race.

However, it's rare (certainly in modern times) for one pitcher to go the distance for either the winning or the losing team. Therefore, some attention must be given to deciding which pitcher gets credit for a win, and which pitcher gets charged with a loss, even in relatively simple cases.

FOR EXAMPLE: After 7½ innings have been played, the score is tied at 1–1.

The starting pitcher for the home team has pitched all eight of the visiting team's frames.

In the bottom of the eighth inning, the starting pitcher for the home team leaves the game for a pinch-hitter. The home team scores a run to make the score 2–1 in its favor.

In the top of the ninth inning, the pitcher who takes the mound in relief of the home team's starting pitcher manages to strike out the first three batters he faces and thereby ends the game.

The home team's starting pitcher is properly considered the winning pitcher, even though he wasn't in the game (in a sense) when the game was won by his team.

WHAT IT MEANS: Note that when the home team's pitcher threw his last pitch, his team was not ahead. However, before another pitcher took over the pitching duties from him, the home team took a lead that held up until the conclusion of the game. Consequently, the win goes to the home team's starter, just as it would have if the home team had assumed the lead in the first inning and the visiting team never tied the score during the balance of the game.

That said, special note should be taken of the two major exceptions stated in the preliminary text of Rule 9.17 concerning the restrictions placed upon the selection of winning pitchers. The first is found in Rule 9.17(b), dealing with how many innings a starting pitcher must pitch in order to qualify for being deemed the winning pitcher. The second is found in Rule 9.17(c), in regards to situations where more than one relief pitcher qualifies to receive credit for the "win."

THE INITIAL PREMISE RESTATED

Rule 9.17(a) Comment: Whenever the score is tied, the game becomes a new contest insofar as the winning pitcher is concerned. Once the opposing team assumes the lead, all pitchers who have pitched up to that point and have been replaced are excluded from being credited with the victory. If the pitcher against whose pitching the opposing team gained the lead continues to pitch until his team regains the lead, which it holds to the finish of the game, that pitcher shall be the winning pitcher.

FOR EXAMPLE: It's the bottom of the ninth, and the home team is behind by one run.

Both teams have used multiple pitchers leading up to this point. However, that's of no consequence (in terms of who might end up being the winning pitcher in the game) because the home team ties the score to take the game into extra innings.

That being the case, all the pitchers who previously appeared in the game are eliminated from consideration for being deemed the winning pitcher (with the exception of the pitchers who finished for their team in the ninth inning if either of them come back to pitch in the tenth inning).

WHAT IT MEANS: The comment to Rule 9.17(a) is nothing more than an interpretation—an alternative rendition—of the main text of Rule 9.17(a), and it doesn't substantially add anything to what has been stated in Rule 9.17(a). After all, it logically follows that once the score in a game is tied, one team or the other will thereafter have to assume the lead in order to win, and the pitcher who is pitching for the team that assumes the lead—which lead is held until the game is completed—will be the winning pitcher (generally speaking) and all the pitchers that came to the mound for the winning team prior to that point in the game (if any) are therefore, logically, ineligible for being credited with the win.

In other words, the comment to Rule 9.17(a) could very well begin by saying "in other words." It's simply stating the same premise as Rule 9.17(a) does, just in a different manner.

A SPECIAL PREREQUISITE FOR STARTING PITCHERS IN TERMS OF WINS

Rule 9.17(b)   If the pitcher whose team assumes a lead while such pitcher is in the game, or during the inning on offense in which such pitcher is removed from the game, and does not relinquish such lead, is a starting pitcher who has not completed

(1) five innings of a game that lasts six or more innings on defense, or

(2) four innings of a game that lasts five innings on defense,

then the official scorer shall credit as the winning pitcher the relief pitcher, if there is only one relief pitcher, or the relief pitcher who, in the official scorer's judgment was the most effective, if there is more than one relief pitcher.

FOR EXAMPLE: The visiting team scores one run in the top of the first inning, and no more runs are scored by either team after nine full innings have been played, leading (obviously) to a victory for the visiting team.

The starting pitcher for the winning (visiting) team was replaced with two outs in the bottom of the fifth inning, (i.e., replaced after having pitched 4⅔ innings).

Initially, it would appear that the starting pitcher for the visiting team would qualify to be the winning pitcher inasmuch as his team assumed the lead that held up for the balance of the game while he was pitching, but because he didn't pitch a full five innings, he is disqualified from being credited with the win under Rule 9.17(b).

If only one relief pitcher was used for the balance of the game, that relief pitcher qualifies for the win (by default, simply because—with the starting pitcher being ineligible for the win—there's no one else to award the win to). However, if more that one relief pitcher was used by the visiting team, the official scorer has to decide which relief pitcher is properly credited with the win.

WHAT IT MEANS: Rule 9.17 takes the position that a starting pitcher who doesn't stay in the game beyond what would normally be more than half the game (in terms of innings completed, as opposed to elapsed time or any other measure of how much a pitcher works) falls inexcusably short of what is expected of that pitcher. Therefore, regardless of whether that pitcher may otherwise qualify for a win, and regardless of how well that pitcher may have pitched during his tenure on the mound, that pitcher can't legitimately be credited with a win.

Notwithstanding whatever the reason may be for doing so, that's the way it is: no exceptions (except for the one narrow exception allowing a starting pitcher to be considered for a win in a game that lasts only "five innings on defensive" if the starting pitcher pitched four innings).

Simple enough.

If only one reliever is used, that reliever gets credit for the win because there's no one else to give the win to: the reliever finished first in a one-man track meet.

That's simple too.

However, if more than one reliever follows the starting pitcher, you have more than one candidate for the win if the winning team's lead holds up for the balance of the game, and that's where things can get a bit tricky.

Uncharacteristically, the rulebook doesn't set down a definitive standard for the official scorer to follow in this regard, because doing so could, and in all likelihood would, lead to a great many injustices. Consequently, the official scorer is given a considerable degree of discretion in that case, although the discretion is to be exercised in conformity with a number of specific guidelines (found in Rule 9.17(b)'s comment, as well as in Rule 9.17 (c)).

Guidelines for Choosing a Winning Pitcher Among Two or More Relief Pitchers

Rule 9.17(b) Comment: It is the intent of Rule 9.17(b) that a relief pitcher pitch at least one complete inning or pitch when a crucial out is made, within the context of the game (including the score), in order to be credited as the winning pitcher. If the first relief pitcher pitches effectively, the official scorer should not presumptively credit that pitcher with the win, because the rule requires that the win be credited to the pitcher who was the most effective, and a subsequent relief pitcher may have been most effective. The official scorer, in determining which relief pitcher was the most effective, should consider the number of runs, earned runs and base runners given up by each relief pitcher and the context of the game at the time of each relief pitcher's appearance. If two or more relief pitchers were similarly effective, the official scorer should give the presumption to the earlier pitcher as the winning pitcher.

Rule 9.17(b)'s comment is entirely a product of the 2007 revisions. Obviously, the rules committee considered this corner of scorekeeping to be important enough to devote a considerable amount of verbiage to giving an official scorer a number of fairly specific parameters in deciding between multiple relief pitchers, each of whom could—technically—qualify for the "win."

The finer points of Rule 9.17(b) came into play, in rather dramatic fashion, back in 2003 in the "combined no-hitter" that took place at Yankee Stadium on June 11, involving the Houston Astros and the New York Yankees, and a close look at that game serves as an excellent example of the complexities that can arise in dealing with Rule 9.17(b).

Note that the comment to Rule 9.17 had not yet been written at the time of the Astros/Yankees game, but inasmuch as the guidelines found in Rule 9.17(b)'s comment are for the most part nothing more than com-mon sense embellishments of the main text of Rule 9.17(b)—they were followed in the decision made by the official scorer (in the person of my friend, sports reporter and fellow author, Howie Karpin).

◆ ◆ ◆

The Astros scored eight runs in the game: one in the first, one in the second, two in the third, one in the seventh, one in the eighth and two in the ninth. The Yankees (who failed to garner even so much as one base hit) scored no runs at all. Therefore, Houston had the lead even before New York came to bat, and the Astros never came close to giving up that lead at any point in the game.

With that in mind, here's how it all went down for the winning team's pitching.

The starting pitcher for Houston (Roy Oswalt) lasted only one inning. He faced three batters, striking out two and not issuing a walk. In addition, he threw 23 pitches (seven balls and 16 strikes).

Pitcher #2 for the Astros (Pete Munro) worked 2⅔ innings. He faced 13 batters, striking out two and giving up three walks plus one hit batsman, and threw 51 pitches (26 balls and 25 strikes).

Pitcher #3 (Kirk Saarloos) gave his team 1⅓ innings. He dealt with four batters, striking out one without giving up any walks, and he threw 16 pitches (six balls and 10 strikes).

Pitcher #4 (Brad Lidge) contributed two full innings, facing six batters and striking out two of them without issuing a walk. In addition, he threw 23 pitches (eight balls and 15 strikes).

Pitcher #5 (Octavio Dotel) took care of one full inning (the eighth). He faced four batters, striking out all four (as the second batter he faced reached base on a "strike-three wild pitch"). In doing so, he threw 20 pitches (five balls and 15 strikes).

Pitcher #6 (Billy Wagner) finished the game by pitching the bottom of the ninth, striking out the first two of the three batters he faced and getting a "3–1" ground out to finish the game. In the process, he threw 14 pitches (three balls and 11 strikes).

Given all that, the question is who—out of the six pitchers involved— properly gets credit for the win?

For starters, the starting pitcher (Roy Oswalt) is eliminated from consideration for the win because he came nowhere near pitching the five innings required by Rule 9.17(b), but that still leaves five pitchers from which to choose.

Needless to say, the official scorer had a somewhat difficult task in deciding whom to credit with the win inasmuch as all five relief pitchers made legitimate contributions to winning the game, but ultimately, the fourth pitcher (Lidge) was officially credited with the win.

After all, Lidge retired all six batters he faced in the sixth and seventh innings (namely, Jason Giambi, Jorge Posada, Robin Ventura, Hideki Matsui,

Todd Zeile and Raul Mondesi, well-known and respected players all), while the only pitcher who logged more outs than Lidge (namely, Munro) walked three batters and plunked one as well.

All told, this game stands as an excellent example of a game where multiple relief pitchers could qualify for a win and there is no altogether clear and indisputable "correct answer" to the question of who should be considered the winning pitcher. It demonstrates how sometimes the "right call" simply comes down to the official scorer using his or her best judgment.

More About Choosing a Winner Pitcher Among Multiple Relief Pitchers

Rule 9.17(c)   The official scorer shall not credit as the winning pitcher a relief pitcher who is ineffective in a brief appearance, when at least one succeeding relief pitcher pitches effectively in helping his team maintain its lead. In such a case, the official scorer shall credit as the winning pitcher the succeeding relief pitcher who was most effective, in the judgment of the official scorer.

Rule 9.17(c) Comment: The official scorer generally should, but is not required to, consider the appearance of a relief pitcher to be ineffective and brief if such relief pitcher pitches less than one inning and allows two or more earned runs to score (even if such runs are charged to a previous pitcher). Rule 9.17(b) Comment provides guidance on choosing the winning pitcher from among several succeeding relief pitchers.

Rule 9.17(c), along with its "comment," constitute nothing more than additional guidance in regards to situations where an official scorer is called upon to exercise judicious reasoning in deciding on a winning pitcher among multiple relievers (with the comment to Rule 9.17(c) having been added—in its entirety—as part of the 2007 revisions).

Because this is one of the few areas in scorekeeping—aside from deciding between base hits and errors—in which an official scorer is not more or less locked into a "right" choice, the rules committee apparently felt it necessary to "pile it on" a bit, but in any case, one can safely assume that conscientious scorekeepers welcome the extra help.

Better too much than too little.

Deciding Who Gets the Loss

Rule 9.17(d)   A losing pitcher is a pitcher who is responsible for the run that gives the winning team a lead that the winning team does not relinquish.

Rule 9.17(d) Comment: Whenever the score is tied, the game becomes a new contest insofar as the losing pitcher is concerned.

Most of the changes made in the 2007 revisions were either "tweaks," renumberings or additional comments of one sort or the other, with little changed in terms of the language employed by the "former"rules. However, Rule 9.17(d), together with its comment, represent something quite different: a wholesale deletion of the former Rule 9.19(e) and a substitution of an entirely new text.

Here's how the former rule concerning losing pitchers—Rule 10.19(e) before the 2007 revisions—read.

Regardless of how many innings the first pitcher has pitched, he shall be charged with the loss of the game if he is replaced when his team is behind in the score, or falls behind because of runs charged to him after he is replaced, and his team thereafter fails either to tie the score or gain the lead.

Obviously, the new rule is markedly better than the prior one inasmuch as—among other things—it remedies the fact that the old rule spoke only in terms of "the first pitcher," and therefore how to determine which relief pitcher for a losing team might be charged with a loss required extrapolation from the text of the old rule.

Be that as it may, the most significant difference between determining losing pitchers and winning pitchers is (and was) that there is no requirement that the starting pitcher for the losing team pitch a certain number of innings to be charged with the loss.

That said, the "new" rule is easy to apply. At the same time, it also tacitly touches upon the concept of a pitcher being the "pitcher of record" (a term that is in common use in baseball, even though it is never used—let alone defined—in the rulebook).

For example: It's the bottom of the ninth inning with the score tied, and the visiting team's pitcher (P1) has loaded the bases.

As a result, P1 is relieved by P2.

P2 walks in the winning run.

Although P1 was no longer in the game when the winning run scored, he is nevertheless properly considered the losing pitcher.

What it means: P1 was the pitcher responsible for the home team's runner at third base. Therefore, given the fact that the winning run (i.e., the run that gave the winning team the lead it did not relinquish) was scored by the runner at third, P1 is properly deemed the losing pitcher.

The fact that P1 was not actually pitching when the game was lost is not relevant: P1 was the "pitcher of record" in terms of being eligible to be charged with the loss (even though he was no longer in the game) because the runner who scored the winning run was his responsibility.

At the same time, note that a winning pitcher can also be a "pitcher of record" when (for instance) that pitcher leaves the game with his or her team in the lead, another pitcher or pitchers finish the game, and the pitcher's team holds on to the lead until the conclusion of the game. In other words, while that pitcher was in the dugout waiting for the game to be finished, that pitcher was the "pitcher of record" in line to be credited with the win.

Special Circumstances

Rule 9.17(e)   A league may designate a non-championship game (for example, the Major League All-Star Game) for which Rules 9.17(a)(1) and 9.17(b) do not apply. In such games, the official scorer shall credit as the winning pitcher that pitcher whose team assumes a lead while such pitcher is in the game, or during the inning on offense in which such pitcher is removed from the game, and does not relinquish such lead, unless such pitcher is knocked out after the winning team has attained a commanding lead and the official scorer concludes that a subsequent pitcher is entitled to credit as the winning pitcher.

Strict application of the rules governing the selection of winning pitchers—specifically the requirement that the starting pitcher for the winning team pitch a certain number of innings to qualify for being credited with a win—would be foolish in "non-championship" games (i.e., games that are not official regular season or post-season games: games that don't "count," so to speak) because starting pitchers in games like that rarely pitch more than an inning or two. Therefore, Rule 9.17(e) suggests an alternative methodology that simply makes much more sense in those situations.

In any case, note that the determination of a losing pitcher (as per Rule 9.17(d)) in non-championship games remains the same as it does in regular and post-season games: there is no minimum inning requirement associated with losing pitchers, and there is no good reason not to apply the provisions of Rule 9.17(d) in non-championship games.

◆ ◆ ◆

Rule 9.18—Shutouts

A shutout is a statistic credited to a pitcher who allows no runs in a game.

STATING THE OBVIOUS—MORE OR LESS

One approach that is manifestly evident in the 2007 revisions of then Rule 10 is a desire to condense the numbering of Rule 10's major sub-sections from what they were prior to the revisions.

For example, what was previously Rule 10.05 (enumerating cases when base hits are to be scored) and what was Rule 10.06 (enumerating cases when base hits are not to be scored) were consolidated into one major sub-section: the "new" Rule 10.05, now Rule 9.05. Similarly, what was Rule 10.13 (enumerating cases where errors are to be charged) and what was Rule 10.14 (enumerating cases where errors are not to be charged) were consolidated into the "new" Rule 10.12, now Rule 9.12.

Although it would seem a logical thing to do, it was not an altogether great idea as it created the rather awkward necessity of referring to the previous version of a "revised" rule by citing an altogether different rule number in many instances. And (in my opinion, most tragically) it ruined the rather cool fact that in the "old" rules, the subject of errors arose under the widely regarded as unlucky and otherwise infamous number 13, which made it very easy to remember where the subject of errors could be found in the rulebook.

Another odd thing is that what is Rule 10.18 (now Rule 9.18) used to be just a minor part of, a virtual footnote to the old Rule 10.19 (i.e., Rule 10.19(f), with the old Rule 10.19 being generally devoted to issues regarding winning and losing pitchers).

All that being so, one has to wonder why this quite narrow scorekeeping provision was given an entire section all to itself, divorced from any other larger subject matter.

In any event, the "new" Rule 10.18 (now Rule 9.18), after its initial text, goes on to put a finer edge on exactly what a shutout means, as follows.

TRUST ME, I'M NOT MAKING THIS UP:
IT REALLY HAPPENED

No pitcher shall be credited with pitching a shutout unless he pitches the complete game, or unless he enters the game with none out before the opposing team has scored in the first inning, puts out the side without a run scoring and pitches the rest of the game without allowing a run.

The first part of the second sentence of Rule 9.18 needs no clarification.

It's as simple as it can be: a pitcher needs to pitch the "entire" game in order to get credit for a shutout.

At the same time, there is no need to construct an artificial example of what the exception to the main proposition to Rule 9.18's second sentence is all about because a perfect example of it happened—for real—in a major league game, one that involved the most famous and celebrated baseball player of all time.

FOR EXAMPLE: On June 23, 1917, the Red Sox were scheduled to play a doubleheader in Boston against the visiting Washington Senators, and no less than the legendary Babe Ruth was the starting pitcher for the home team in the first game.

As luck would have it, Ruth walked the first batter he faced, and he ended up being tossed from the game before facing another batter for arguing with the home-plate umpire.

Right after the relief pitcher for Boston came to the mound—one Ernie Shore—the Washington runner that Ruth had allowed to reach first base was put out trying to steal second, and subsequently all of the next 26 Washington batters that Shore faced were retired without reaching base in the nine-inning Red Sox victory.

Although in a very real sense Shore didn't pitch the entire game, he nevertheless qualified for being credited with a shutout under Rule 9.18's quirky "exception."

WHAT IT MEANS: An achievement such as the one that Ernie Shore pulled off ought not to be overlooked, and aside from any cogent arguments one might care to make that he should be deprived of the honor of having pitched a "bona fide" shutout, denying him credit for the shutout (under these quite narrow and highly unusual circumstances) cannot, all things considered, be considered fair. But whether one agrees with that proposition or not, Rule 9.18 says what it says, and although he wasn't the starting pitcher, Shore pitched a shutout because every out that had to be made to win the game for Boston was made while he was pitching, and no runs scored during his tenure on the mound.

Case closed.

GOING BEYOND THE OFFICIAL SCORER'S REPORT

When two or more pitchers combine to pitch a shutout, the league statistician shall make a notation to that effect in the league's official pitching records.

Note that this last portion of Rule 9.18 calls upon "the league statistician" to note a shared shutout. This is because, under Rule 9.02, the official scorer is not required to include whether or not any two or more pitchers qualified for being credited with a combined shutout, let alone whether any one pitcher qualified for a shutout either.

Note, however, that the official scorer is obliged to report the total runs allowed by each pitcher (under Rule 9.02(c)(5)), as well as the total of earned runs allowed by each pitcher under Rule 9.02(c)(6). Therefore, whether any pitcher—or pitchers—pitched a shutout could be easily gleaned from any official scorer's report under any circumstances, regardless of whose responsibility it might be to make official note of the fact.

◆ 15 ◆

Saving the Day
Rule 9.19

Rule 9.19—
Saves for Relief Pitchers

A save is a statistic credited to a relief pitcher, as set forth in this Rule 9.19.

The Origin of Saves: The Underlying Aim

Prior to 1969, "saves" were not an official statistic recognized by MLB.

Before then—as now—pitchers could qualify for a win or a loss. However, relief pitchers, especially "closers," rarely got the chance to be considered the winning pitcher, no matter how well they pitched, because they would often come into a game with their team already in the lead.

In other words, there was no commensurate statistical award for pitchers who substantially or significantly contributed to winning a game after another (preceding) pitcher fulfilled the criteria for the win, even though those "late-inning" pitchers might often be called upon to preserve a lead in situations far more difficult and pressure-packed than what any preceding pitcher or pitchers may have had to face.

That being so, awarding "saves" to pitchers who "sealed the deal" came into being, in large part to address that inequity.

The official scorer shall credit a pitcher with a save when such pitcher meets all four of the following conditions:
  (a) He is the finishing pitcher in a game won by his team;
  (b) He is not the winning pitcher;

(c) He is credited with at least ⅓ of an inning pitched; and

(d) He satisfies one of the following conditions:

(1) He enters the game with a lead of no more than three runs and pitches for at least one inning;

(2) He enters the game, regardless of the count, with the potential tying run either on base, or at bat or on deck (that is, the potential tying run is either already on base or is one of the first two batters he faces); or

(3) He pitches for at least three innings.

A Relatively Simple Rule That's Not So Simple in Many Respects

For example: In the top of the seventh inning, with no outs, the home team brings in a pitcher to relieve the starting pitcher.

The score is 3–0 in the home team's favor. In addition, the visiting team has a runner on base.

The home team's relief pitcher retires all three batters he faces in the top of the seventh, and he retires all the subsequent visiting team batters—in order—in the top of the eighth and the ninth inning as well.

Under these circumstances, the home team's relief pitcher is properly credited with a save under the provisions of Rule 9.19.

What it means: The relief pitcher in this case met *all* of the required criteria: he was the finishing pitcher in the game won by his team, he was not the winning pitcher (the starting pitcher for his team qualified for the win under Rule 9.17), and he was credited with ⅓ of an inning pitched (plus another 2⅔ innings).

Moreover, he entered the game with his team leading by less than four runs. In addition, the potential tying run was "on deck" when he came into the game, and he pitched three full innings.

In sum, even though the pitcher in question needed to fulfill the criterion of only one of the three subsections of Rule 9.19(d)—along with the criteria set forth in the preceding sub-sections of Rule 9.19—in order to qualify for the save, *all* the criteria of Rule 9.19's requirements were clearly met in this case.

A Closer Look at Rule 9.19's Particulars

He is the finishing pitcher in a game won by his team.

For example: With the bases loaded in the bottom of the ninth, no outs, and the home team behind by only one run, a relief pitcher is brought to the mound for the visiting team.

He strikes out the first two batters he faces, and he takes the third batter to an 0–2 count.

At this point, he is relieved by another pitcher, and that pitcher deals strike three to end the game with a victory for the visiting team.

As laudable as the efforts of the first relief pitcher in this example were (striking out the first two batters he faced and putting the third batter as far behind in the count as a batter can possibly be, all with the bases loaded in the bottom of the ninth), he cannot be properly credited with a save because he was not the "finishing pitcher," and the pitcher who relieved him (who ironically threw only one pitch) gets credit for the save in this case.

WHAT IT MEANS: The official scorer cannot consider anyone other than the last pitcher for the winning team as being qualified for a save, no matter how secondary and inferior—as compared to another pitcher's efforts—the finishing pitcher's contributions to winning the game may have been.

In short, as is often the case in Rule 9, the official scorer's discretion is strictly circumscribed so as to promote consistency in scorekeeping.

He is not the winning pitcher.

FOR EXAMPLE: With the score tied in the top of the ninth, no outs and the bases loaded, the home team brings in a relief pitcher to face the third, fourth and fifth batters in the visiting team's lineup (each of whom is in the league's top three in terms of batting average, on-base percentage, slugging percentage and runs batted in).

The relief pitcher strikes out each of the batters he faces, throwing only nine pitches in the process.

Then, in the bottom of the ninth, the home team squeezes out a run to win the game.

Although in a very real sense the home team's relief pitcher "saved" the game, he nevertheless does not get credit for a save.

WHAT IT MEANS: Under these circumstances, the pitcher in issue qualifies for the win because his team "assumed the lead that was held to the game's conclusion" while he was the pitcher of record for his team. Therefore, because he is properly considered the winning pitcher, a save cannot be credited to him, and since he was the finishing pitcher for his team—the only pitcher who can qualify for a save—no save is awarded to anyone.

He is credited with at least ⅓ of an inning pitched.

This portion of the save rule was inserted as part of the 2007 revisions so as to withhold credit for a save from a pitcher who might otherwise qualify for a save, but in reality pitched quite poorly (as in when, for instance, an official game is called after the finishing pitcher for the winning team, who came into the game in a save situation, walks the bases full before logging so much as a single out). In any instance, the pitcher would have to retire a batter.

He enters the game with a lead of no more than three runs and pitches for at least one inning;

He enters the game, regardless of the count, with the potential tying run either on base, or at bat or on deck (that is, the potential tying run is either already on base or is one of the first two batters he faces); or

He pitches for at least three innings.

The last of the four elements necessary to qualify a pitcher for a save consists of three alternative scenarios that are not mutually exclusive (more than one can apply at the same time, as was the case in the initial example given in this chapter).

The first two are well known, and they are so common that illustration of them is not necessary: one can easily envision cases where they apply. In fact, there are countless examples in modern MLB games where at least one, if not both, of these two provisions came into play.

However, the third is far less well known, to the point that it can be overlooked.

FOR EXAMPLE: The home team's starting pitcher has dominated the visiting team's batters to the point of absurdity: after pitching six full innings, only one batter for the visitors has reached base (by way of a bloop single), and—as should come as no surprise—no runs have been scored by the visiting team.

At the same time, the home team has amassed 18 runs during the course of the same six innings.

Although it appears that the home team's pitcher could continue to pitch the rest of the game sitting in a rocking chair while smoking a cigar and still win the game handily, he is nevertheless pulled at the start of the seventh inning.

One would think that with an 18-run lead, the home team's relief pitcher would have no difficulty getting through the final three innings of the game, but nothing could be further from the truth. In fact, the home team's relief pitcher gives up 17 earned runs before the visiting team makes its final out in the top of the ninth to end the game at 18–17 in favor of the home team.

(Note that the home team manager's decision to pull the starting pitcher and to leave the hapless relief pitcher in the game for the entire last three innings of the game was made in order to give me this extreme example to illustrate the point that I am trying to make.)

When all is said and done, the home team's relief pitcher is properly credited with a save.

WHAT IT MEANS: The exaggerated circumstances in this example demonstrate the fact that when a finishing pitcher qualifies for a save by meeting the first three of Rule 9.19's criteria, and he fulfills the fourth criterion by way of pitching "at least three innings," the score (aside from that pitcher's team being ahead when he enters the game and maintaining that lead) is irrelevant, and the quality of the pitching (in terms of runs given up, or any other measure) is also immaterial.

In other words, Rule 9.19(d)(3) is altogether lacking in any qualifying conditions. Therefore, a pitcher who performed in a manner that would never lead one to consider that pitcher as having "saved" the game for his team (in any ordinary sense of the word) can nevertheless receive the statistical reward of being credited with a save under Rule 9.19(d)(3).

In this regard, note that prior to the 2007 revisions, a pitcher was required to pitch "effectively" for at least three innings in order to be considered for a save under what is now Rule 9.19(d)(3). I believe that the deletion of "effectively" was nothing more than another example of the rules committee attempting to limit the official scorer's discretion in order to foster consistency in scorekeeping (in this case by eliminating the possibility of a scorer deciding not to award a save to a pitcher because that pitcher's performance was judged subjectively by the scorer to be ineffective).

A WORD ABOUT "SAVE SITUATIONS" AND "BLOWN SAVES"

The term "save situation" (a/k/a "save opportunity" and the like) is often heard in current baseball parlance. However, the rulebook does not use the term, let alone define it.

Regardless, whenever a pitcher enters a game under circumstances where he might qualify for a save if he finishes the game, that's a save situation for that pitcher. Note, however, that quite often, people will perceive a "save situation" only when a relief pitcher enters a game in the late innings with that pitcher's team leading by less than four runs (as per Rule 9.19(d)(1)) or with the potential tying run on base, at bat or on deck (as per Rule 9.19(d)(2)), and the existence of a "save situation" is often missed when a pitcher enters the game with his team leading by a wide margin and with three (or more) innings left to be played.

By the same token, although not addressed anywhere in the rulebook, a pitcher is considered as having "blown" a save if that pitcher enters a game in a potential save situation but fails to preserve the lead that the pitcher's team had when the pitcher came into the game.

A Word About Something That Isn't There Anymore

Before the 2007 rulebook revisions, the save rule had a short coda, which read as follows.

No more than one save may be credited in each game.
One might think that the deletion of these 11 words was made because they serve no cogent purpose: no scorer would ever consider giving more than one pitcher credit for a save in any given game since there is always only one finishing pitcher for the winning team, and only the finishing pitcher can qualify for a save. However, those now discarded 11 words did serve a legitimate purpose—one that may not be altogether obvious.

Specifically, a finishing pitcher can qualify for a save in three different ways (as is the case in the primary example given in this chapter). Therefore, one might infer that when a pitcher qualifies for a save in more than one manner, that pitcher might be entitled to credit for more than one save. Consequently, the old save rule addressed that by expressly limiting the official scorer to crediting only one save to the winning team's finishing pitcher in any given game, but in the current version of the rulebook, that is merely implied.

♦ ♦ ♦

Holds—The Widely Recognized and Often Cited Statistic That's Not a Part of the Rulebook at All

Starting pitchers stand a chance of getting credit for a win, and closers (since 1969) can hope for a save, but "middle relievers," "long relievers," "short relievers" and "setup" pitchers (i.e., all the pitchers who appear in games after the starting pitcher but before the closing pitcher) have no statistical award equivalent to a win or a save to strive for, at least as far as MLB's rulebook is concerned.

That being so, a new and special statistic was invented in the 1980s to address that fact—holds.

Not being a statistic officially recognized by MLB, no mention of holds can be found anywhere in the rulebook, even after the 2007 revisions. Nonetheless, MLB's official web site defines a "hold" as follows.

If a reliever comes into a game to protect a lead (that is to say, comes into the game with his team in the lead), **gets at least one out and leaves** (the game) **without giving up that lead, he gets a hold. But you can't get a save and a hold at the same time.**

As loose as this definition is, other definitions of a hold do not require a pitcher getting even one out, and there are other variations on the concept as well.

In any case, a number of strange results can arise when the concept of holds is applied to game situations, and it is not uncommon for a pitcher undeserving of any statistical award (because that pitcher in fact pitched quite poorly) nevertheless getting credit for a hold.

FOR EXAMPLE: A relief pitcher comes into the game with his team enjoying a five-run lead.

He strikes out the first batter he faces, but goes on to load the bases by issuing three straight bases on balls.

That's followed by a grand slam home run that cuts the pitcher's team's lead down to a single run, which in turn results in the pitcher being removed from the game in disgrace by his manager.

If the pitcher's team is able to maintain the lead that was almost entirely squandered by him, the relief pitcher would qualify for a hold regardless of the fact that the performance on the mound was far from stellar.

(Note that if the pitcher in this case had not struck out the first batter, that pitcher would nevertheless still qualify for a hold under the definitions of a hold that don't require the pitcher to log as much as a single out.)

WHAT IT MEANS: Regardless of the potentially bizarre results that can arise from employment of any definition in general circulation of a hold, the statistic nonetheless does serve to fill a gap in baseball statistics, and it's therefore worthy of some degree of deference. However, unless and until holds become an official part of the rulebook, with standardized "official" criteria that minimize (as much as possible) the potential for erroneous outcomes, holds will be what they are—essentially a well-intentioned device with a good degree of merit, but nonetheless a somewhat awkward appendage to the official statistics of baseball.

◆ 16 ◆

Stats and Streaks
Rules 9.20–9.23

Rule 9.20—Statistics

MUCH ADO ABOUT NOTHING (INSOFAR AS
THE OFFICIAL SCORER IS CONCERNED,
BUT NONETHELESS RELEVANT TO DETERMINING
WHETHER A PLAYER "PLAYED" IN A GAME OR NOT)

The League President shall appoint an official statistician. The statistician shall maintain an accumulative record of all the batting, fielding, running and pitching records specified in Rule 9.02 for every player who appears in a league championship game or post-season game.

The statistician shall prepare a tabulated report at the end of the season, including all individual and team records for every championship game, and shall submit this report to the League President. This report shall identify each player by his first name and surname and shall indicate as to each batter whether he bats righthanded, lefthanded or both ways, and as to each fielder and pitcher, whether he throws righthanded or lefthanded.

This first portion of Rule 9.20 isn't really a rule at all; it's more along the lines of an interoffice memo.

It doesn't convey anything in the way of instructions, rules, guidelines or precepts for an official scorer to follow. Rather, it simply directs the "League President" to name someone as an official statistician, and then goes on to delineate what that official statistician is obligated to do.

(Note that the Elias Sports Bureau in NYC—a long-established, well-

235

known, respected and sophisticated business organization, whose involvement in professional sports goes far beyond baseball—is currently the official statistician for MLB, and has served in that capacity since the early 20th century).

In any case, Rule 9.20 goes on to spell out instructions regarding how to determine which members of any given team are to be credited with a "game played" in the official scorer's report.

When a player listed in the starting lineup is substituted for before he plays on defense, he shall not receive credit in the defensive statistics (fielding) unless he actually plays that position during the game.

In other words, if a player's name appears on that player's team's lineup card at the beginning of a game, but he never goes onto the field and actually "plays," that player is not considered as having played in terms of defense.

All such players, however, shall be credited with one game played (in batting statistics) so long as they are announced into the game or listed on the official lineup card.

In other words, a player (notwithstanding the sentence that proceeded this one in Rule 9.20) is properly considered as having participated in a game—in the context of batting statistics—if that player is "announced into the game" or "listed" on the lineup card given to the umpire in charge of the game, regardless of whether that player actually played in the field or not.

Rule 9.20 Comment: The official scorer shall credit a player with having played on defense if such player is on the field for at least one pitch or play. If a game is called (for example, because of rain) after a substitute player enters the field but before a pitch is thrown or a play is made, the official scorer shall credit such player with a game played in the batting statistics but shall not credit such player in any defensive statistics. If a game is called (for example, because of rain) after a relief pitcher enters the field but before a pitch is thrown or a play is made, the official scorer shall credit such pitcher with a game played in the batting statistics but shall not credit such pitcher in any defensive statistics or with a game pitched.

Any games played to break a divisional tie shall be included in the statistics for that championship season.

But for Rule 9.20's preliminary text concerning the responsibilities of the official statistician that the league president is obliged to appoint, Rule

9.20 could simply be labeled "Determining Games Played by Individual Players," and in that regard, it goes to considerable lengths to address that issue.

That said, Rule 9.20 (from the perspective of a scorekeeper) is ultimately nothing more than a roadmap for deciding issues that may arise in the context of determining whether a particular member of a team officially participated in any given game or not, when (in rare instances) how to do so is not altogether obvious.

♦ ♦ ♦

Rule 9.21—
Determining Percentage Records

Before computers transformed the world, sophisticated statistical analysis of anything required a substantial amount of effort. That being so, for quite some time, baseball statistics were quite rudimentary. However, with the advent of modern technology, and databases that grow larger every day, coupled with the profusion of highly sophisticated analytical tools that have been developed in recent years (commonly known as and referred to as sabermetrics), there is virtually no end to the number crunching that goes on in baseball these days.

In spite of that, MLB—for better or worse—has chosen to remain faithful to only the most basic and familiar statistical categories that have been the mainstay of baseball statistics seemingly forever. Consequently, no new or novel "modern" statistics have yet to find a place in baseball's rulebook, even with the 2007 revisions.

That being so—and regardless of their shortcomings in the minds of many—Rule 9.21 concerns itself only with the most time-honored (albeit antiquated) pillars of baseball statistics: namely, games won and lost; batting averages; slugging percentages; fielding averages; earned run averages and on-base percentages, and it simply lays out how to compute them without elaboration.

Rule 9.21(a)   To compute percentage of games won and lost, divide the number of games won by the sum of games won and games lost.
Duh!

In other words, if five games are played, and two of those games are won and three are lost, the "percentage of games won and lost" is 40 percent.

The Venerable Cornerstone of Baseball Statistics, Regardless of Its Faults

Rule 9.21(b)   To compute batting average, divide the total number of safe hits (not the total bases on hits) by the total times at bat, as defined in Rule 9.02(a).

"Times at bat" are plate appearances that do not culminate in a batter being credited with a sacrifice bunt or a sacrifice fly, or in the batter reaching base on a walk, being hit by a pitch, or by virtue of a call of interference or obstruction.

Consequently, Rule 9.21(b) is all about plate appearances where the batter reaches base by way of a base hit, a fielding error or a fielder's choice, or when the batter is put out before reaching base at all.

That said, the main criticism voiced in many quarters in regards to using a batting average as a measure of a batter's abilities is that it is far too narrow a gauge of a batter's contributions to his team to be truly meaningful: it doesn't take into account the benefits to a team that come from a batter getting on base without a base hit.

Moreover, a batter's accomplishments in terms of doubles, triples and home runs are also overlooked. In the context of batting average, all base hits are equal; a single is looked upon and measured exactly the same as a double, triple or home run (which, significantly, is not the case when it comes to computing a batter's slugging percentage, as set forth in the following provision of Rule 9.21).

As a result, a more "sophisticated" statistic, "OPS" (which is simply on-base percentage and slugging percentage added together), is widely regarded as being superior to "BA," even though OPS is not recognized or even referred to by the rulebook.

Be that as it may, note that batting averages (as well as on-base percentages and slugging percentages) are traditionally expressed as three-digit or four-digit decimals. In other words, a batter who gets on base in one of four official "at-bats" is said to have a batting average of .250 (as opposed to a batting average of 25 percent), and a batter who goes "one-for-one," "two-for-two" or "three-for-three" (and so forth) is considered as "batting 1.000."

Power Gets Its Due

Rule 9.21(c)   To compute slugging percentage, divide the total bases of all safe hits by the total times at bat, as defined in Rule 9.02(a).

"Slugging" is all about what its name suggests: a batter's ability not just to get on base by way of singles, but rather the ability to whack a pitch well enough to tally doubles, triples and home runs. Consequently, under Rule 9.21(c)—in marked contrast to batting average—the number of bases attained by a batter by virtue of base hits are counted, and they constitute the essence of slugging percentage.

FOR EXAMPLE: A batter has four "at-bats" during the course of a game.

To the delight of everyone (except, of course, the opposing team, its fans and sundry supporters), the batter "hits for the cycle" (i.e., the batter is credited with a single, a double, a triple and a home run in four times at bat, a feat as rare as a pitcher throwing a no-hitter). Therefore, the batter's batting average for the day is 1.000, having "gone four-for-four." However, the slugging percentage is 2.500 because the single counts as one base, the double as two bases, the triple as three bases and the home run as four bases.

In other words, one plus two plus three plus four equals ten, and ten divided by four equals 2.5, which (in the aforementioned parlance of baseball) is stated as 2.500.

Note that if all four times at bat had been home runs, the slugging percentage in this case would be 4.000—the max.

WHAT IT MEANS: It is only logical for the rulebook to acknowledge the fact that a batter who knocks out an extra-base hit contributes more to the cause of his team than a batter who merely manages to eke out a single. Therefore, logically, you have slugging percentage as a recognized measure of achievement set forth by the rulebook.

In passing, it can be noted that the highest career slugging percentage in the history of MLB (to date) is that of Babe Ruth, whose ability not only to get on base was extraordinary, but whose proficiency in knocking the snot out of the ball consistently was remarkable as well (as virtually everyone with any contact with, or even cursory knowledge of baseball knows quite well). Specifically, his career batting average was .342. At the same time, his career slugging percentage was .690 (with a zaftig slugging percentage in the 1920 season of .847, inasmuch as he attained 388 bases in the course of 458 at-bats that year).

A SUSPECT STATISTIC, IF THERE EVER WAS ONE

Rule 9.21(d)   **To compute fielding average, divide the sum of putouts and assists by the sum of putouts, assists and errors (which shall be called chances).**

Objectively measuring the abilities of fielders has always been problematic, and it continues to be so. That is because fielding is far less cut and dried than batting—or even pitching for that matter—in terms of having objective or quasi-objective things to "count."

For instance, if a batter hits a home run, there is no doubt that the batter performed his job in a manner that unequivocally deserves special statistical credit over and beyond what a batter who only hits a single merits, and it can be quantified relatively easily. On the other hand, if a fielder makes a play to put out a batter that draws gasps from the people observing the play for the skill and athletic artistry exhibited, it is nonetheless treated in the same manner (from a statistical perspective) as if the fielder had caught a lazy routine popup for an easy, run-of-the-mill putout, because a number cannot be readily ascribed to the brilliant play compared to the routine play.

The point is that simply counting a fielder's putouts, assists and errors, and subjecting the numbers to the formula set forth in Rule 9.21(d), sheds some degree of light on that player's fielding abilities, but is flawed as far as being an altogether accurate barometer of fielding abilities.

In that regard, note also that a fielder may be charged with an error on a "play" where there was no possibility of the fielder getting credit for a putout or an assist (e.g., simply returning the ball to the pitcher after a base hit in a somewhat sloppy manner, thereby allowing a runner to advance along the base paths) and that skews and otherwise distorts fielding statistics beyond even the inherent problems that come from simply counting putouts, assists and errors in order to judge how good—or bad—any given player's fielding may be.

Add to that the intrinsic subjectivity in scorers deciding between base hits and errors in borderline situations.

Regardless, "fielding average" is the rulebook's only barometer for measuring fielding abilities and accomplishments.

ANOTHER PLAIN AND SIMPLE EXERCISE IN ARITHMETIC, BUT ONE WITH "INFINITE" IMPLICATIONS

Rule 9.21(e)   To compute pitcher's earned-run average, multiply the total earned runs charged against such pitcher by 9, and divide the result by the total number of innings he pitched, including fractions of an inning.

Rule 9.21(e) Comment: For example, 9⅓ innings pitched and 3 earned runs is an earned-run average of 2.89 (3 earned runs times 9 divided by 9⅓ equals 2.89).

For anyone who has a grasp of fundamental grade school mathematics, Rule 9.21(e) is not something hard to understand or apply: it simply calculates how many earned runs a pitcher has averaged over the course of each nine innings that the pitcher has pitched (if nine or more innings of pitching are plugged into the equation) or how many earned runs that pitcher would be charged with if that pitcher had pitched nine innings (if less than nine innings of pitching are counted).

(Note that in leagues other than those where nine inning games are the norm, earned run averages are often computed based on less than nine innings. Therefore, in NCAA Softball, for example, instead of multiplying earned runs by nine, earned runs are multiplied by seven because NCAA Softball games, other than games that go into extra innings, end after seven innings.)

That said, a most intriguing aspect of Rule 9.21(e) arises when a pitcher comes into a game, gives up one or more earned runs, but fails to log any outs before leaving the game.

FOR EXAMPLE: The home team's starting pitcher begins the game by issuing three straight walks to the first three batters he faces. That's followed by the visiting team's clean-up batter belting a bomb over the fence in fair territory to score four runs for his team with one swing of the bat.

Logically, the ill-fated starting pitcher for the home team is (mercifully) pulled from the game at this point.

Applying the formula set out in Rule 9.21(e), the home team's starting pitcher's ERA for this game is infinity.

WHAT IT MEANS: Conceptually, if this pitcher had continued to pitch in the same manner that he did during the course of the plate appearances of the four batters he faced, the visiting team would have scored run after run after run forever: earned runs would score against him without end and in perpetuity. Therefore, the pitcher's ERA would be "infinite."

At the same time, if the pitcher in this case had (for instance) struck out the first batter he faced, loaded the bases, given up a home run, and was then pulled from the mound, his ERA for the game would be less than infinite: it would be 108.00 (because 4 times 9 [36] divided by ⅓ equals 108), and although that's an ERA that's nothing to be proud of, it's infinitely better than infinity.

THE LAST OF THE "STATS" LAID OUT IN RULE 9.21, AS SIMPLE AS THE REST BUT CONTAINING ONE OF THE ODDEST THINGS IN ALL OF BASEBALL SCOREKEEPING

Rule 9.21(f)   To compute on-base percentage, divide the sum of hits, bases on balls and times hit by pitch by the sum of at-bats, bases on balls, times hit by pitch and sacrifice flies.

Rule 9.21(f) Comment: For the purpose of computing on-base percentage, ignore instances of a batter being awarded first base on interference or obstruction.

It's simple to calculate a batter's on-base percentage.

For instance, if a batter comes to bat four times in a game, and he strikes out once, reaches base on a base hit once, draws a walk once and is hit by a pitch once, that batter's batting average is .500. That's because the walk and HBP are not counted in calculating batting average, and that leaves only two "official at-bats" to consider in terms of calculating batting average. Of those two at-bats, one was successful and the other was not, so he "batted .500."

At the same time, in computing on-base percentage, all of the plate appearances in this case are counted, and of the four plate appearances, the batter reached base three times. Therefore, the same batter's on-base percentage is .750.

(Note that it's irrelevant whether the base hit was a single or an extra-base hit; it is only in computing slugging percentage that the number of bases attained on a base hit are factored into the equation.)

Consequently, one does not have to have a Ph.D from MIT in order to determine what a particular batter's on-base percentage might be: the methodology is fairly uncomplicated (as is the case with all the other formulas that make up Rule 9.21).

At the same time, there is a curious aspect to on-base percentage that's illustrated by the following.

FOR EXAMPLE: A batter comes to bat three times in a game.

The first time, the batter strikes out. The second time, the batter reaches base on a base hit. The third time, the batter hits a sacrifice fly.

In terms of his batting average for this game, the batter is "one-for-two" because a sacrifice fly is not counted in the context of computing batting averages, and that translates to a batting average of .500.

At the same time, the batter's on-base percentage is only .333 (!) because sacrifice flies are not overlooked in tabulating on-base percentage, and therefore—in that context—the batter is "one-for-three."

WHAT IT MEANS: When it comes to a player's batting average, the focus is fundamentally on how many times the batter put the ball into play and reached base (without the benefit of an error committed by the defensive team, or by virtue of a fielder's choice). Walks, being hit by a pitch, awards of first base by way of interference or obstruction, sacrifice bunts and sacrifice flies are all disregarded entirely.

At the same time, in terms of on-base percentage, sacrifice bunts are overlooked, just as they are in the context of batting averages. Notwithstanding, reaching base on a walk or by being hit by a pitch is taken into account, but failing to reach base on a sacrifice fly (or reaching base on a fielding error or fielder's choice where a sacrifice fly is nonetheless scored) is not disregarded. Consequently, a batter's on-base percentage can be lower than his batting average, as it is in the example given.

The reason behind this rather odd aspect of baseball statistics is that a batter being credited with a sacrifice fly is not dependant on the batter having purposefully allowed himself to be put out so as to advance a runner on base (as contrasted to a sacrifice bunt, where that is the case). Therefore, in terms of on-base percentage (i.e., measuring a batter's "rate of success" in reaching base) one cannot fairly consider a fly ball—or line drive—hit to the outfield that is caught to put out the batter (or which would have been caught but for an error) that allows a runner on base to score as being anything less than a batter's failure to reach base (divorced from errorless play or a fielder's choice).

In sum, a blind eye is not turned to sacrifice flies in the context of computing on-base percentage. Therefore, the rather odd outcome, in which a batter may have a batting average that is higher than his on-base percentage, can happen.

◆ ◆ ◆

Rule 9.22—Minimum Standards for Individual Championships

To assure uniformity in establishing the batting, pitching and fielding championships of professional leagues, such champions shall meet the following minimum performance standards.

Deciding Who (Really) Had the Best Batting Average, Slugging Percentage, On-Base Percentage and Fielding Average During the Course of a Given Season

Inasmuch as the rulebook concerns itself—in Rule 9.21—with the computation of batting averages [Rule 9.21(b)], slugging percentages [Rule 9.21(c)], fielding averages [Rule 9.21(d)], earned-run averages [Rule 9.21(e)] and on-base percentages [Rule 9.21(f)], it should come as no surprise that the rulebook addresses how to determine which player in any given league qualifies as being the best in each of those categories at the end of a season.

That said, one might wonder why an entire section of Rule 9 is devoted to the topic; after all, isn't it just a matter of simply pointing to the player with the best numbers in any given category?

Not quite.

The problem is that you can have (for instance) a player come to bat only once during the course of an entire season and hit a home run. Consequently, that player would automatically have the highest batting average that anyone could possibly have (1.000), the highest on-base percentage (1.000) as well, and the highest slugging percentage (4.000) in that league in that season, but to consider that player as being the "best" in any of those categories would of course be a grave injustice to all the players in that league who played day in and day out, and contributed far more to whatever success their respective teams may have achieved than a player who showed up for nothing more than a "cup of coffee."

In short, the rulebook recognizes that a player must participate in multiple games to a meaningful degree during the course of a season in order to be honestly and fairly worthy of being considered the best batter in any of the three batting statistics that the rulebook recognizes, the best pitcher (in terms of ERA), or the best fielder (in terms of fielding average), and exactly what degree of participation is required to do so is what Rule 9.22 is all about.

That said—to its credit—Rule 9.22 lays out its criteria in a relatively plain and simple manner, and it does so with examples that suffice to make clear how to apply its "finer points."

(Note that "league championship games"—as repeatedly referred to in Rule 9.22—are just regular season games: games that "count" in terms of determining which teams qualify for "post-season" play. Note also that references to the "National Association" are references to professional baseball leagues that compete at levels "below" that of Major League Baseball that are nonetheless affiliated with Major League Baseball, such as "Triple A," "Double A," and so forth and so on: leagues that are commonly referred to as the "minor leagues."

Rule 9.22(a)   The individual batting, slugging or on-base percentage champion shall be the player with the highest batting average, slugging percentage or on-base percentage, as the case may be, provided the player is credited with as many or more total appearances at the plate in league

championship games as the number of games scheduled for each club in his club's league that season, multiplied by 3.1 in the case of a Major League player and by 2.7 in the case of a National Association player. Total appearances at the plate shall include official times at bat, plus bases on balls, times hit by pitcher, sacrifice hits, sacrifice flies and times awarded first base because of interference or obstruction. Notwithstanding the foregoing requirement of minimum appearances at the plate, any player with fewer than the required number of plate appearances whose average would be the highest, if he were charged with the required number of plate appearances shall be awarded the batting, slugging or on-base percentage championship, as the case may be.

Rule 9.22(a) Comment: For example, if a Major League schedules 162 games for each club, 502 plate appearances qualify (162 times 3.1 equals 502) a player for a batting, slugging or on-base percentage championship. If a National Association league schedules 140 games for each club, 378 plate appearances qualify (140 times 2.7 equals 378) a player for a batting, slugging or on-base percentage championship. Fractions of a plate appearance are to be rounded up or down to the closest whole number. For example, 162 times 3.1 equals 502.2, which is rounded down to a requirement of 502.

If, for example, Abel has the highest batting average among those with 502 plate appearance in a Major League with a .362 batting average (181 hits in 500 at-bats), and Baker has 490 plate appearances, 440 at-bats and 165 hits for a .375 batting average, Baker shall be the batting champion, because adding 12 more at-bats to Baker's record would still give Baker a higher batting average than Abel: .365 (165 hits in 452 at-bats) to Abel's .362.

Rule 9.22(b) The individual pitching champion in a Major League shall be the pitcher with the lowest earned-run average, provided that the pitcher has pitched at least as many innings in league championship games as the number of games scheduled for each club in his club's league that season. The individual pitching champion in a National Association league shall be the pitcher with the lowest earned-run average provided that the pitcher has pitched at least as many innings in league championship season games as 80 percent of the number of games scheduled for each club in the pitcher's league.

Rule 9.22(b) Comment: For example, if a Major League schedules 162 games for each club, 162 innings qualify a pitcher for a pitching championship.

A pitcher with 161⅔ innings would not qualify. If a National Association league schedules 140 games for each club, 112 innings qualify a pitcher for a pitching championship. Fractions of an inning for the required number of innings are to be rounded to the closest third of an inning. For example, 80 percent of 144 games is 115.2, so 115⅓ innings would be the minimum required for a pitching championship in a National Association league with 144 games scheduled and 80 percent of 76 games is 60.8, so 60⅔ innings would be the minimum required for a pitching championship in a National Association league with 76 games scheduled.

Rule 9.22(c)   The individual fielding champions shall be the fielders with the highest fielding average at each position, provided:

(1) A catcher must have participated as a catcher in at least one-half the number of games scheduled for each club in his league that season;

(2) An infielder or outfielder must have participated at his position in at least two-thirds of the number of games scheduled for each club in his league that season; and

(3) A pitcher must have pitched at least as many innings as the number of games scheduled for each club in his league that season, unless another pitcher has a fielding average as high or higher and has handled more total chances in fewer innings, in which case such other pitcher shall be the fielding champion.

◆ ◆ ◆

Rule 9.23—Guidelines for Cumulative Performance Records

Dealing with "Streaks"

Rule 9.23 is a fitting coda to all that comes before it: a "dessert" (in a way) to the more complex and weightier issues wrestled with in much of the rest of the official rules governing scorekeeping in baseball.

At the same time, this last section of Rule 9 could fittingly be dedicated to three of baseball's all-time greatest players—Joe DiMaggio, Lou Gehrig and Cal Ripken, Jr.—inasmuch as Rule 9.23(b) cannot be read by anyone even remotely aware of baseball's history and most time-honored records without thinking about the remarkable 56 consecutive game hitting streak that the storied "Joltin' Joe" had in 1941, without some thought being given to the feat of playing in 2,130 consecutive games by the legendary "Pride of the Yankees" between 1925 and 1939, and the subsequent breaking of that seemingly unbreakable record by Baltimore's extraordinary "Iron Man" by playing in 2,632 consecutive games between 1982 and 1998.

That said, Rule 9.23 is very much to the point, and therefore requires little elaboration in order to be understood or applied.

You Don't Have to Bang Out a Hit Every Time You Come to Bat to Keep the Streak Going

Rule 9.23(a)—Consecutive Hitting Streaks

A consecutive hitting streak shall not be terminated if a batter's plate appearance results in a base on balls, hit batsman, defensive interference or obstruction or a sacrifice bunt.

A sacrifice fly shall terminate the streak.

In other words, if a batter's eight consecutive plate appearances consist of—in sequence—(1) a base hit, (2) a walk, (3) another base hit, (4) hit by a pitch, (5) a catcher's interference call, (6) another base hit, (7) a sacrifice bunt and (8) a final base hit, he has a consecutive hitting streak of four (inasmuch as the walk is skipped, being hit by a pitch is skipped, reaching base on catcher's interference is skipped, and the sacrifice bunt is skipped as well, leaving four base hits "in a row").

On the other hand, if that same batter had hit a sacrifice fly instead of the sacrifice bunt in the seventh plate appearance, the consecutive hitting streak would only be three.

In regards to why the rulebook looks upon a sacrifice fly differently than a sacrifice bunt in cases like this, reference may be made to the comments made in connection with calculating on-base percentage under Rule 9.21(f).

You Don't Necessarily Have to Get a Hit in Every Game You Play to Keep the Streak Going

Rule 9.23(b)—Consecutive-Game Hitting Streaks

A consecutive-game hitting streak shall not be terminated if all of a batter's plate appearances (one or more) in a game result in a base on balls, hit batsman, defensive interference or obstruction or a sacrifice bunt.

The streak shall terminate if the player has a sacrifice fly and no hit.

A player's individual consecutive-game hitting streak shall be determined by the consecutive games in which such player appears and is not determined by his club's games.

In other words, if a player goes through a game without being put out (except on a sacrifice bunt) or without reaching base on an error or by virtue of a fielder's choice, but the player doesn't manage a base hit during the course of the game either, it's looked upon as though that player—in a sense—didn't play at all, and that player is not considered as having played a game without getting a base hit.

At the same time, "skipping" a game—or games—altogether doesn't ruin a player's consecutive game hitting streak: it's all about getting hits in consecutive games played by the batter, not in consecutive games played by the batter's team.

What It Means to "Play"

Rule 9.23(c)—Consecutive-Game Playing Streak

A consecutive-game playing streak shall be extended if a player plays one half-inning on defense or if the player completes a time at bat by reaching base or being put out.

A pinch-running appearance only shall not extend the streak.

If a player is ejected from a game by an umpire before such player can comply with the requirements of this Rule 9.23(c), such player's streak shall continue.

In other words, there is a minimum amount that a someone must "play" in order to be officially considered as having played in a game, but it really isn't all that much in the final analysis.

Illustrative of this is the following.

On Friday, July 13, 1934, in his 1,426th consecutive game played—Lou Gehrig was suffering such severe back pain in Detroit that he had to be assisted from the field.

In the game played the following day, Gehrig was listed in the Yankees batting order as usual, but uncharacteristically not in his customary "clean up" position (batting fourth, as his uniform number would indicate), but rather as New York's leadoff batter.

True to form, the "Iron Horse" singled to start the game, but he was immediately pulled for a pinch-runner and consequently didn't play for the remainder of the game.

The Yankees went on to lose the game that day, but because he completed a time at bat, Gehrig's streak went on (and for nearly another five years, no less).

Reversion Back to a Prior Date in Terms of Determining When Things— Officially—Happened

Rule 9.23(d)—Suspended Games

Rule 9.23(d) is about as uncomplicated and straightforward as any provision in any rulebook could be. That being the case, and in deference to baseball's rulebook, I'll let the rulebook have the last word.

For the purpose of this Rule 9.23, all performances in the completion of a suspended game shall be considered as occurring on the original date of the game.

Index

Numbers in *bold italics* indicate pages with photographs.